EPICS ON
EVEREST

STORIES OF SURVIVAL FROM
THE WORLD'S HIGHEST PEAK

EPICS ON EVEREST

STORIES OF SURVIVAL FROM THE WORLD'S HIGHEST PEAK

EDITED BY CLINT WILLIS

Thunder's Mouth Press
New York
2003

EPICS ON EVEREST:
STORIES OF SURVIVAL FROM THE WORLD'S HIGHEST PEAK

Compilation copyright © 2003 by Clint Willis
Introductions copyright © 2003 by Clint Willis

Adrenaline® and the Adrenaline® logo are trademarks of
Avalon Publishing Group Incorporated, New York, NY.

An Adrenaline Book®

Published by
Thunder's Mouth Press
An Imprint of Avalon Publishing Group Incorporated
161 William Street, 16th floor
New York, NY 10038

Book design: Sue Canavan

frontispiece photo: Climbing Mount Everest, © Galen Rowell/Corbis

Library of Congress Cataloging-in-Publication Data is available.

ISBN 1-56025-499-8

Printed in the United States of America

Distributed by Publishers Group West

For four climbers:
Mike Jewell
Steve Longenecker
Ian Turnbull
Perry Willis

c o n t e n t s

Introduction

Tenzing Norgay and Edmund Hillary reached the summit of Mount Everest at about 11 o'clock in the morning on May 29, 1953. Tenzing buried some food as a gift to the mountain's gods. Hillary buried with the food a small crucifix. After 32 years and 16 expeditions—and at the cost of more than 20 lives—men had finally reached the summit of the world's highest peak.

The year 2003 marks the 50th anniversary of the first ascent of Mount Everest. *Epics on Everest: Stories of Survival from the World's Highest Peak* celebrates that achievement and the struggles that led to it. The book also makes clear that those early expeditions were a prelude to a half-century of even more extreme climbing. The mountain has been climbed by more than 1,000 individuals since Hillary and Norgay's summit day, and by more than a dozen different routes.

Modern Everest climbers have endured scores of epics and dozens of tragedies. Another 162 men and women have died on Everest during these 50 years—57 during the past decade alone. The mountain's fascination for climbers and armchair mountaineers transcends its altitude (29,035 feet, or 8,850 meters) and grows with every mystery, every tragedy, every achievement.

Everest is known to most of us as a mosaic of overlapping or disparate stories. The mountain is a leading figure—not merely a setting, but a character—in many of the past century's best accounts of friendship, adventure, hardship, danger, courage, disaster and death. It is not hard to imagine that Everest was put upon the earth to show us some ways to experience certain kinds of authenticity and intensity, whether firsthand or by way of stories.

Men and women who go to Everest in search of insights or discoveries often find what they don't know they are looking for. Some come away with more than they sought—new stories and new notions—with their identities somehow stripped bare and washed clean. Is the possibility of such transformation worth the risk of dying on the mountain? The answer may depend upon what you think you are risking—how you see your life and your attachments, and how you live. What do our lives mean, and what are they worth to us or to anyone? How should we live them?

The stories in this book at times suggest that the mountain is a gift meant to help us unravel such mysteries. The stories are drawn from a universe of hundreds of accounts, and present nothing like an orderly survey of mountaineering on Everest. They're just some of the best stories about Everest that I have come across in 35 years of reading about the mountain and its history.

British surveyors in India 151 years ago used a 100-pound theodolite to take 38 observations of a mountain locals knew by various names. The Tibetans called it *Chomolungma,* or Goddess Mother of the Earth. The British employed their theodolite—which took 11 men to carry—at distances of 100 to 118 miles from the peak. They collected data that told them they had stumbled upon the world's highest known mountain. They named it Everest after Sir George Everest, surveyor general of India from 1823 to 1843.

The first British to approach Everest were drawn by its secrets as much as by the more tangible fact of its extreme altitude. The mountain lay on the border of two hidden kingdoms, Tibet and Nepal. Both countries had been closed to Westerners for many years when Captain John Noel made his 1913 attempt to approach the mountain through Tibet:

> Everest! Hitherto unapproached by men of my race; guarded, so fantastic rumor said, by the holiest lamas dwelling in mystic contemplation of the soul of the giant peak, communicating with its demons and guardian gods! It was an alluring goal.

Noel assembled a small party of hillmen from the borders of Tibet and India, and darkened his skin and hair. He hoped to pass as a Muslim from India. He traveled to Tibet, and was just 40 miles from Everest when soldiers turned him back.

World War I interrupted such ventures, but Noel in 1919 told to England's Royal Geographical Society the story of his Tibetan journey. The Society agreed to sponsor an expedition to Everest, pending approval to enter Tibet, which the Dalai Lama granted in December 1920.

The 1921 British reconnaissance entered Nepal and discovered an approach to the mountain's North Col, a key to early attempts on the peak. The British returned to the mountain in 1922. George Finch and Geoffery Bruce reached 8,320 meters (27,297 feet), but the expedition lost seven porters—all of them Sherpa villagers—to an avalanche.

The British tried yet again in 1924. Expedition leader General Charles Bruce died from malaria on the way to the mountain. Edward Norton reached 8,580 meters (28,150 feet) without supplementary oxygen. George Leigh Mallory—a member of both previous expeditions—and young Andrew Irvine then made their summit attempt, setting out from the high camp on June 8. They were last seen high on the mountain's Northeast Ridge.

The British didn't return to the mountain until the '30s, when four formal expeditions fell far short of the summit. Englishman Maurice Wilson—who had no mountaineering experience—flew to India and made an audacious solo attempt on the mountain in 1934. Wilson struggled as far as the Rongbuk glacier at 6,363 meters (20,875 feet), where his body was found by the 1935 British Reconnaissance Expedition.

The mountain once again receded from interest during World War II. When that conflict ended, the situation had changed. The Chinese occupation of Tibet had closed that country to Westerners. Meanwhile, Nepal had opened its borders, clearing the way for attempts from the south side of the peak.

The explorer Eric Shipton—an early and influential proponent of fast, lightweight climbing expeditions—led a party to find a new approach to the peak. They explored the Khumbu glacier, and managed to climb a shifting mass of crevasses and ice towers that came to be known as the icefall. The icefall eventually proved a key to the first route up the peak.

Two Swiss expeditions attempted Everest the following year. The first came tantalizingly close, with Sherpa Tenzing Norgay (on his sixth Everest expedition) and Robert Lambert reaching 8,595 meters—28,363 feet. A year later—almost to the day—Tenzing and Edmund Hillary as members of the ninth British expedition reached the summit by way of the South Col route.

That first summit climb ended the first epoch in the history of mountaineering on and around Everest. The single-minded effort to get up the peak gave way to a hunt for new routes.

A review of some highlights of the past half-century on Everest might start with four Swiss climbers who in 1956 followed the South Col route to the summit. Four years passed before the Chinese in 1960 claimed the first complete ascent of the North Col route pioneered by the British before World War II. An American team climbed the

South Col route in 1963, and two members—Tom Hornbein and Willi Unsoeld—made the first traverse of the entire peak. Their climb took them up the previously unclimbed West Ridge and then down by way of the South Col.

A series of large expeditions from various countries visited the mountain during the '60s and early '70s. A woman—Junko Tabei of Japan—reached the summit in 1975. The same year, an 18-member expedition led by British climber Chris Bonington claimed the coveted first ascent of the peak's Southwest Face. The expedition got at least four members to the top of Everest; climber and cameraman Mick Burke vanished on his summit bid.

Tyrolians Reinhold Messner and Peter Habeler upped the ante in 1978, making the peak's first ascent without artificial oxygen. Messner returned in 1980 to make a solo ascent from the North side. Two years later, a tiny British expedition led by Chris Bonington attempted the daunting Northeast Ridge. The expedition ended when Peter Boardman and Joe Tasker disappeared high on the climb.

Six Americans got up the imposing Kangshung Face of Everest in 1983. Their route included 3,000 feet of difficult rock climbing, and may be the most difficult route done to date on the mountain. Five years later, a four-man Anglo-American team created a new route up the Kangshung Face, and team member Stephen Venables continued to the summit, alone and without oxygen.

Texas businessman Dick Bass, 55, paid American David Breashears to guide him up Everest in 1985, ushering in an era of commercial climbing on the peak. A decade later, the business of guiding on Everest was in full bloom. Some 240 climbers arrived at the mountain in the spring of 1996. Two guides and six members of their respective expeditions died when a storm caught them high on the mountain. The epic inspired several best-selling books and much debate over the role of guides on Everest—and the publicity attracted to the peak even greater numbers of affluent but underqualified climbers.

Still, the mountain refused to give up all its secrets. A 1999 expedition set out to discover evidence about the fate of British pioneers George Mallory and Andrew Irvine, and came upon Mallory's 75-year-old corpse. Their discovery offered no conclusive answers to the question of whether the two men reached the summit in 1924, let alone what they did or said or believed or experienced.

The story isn't over. The mountain's most popular routes continue to swarm with climbers. The climbers arrive with their agendas: to add lines to their resumes or make a few bucks guiding or prove their strength or courage or learn what they can. Everest has no plans. It stands aloof from our ambitions, luminous and unknowable, like everything else on earth.

—CLINT WILLIS
SERIES EDITOR, ADRENALINE BOOKS

from The Lost Explorer
by Conrad Anker
and David Roberts

David Roberts (born 1943) wrote this sketch of the first British attempts to climb Everest in 1921 and 1922. He offers perspective on the task the climbers faced, as well as an introduction to George Mallory. Mallory went back to the mointain in 1924, and disappeared high on its Northeast ridge.

The 1921 reconnaissance of Everest, pursued through the monsoon summer and into the autumn season, was in many respects a colossal mess. The party's talents were wildly uneven, with several over-the-hill, out-of-shape veterans in leadership positions. Entrusted with choosing a team, the Everest Committee—a national board of exploratory experts formed for the express purpose of claiming the "Third Pole" for the Empire—valued years of hill-walking and Himalayan rambling over technical mountaineering skills.

From the start, Mallory was at serious odds with the team's leader, Charles Howard-Bury, and its climbing leader, Harold Raeburn, both much older than he. Of the former, he wrote Ruth, "He is not a tolerant person. He is well-informed and opinionated and doesn't at all like anyone else to know things he doesn't know. For the sake of peace, I am being very careful not to broach certain subjects of conversation."

Of Raeburn: "He is dreadfully dictatorial about matters of fact, and often wrong."

Before the party even got near Mount Everest, the well-liked but fifty-year-old Scottish doctor, A. M. Kellas, died of dysentery. His teammates buried him on a stony hillside, in what Mallory called "an extraordinarily affecting little ceremony."

In view of the 1999 controversy over scoops on the Internet and secrets guarded by Simonson's teammates, it is interesting to note that the same kinds of worries afflicted the first expedition to approach the world's highest mountain. The Everest Committee had made a deal with the *Times* of London for exclusive coverage, irritating rivals such as the *Daily Telegraph*. Even before the team had found Everest, one of the committee's potentates wrote the surveyor-general of India, expressing his fears about "unexpected leakage," and fingering a reporter for the Calcutta *Morning Post* as a particularly dangerous suspect. A kindred paranoia had dictated an oath that all the team members had been required to sign before leaving England, enjoining them "not to hold any communication with the press or with any press agency or publisher, or to deliver any public lecture" without the approval of the Everest Committee.

So a motley assortment of mountaineers and travelers, already torn by jealousies and disparate ambitions, stumbled toward Everest in the wrong season. George Bernard Shaw later memorably characterized a group portrait of the team as looking "like a picnic in Connemara surprised by a snowstorm."

By mid-June, with the party still far from the mountain, with Kellas dead and Raeburn laid low by diarrhea and injuries incurred in twice falling off his horse, the number of able mountaineers left on the expedition had dwindled to two: Mallory and Guy Bullock. This pair virtually by themselves would accomplish what in the long run amounted to a brilliant reconnaissance of Everest. During the following months, the other members puttered off in various directions, performing botanical and topographical missions that had little bearing on finding a route up the mountain.

As always, Mallory's mood swung wildly between giddy enthusiasm and leaden disenchantment. By the beginning of 1921, as he prepared for Everest, now thirty-four years old, he had reached a gloomy crossroads in life. He had quit his teaching job at Charterhouse, with no clear notion of what to do next. Ideally, he would have become a writer, but he lacked confidence, complaining to Robert Graves in a letter from shipboard, "I can't think I have sufficient talent to make a life-work of writing, though plenty of themes suggest themselves as wanting to be written about. Perhaps I shall get a job at a provincial university." At the moment, he was reading that masterpiece by his Bloomsbury admirer, *Queen Victoria:* no doubt Lytton Strachey's sardonic command of prose set a daunting example to Mallory of what a real writer could do.

On June 13, Mallory caught his first sight of Everest—like "a prodigious white fang excrescent from the jaw of the world," as he would write in the expedition book. The distant vision was daunting in the extreme: in a letter to Ruth, he recorded "the most stupendous ridges and appalling precipices that I have ever seen. . . . All the talk of easy snow slope is a myth." Yet while the sight intimidated Mallory, at the same time it captivated him. The man's obsession with Everest can be said to date from that first glimpse, still fifty-seven miles away from the mountain. As he wrote Ruth, during the subsequent days, "The problem of its great ridges and glaciers began to take shape and to haunt the mind, presenting itself at odd moments and leading to definite plans. Where can one go for another view, to unveil a little more of the great mystery?"

Part of Mallory's genius was a deeply analytical grasp of the shape and structure of mountains. Other climbers might be content to stare with field glasses at a single aspect of the mountain, seeking routes; Mallory was eager, in effect, to create a three-dimensional model in his mind. As he wrote in the official report, "Our reconnaissance must aim at . . . a correct understanding of the whole form and structure of the mountain and the distribution of its various parts; we must distinguish the vulnerable places in its armour and finally pit our skill against the obstacles."

As Mallory and Bullock trudged up one snow-struck valley after another, with the monsoon now in full force, the power of that visionary goal drove them across a succession of bleak landscapes. Mallory described one such clime in *Mount Everest: The Reconnaissance:*

> It was a desolate scene, I suppose; no flowers were to be seen nor any sign of life beyond some stunted gorse bushes on a near hillside and a few patches of coarse brown grass, and the only habitations were dry inhuman ruins; but whatever else was dead, our interest was alive.

By June 25, Mallory and Bullock had reached the terminus of the Rongbuk Glacier, the massive ice stream that drains the whole north side of Everest. For a month, the indefatigable duo would explore approaches, only to be stymied and puzzled again and again. Few Europeans had yet traveled on any of the colossal Himalayan glaciers: used to the easy highways such rivers of ice formed in the Alps, the two British climbers were severely frustrated by the jumbled séracs, the crevasse-riddled icefalls, and the weird ice pinnacles, called *nieves penitentes*, that the Rongbuk threw in their path. The glacier was, Mallory wrote, "not a road but an obstacle"; and, "The White Rabbit himself would have been bewildered here." Part of the time, the men hiked in snowshoes, but even so, in the soggy monsoon conditions they often could not avoid wading knee-deep through slush pools.

All the while, Mallory kept staring at the mountain, analyzing it. Early on, he had decided, as he jotted in his diary, "Last section of East arête should go." Here was a pregnant observation, for on that last section of what would come to be called the northeast ridge, Mallory and Irvine would vanish three years hence.

Just as early, Mallory recognized that the key to reaching the northeast ridge was gaining the 23,000-foot saddle of snow and ice that he and Bullock named the Chang La, or North Col. The approach to the col from the main Rongbuk Glacier, however, looked impossible. For weeks, the two men reconnoitered, climbing lower peaks just to acclimatize and to gain new views of Everest, teaching their "coolies" (as they called the porters) the rudiments of mountaineering.

In the course of these explorations, the men climbed to another col on the west of Everest, called the Lho La. From here, the two became the first Europeans to behold the Khumbu Glacier and its upper basin, the Western Cwm (pronounced "Coom"), which Mallory named, slapping a Welsh term for an alpine basin onto a Himalayan landscape. The Khumbu and the Western Cwm would prove the route by which Hillary and Tenzing would make the first ascent of Everest, thirty-two years later. From the Lho La, however, the 1,500-foot drop to the Khumbu unfolded as a "hopeless precipice." The question was moot, in any event, for at the pass, the men stood on the border of Tibet and Nepal, and they were forbidden to enter the latter country.

Always Mallory's eye was fixed on the dotted line his imagination had already drawn from the North Col to the summit. "We saw the North Col quite clearly today," he told his diary on July 15, "and again the way up from there does not look difficult."

Thus the immediate task of the reconnaissance was to see if the North Col could be gained from the opposite, or eastern side. Later Mallory, that geographical perfectionist, would castigate himself for not discovering in 1921 that the East Rongbuk Glacier, a tributary ice stream that enters the Rongbuk proper by a V-shaped side valley two and a half miles above the terminus, would prove the royal road to the North Col. (Virtually all modern expeditions to Everest's north side, including Simonson's in 1999, haul their loads up a succession of camps on the East Rongbuk, establishing Camp IV on the North Col.) But that narrow, V-shaped entry of the East Rongbuk into the main glacier is all too easy to miss; and the existing Royal Geographical Society maps Mallory was using argued an entirely different structure of ridges on the northeast side of Everest.

To gain the North Col, then, Mallory and Bullock undertook a heroic end run to the north and east, skirting dozens of nameless subsidiary peaks, until they could find and ascend the Kharta Glacier. Before they could launch that effort—the second great prong of the reconnaissance—during a brief reunion with team leader Charles Howard-Bury, Mallory received some devastating information. The photographic plates he had labored for more than a month to expose, lugging a large camera to distant heights, were all blank, for he had been inserting them backwards. Once more, Mallory's chronic mechanical ineptitude had taken its toll. This "hideous error," as he called it in the expedition report, came as "an extremely depressing piece of news."

Mallory's attitude toward the "coolies" who were his only support in the reconnaissance, and without whom it could not have been undertaken, was a mixture of sympathetic curiosity and the cultural condescension that was endemic in his day. Recognizing the importance of being able to speak the porters' own language, he set himself to learning Tibetan. He shared with them the precious chocolates and nuts he received in the occasional parcel from England that made its way to Base Camp. Yet, as he watched the porters whom he had taught the basics of ice-craft apply their lessons for the first time, he wryly concluded, "It was not a convincing spectacle, as they made their way up with the ungainly movements of beginners." The sirdar, or head porter, Mallory dismissed in exasperation as "a whey-faced treacherous knave, whose sly and calculated villainy" (a matter of selling food rations for personal profit) threatened to wreck the reconnaissance.

The reunion with Howard-Bury and Raeburn, who had done little to help the expedition, only exasperated Mallory further. "I can't get over my dislike of him," he wrote Ruth of the team leader; and with regard to Raeburn, who had arrived grizzled and weak, "When he is not being a bore I feel moved to pity, but that is not often." The high-strung Mallory had even grown irritated with Bullock, his faithful partner in the reconnaissance. "We had rather drifted into that common superficial attitude between two people who live alone together," he wrote Ruth—"competitive and slightly quarrelsome, each looking out to see that he doesn't get done down in some small way by the other."

In early August, Mallory and Bullock worked their way up the

Kharta Glacier. So poor was local knowledge of this terrain that the team started southward on what would have been a wild goose chase, lured by a local tribesman's assertion that Chomolungma ("Mother Goddess of the Snows"), the Tibetan name for Everest, lay five days away in that direction. With his keen sense of direction, Mallory grew skeptical, and a cross-examination revealed that in local parlance, there were *two* Chomolungmas: the tribesman had directed the party toward Makalu, the world's fifth-highest mountain.

On August 7, Mallory fell ill, succumbing to a "weariness beyond muscular fatigue." For several days, Bullock and the porters pushed ahead, while Mallory tried to recuperate, lying in his sleeping bag, agonizing over the thought of Bullock reaching the North Col without him. His veering spirits plunged: at such moments, he wrote later, "I hated the thought of this expedition."

To Mallory's further dismay, it turned out the Kharta Glacier did not head on the slopes of Everest after all: the party would have to find and cross another high pass simply to get to the East Rongbuk Glacier. Finally in mid-August, buoyed by the unexpected addition of another climber, H. T. Morshead, who had hitherto been off on a lowland surveying mission, a rejuvenated Mallory and the steady Bullock crested the Lhakpa La, at 22,500 feet. At last they could see, only three miles away, across easy glacier, the slopes leading up to the North Col from the east. They looked climbable.

By now the monsoon hung so heavy on the Himalaya that it was snowing from eight to ten hours a day. On this interminable expedition, it would turn out to be a major accomplishment simply to reach the North Col, and thus pave the way for a true attempt in some future year. Yet now Mallory's spirits soared wildly, as he anticipated making an assault on the summit in September.

It can be argued that on all three Everest expeditions, Mallory underestimated the mountain. It was a common foible: during the early years, one crack European mountaineer after another misjudged the Himalaya in general. In 1895, Alfred Mummery, the finest British climber of the last quarter of the nineteenth century, a genius in the

Alps, had tried to climb 26,660-foot Nanga Parbat with only two team-mates and a pair of Gurkha porters. From the mountain, he jauntily wrote his wife, "I don't think there will be any serious mountaineering difficulties on Nanga. I fancy the ascent will be mainly a question of endurance." Treating the massive peak as though it were merely a slightly outsized version of Mont Blanc, Mummery vanished with the two Gurkhas on a reconnaissance of the west face. Their bodies were never found. Nanga Parbat would not be climbed until 1953.

Almost never during subsequent decades would a Himalayan mountain fall to the same expedition that first reconnoitered it (the glorious exception being the French on Annapurna in 1950). In his more judicious moments, Mallory recognized how weak the 1921 party was, how formidable Everest's defenses; but then he would stare again at his dotted line from the North Col to the summit and imagine himself sailing past each easy obstacle . . .

In topping the Lhakpa La, the trio of climbers had found the key to the mountain. But now, snow conditions were so atrocious that the party dared not attempt those three miles separating their farthest push from the North Col. For a full month, they played a demoralizing waiting game.

At last, on September 16, the weather changed, as the monsoon began to peter out. In the meantime, the full team had finally assembled on the Kharta Glacier. Mallory organized a carry that got eleven loads of supplies to the top of Lhakpa La. Four days later, he set out with Bullock and Edward Wheeler, the expedition's chief surveyor, to cross the East Rongbuk and climb to the North Col. By now, it had been four months since the party had set out from Darjeeling on horseback.

All through these latter weeks, Mallory's mood had characteristically swung between joy and despair. In his letters home, sometimes the expedition was "a thrilling business," at others "a fraud." "Our present job is to rub our noses against the impossible," he wrote in a despondent moment. Yet in a hopeful one, he blithely predicted, "It is now only a question of waiting for the weather and organizing our push to the summit."

On the morning of September 24, Mallory, Bullock, Wheeler, and three porters got a late start from the Lhakpa La: only Mallory had slept well the night before. The crossing of the East Rongbuk, however, and the climb to the North Col, was mostly a matter of "straightforward plugging," with the leader cutting about 500 steps in the ice just below the Col. They reached the saddle—that prized and elusive goal Mallory had been gazing at for almost three months—at 11:30 a.m.

The climb had been easy enough, but now the six men stood fully exposed to a bitter gale that tore across the gap: it "came in fierce gusts at frequent intervals, blowing up the powdery snow in a suffocating tourbillon." Wheeler was resolute about turning around at once; Bullock, though exhausted, knew how much the effort mattered to Mallory, and was willing to follow him a little farther. After a shouted discussion, the men staggered a few feet on, leaning against the gale, then "struggled back to shelter" on the lee side of an ice cliff. "The wind had settled the question," Mallory later wrote. Yet he felt in retrospect that he could have climbed another 2,000 vertical feet that day, wind or no wind.

As it was, Wheeler came close to serious frostbite, with his circulation restored in camp only by Mallory's rubbing his feet for hours; and Bullock lagged behind on the descent, stumbling into camp two hours after his friends, completely played out.

Thus ended the reconnaissance of 1921. As the party meandered back toward Darjeeling, Mallory was filled with a sense of failure. "We came back without accident, not even a frostbitten toe," he reported to Geoffrey Winthrop Young, trying to look on the bright side; but in the next breath, "It was a pitiful party at the last, not fit to be on a mountainside anywhere." Young wrote back, telling his protégé that "this end of the world is only using the word *success*," and putting Mallory's extraordinary achievement in the perspective that posterity has since granted it: "I can assure you that the colossal effort of lifting an entirely unsuitable party, at the first attempt, on a single pair of shoulders, not only onto the right line but well up it, against hopeless conditions, forms an episode by itself in the history of mountain exploration, and will only be the more appreciated the more time goes on."

On the voyage back to England, Mallory was burnt out and home-sick. "I'm tired of travelling and travellers," he wrote David Pye. "What I want to see is faces I know, and my own sweet home; afterwards, the solemn facades in Pall Mall, and perhaps Bloomsbury in a fog; and then an English river, cattle grazing in western meadows."

There was already talk of another expedition in the spring of 1922. The long summer reconnaissance had convinced Mallory that the only time to go to Everest was in April and May, before the monsoon. He also judged that "it's barely worth while trying again . . . without eight first-rate climbers."

Of a 1922 assault, however, at the moment he wanted no part. "I wouldn't go again next year . . . ," he wrote his sister Avie, "for all the gold in Arabia."

As it was, George Mallory would spend only three months at home before setting out on the second Everest expedition.

During those three months, Mallory gave some thirty lectures on Everest, and hurriedly wrote six chapters of the official expedition book. The mountain was never far from his mind, and as he penned the last chapter, called "The Route to the Summit," offering a step-by-step logistical brief for success on Everest, the obsession reclaimed him. At only thirty-five, Mallory was beginning to worry that he was past his climbing prime. And that vision, of the relatively easy stages by which a climber might angle up the north face to the northeast shoulder, then along the ridge to the summit, haunted his domestic hours.

By late winter, the Everest Committee had put together a team for the pre-monsoon season of 1922. Once more the pundits opted for leaders long in tooth and short on technical ability. General Charles Bruce, who had served much of his career in the army in India, was made leader, at the age of fifty-six. Colonel Edward Strutt, who was forty-eight, also an ex-soldier, was drafted as climbing leader. (In the 1930s, Strutt would become infamous as the curmudgeonly spokesman for a wholesale British retreat into climbing conservatism, as he deplored the bold technical breakthroughs being promulgated by Germans, Austrians, and Italians in the Alps, which culminated in the first ascent of the north face of the Eiger in 1938.)

Also on board, and well past his salad days, was Tom Longstaff, who held the record for the highest summit yet attained, when he had topped out on 23,360-foot Trisul, in the Garhwal Himalaya, in 1907. (No higher peak would be climbed for the next twenty-one years.)

In view of his brilliant performance the year before, it may seem odd that Mallory was not made climbing leader in 1922. Knowledge of the man's absentmindedness seems to have dimmed his prospects for an official leadership position. As Longstaff mordantly wrote to a colleague after the expedition, "Mallory is a very good stout hearted baby, but quite unfit to be placed in charge of anything, including himself."

Among the younger team members were Teddy Norton and Howard Somervell, who would prove so staunch in 1924, and Geoffrey Bruce, the general's game but inexperienced nephew. Rounding out the party was George Finch, a remarkable climber who would prove the equal of Mallory on this, his only shot at Everest. Finch had been rejected on spurious medical grounds in 1921, and he would later so alienate the Everest Committee as to preclude any chance of being invited in 1924. Chroniclers attribute much of Finch's difficulties to a vague sense on the committee's part that he had too heartily embraced the more ambitious European ideals of climbing in the Alps; in addition, Finch was not a member of the Alpine Club, and, having been educated in Switzerland, had thus by definition not attended the "right" schools.

In the months leading up to the 1922 expedition, the great debate was over the use of bottled oxygen. Finch, a born tinkerer, was the most avid proponent of using gas; Mallory, with his distrust of all things mechanical, the most ardent opponent, deriding what he called the "damnable heresy" of certain physiologists who theorized that humans would never ascend Everest without supplementary oxygen.

All in all, the 1922 party was many times stronger than the ragtag team of 1921. And at first, everything went like clockwork. Mallory and Bullock's 1921 reconnaissance had been so thorough that it had left only one side of Everest unexplored—the southern approaches, ranging out of forbidden Nepal. Mallory's analysis of the possible routes on the other three sides was so penetrating that the 1922 party needed to waste no further time in exploration.

Moving loads and camps steadily up the East Rongbuk Glacier, with an entourage not only of Tibetan porters but of Sherpas from Nepal, the team reached the North Col by May 13. Only six days later, all the necessary supplies were stocked at Camp IV, ready for a pair of summit pushes. At least two weeks of good weather, and maybe three, loomed before the monsoon would close down the mountain.

The plan called for Mallory, Somervell, H. T. Morshead, and Norton to make a first attempt without oxygen, to be followed, if they were unsuccessful, by Finch and Geoffrey Bruce breathing bottled gas. On May 20, the first quartet set out with porters from the North Col at 7:30 a.m. Every step they climbed probed ground where no one had ever been.

At once the cold assailed all four men. Modern climbers have long been dumbfounded on contemplating the primitive gear and clothing with which Mallory and his partners assaulted Everest in the 1920s. The sense of the inadequacy of that equipage was perhaps the single most powerful perception that struck the five climbers on May 1, 1999, when they beheld Mallory's body at 26,700 feet. It is thus worth pausing to note the passage in *The Assault on Mount Everest, 1922*, in which Mallory narrates the break the four men took at 24,200 feet to put on spare clothes and try to get warm:

> For my part, I added a light shetland "woolly" and a thin silk shirt to what I was wearing before under my closely woven cotton coat. As this outer garment, with knickers to match, was practically windproof, and a silk shirt too is a further protection against wind, with these two extra layers I feared no cold we were likely to meet. Morshead, if I

remember right, troubled himself no more at this time than to wrap a woollen scarf round his neck.

In general, Mallory's passages in the 1922 expedition book are full of details that, in light of what came to pass two years later, seem eerily to foreshadow the great drama of 1924. On the way up into the unknown that day in 1922, the four men came to a dicey slope where crampons would have been useful. (Modern climbers carry and usually wear crampons all the way to the summit.) Yet the men had left theirs at the North Col. Explains Mallory, "We sorely needed them now. And yet we had been right to leave them behind; for with their straps binding tightly around our boots we should not have had the smallest chance of preserving our toes from frostbite." (The leather boots of Mallory's day were soft and pliable. Modern climbers use plastic or nylon double boots so stiff that tightened straps pose no circulation problem.) The fact that, in 1924, Mallory and Irvine again left their crampons at the North Col bears crucially on their fate.

Similarly, as he described the route to the summit he had scouted for months in 1921, Mallory worried aloud, in the expedition book, about "the possibility of turning or of climbing direct certain prominent obstacles" along the summit ridge. Most prominent of all such obstacles would prove to be the ninety-foot-tall Second Step, at 28,230 feet. Climbing higher on May 20, Mallory could see that step as an unmistakable bump on the skyline far above him.

Not only the cold bothered the men; the thin air made them fuzzy-brained. In a clumsy moment, the rope dislodged Norton's pack, which he had laid in his lap during a rest stop. In Mallory's words:

> He was unprepared, made a desperate grab, and missed it. Slowly the round, soft thing gathered momentum from its rotation, the first little leaps down from one ledge to another grew to excited and magnificent bounds, and the precious burden vanished from sight.

• • •

With the pack was lost critical extra clothing.

At 2:00 p.m., around 25,000 feet, the tired men stopped to pitch camp. There was no level shelf, and the climbers wasted hours piling up stones to make tent platforms, only to abandon one site after another. Ever since 1922, climbers on the north side have had the greatest trouble establishing Camp V; even for Simonson's party in 1999, this was the camp the climbers dreaded, knowing a night there meant a struggle to catch any sleep.

At last the men got two tents droopily pitched, their floors so sloping that the upper climber in each tent rolled all night on top of the lower. Mallory took stock of his comrades. Worst off was Morshead, whose fingers and toes were in the first stages of serious frostbite. Though Morshead made no complaint, "He was obliged to lie down when we reached our camp and was evidently unwell." Mallory himself had frost-nipped his fingers as he cut steps up the slope where the men could have easily walked in crampons, and Norton had a frostbitten ear.

After a nearly sleepless night, the men set out at 8:00 a.m. on the twenty-first, still hopeful of reaching the summit. At once, the debilitated Morshead realized he could go no farther: he pleaded that his teammates continue, while he rested through the day in camp. The cold was even worse than the day before; Mallory had to stop, take off one boot, and let Norton rub his foot back into feeling. The going, across downward-tilting plates of dark shale, was made more treacherous by four to eight inches of fresh snow.

By midday, Mallory knew that he and his partners were going too slowly. At their very best, they were capable of gaining only 400 vertical feet an hour (in the Alps, Mallory was used to climbing 1,500 feet per hour without breaking a serious sweat). Their progress would only slow as the air got thinner. A simple "arithmetical calculation" made it plain that night would fall before the men could reach the summit.

Resolving to turn around at 2:15 p.m., the men accepted the mountain's victory. In the expedition narrative, Mallory seems gallantly resigned to defeat: "We were prepared to leave it to braver men to climb Mount Everest by night."

Again, how those words foreshadow! For in 1924, in all likelihood, Mallory and Irvine became those braver men.

At their high point, the three men ate a small lunch of chocolate, mint cake, raisins, and prunes; one of them (whose identity Mallory coyly camouflages in *The Assault on Mount Everest*) produced a pocket flask of brandy, from which each of them took a restorative nip. Then they started down.

With a barometer reading adjusted by a theodolite observation, Mallory fixed his high point at 26,985 feet. In *First on Everest: The Mystery of Mallory & Irvine*, Audrey Salkeld and Tom Holzel argue cogently that the true altitude the three men reached on June 21 was only about 26,000 feet. No matter: it was the highest anyone had yet been on earth.

The prudence of their turnaround would emerge late that afternoon. By 4:00 p.m., Norton, Somervell, and Mallory had regained Camp V. There Morshead declared he was feeling well. The four men roped together, then headed down the 2,000 feet toward Camp IV on the North Col. Mallory took the lead, for, as the strongest of the four men, he readily assumed the tiring task of cutting steps for his partners (a much more awkward task going down than ascending).

Suddenly Morshead, coming third on the rope, slipped on a steep slope. His fall pulled an unprepared Norton, last on the rope, out of his steps, and the two of them pulled Somervell loose. The three plunged helpless toward the void 3,500 feet above the East Rongbuk Glacier.

On the verge of cutting a step, Mallory had time only to drive the pick of his axe into the snow and pass the rope over its head, and time to anticipate one of two outcomes. As he put it in the expedition book, "In ninety-nine cases out of a hundred either the belay will give or the rope will break." Miraculously, neither happened now. The pull came not in one tremendous jerk, but accordion-fashion, as each falling climber absorbed the pull of the one below. Mallory belayed with grim resolve: the rope "gripped the metal like a hawser on a bollard," but the pick held.

Almost never in mountaineering history has one man held three falling companions with nothing more solid than an ice axe belay. The rare instances have become legendary deeds. Mallory's astounding belay has not—in part because he was excruciatingly modest about the accident. In *The Assault on Mount Everest*, he not only avoided identifying the man who slipped, he disguised his own identity as the miracle belayer. The four climbers were tagged only as "the third man," "the leader," etc. Only in a letter to Ruth did Mallory make clear who played which role. Even then, he blamed himself as much as his teammates: "I hadn't realised then how shaky Morshead was and had cut rather poor steps."

Though no one was hurt in the all-but-fatal fall, as they staggered in to Camp IV, at 11:30 p.m., Morshead was ravaged with exhaustion. He had been taking ten-minute rests after feeble two-minute bursts of clumping downward, until Norton and Mallory had to take turns propping him up with a shoulder for his arm and a hand around his waist, all but doing his walking for him.

By the time the four men made it back to Camp III the next day, Morshead's fingers had swollen and turned black with frostbite. The men had also become severely dehydrated. Somervell confessed to downing seventeen mugsful of tea; Mallory guessed the man had drunk even more.

Two days later, on May 24, George Finch set out on a second attempt, using oxygen. Because of the physical conditions of all the other team members, he had only one choice for partner—the plucky Geoffrey Bruce, who had climbed no real mountains before Everest.

Nonetheless, the two men set out full of optimism, telling each other, "Of course, we shall get to the top." Finch believed oxygen would make all the difference.

In the end, the pair's struggle up the north face turned into a fight for their lives. At Camp V, they held on to their tent all night while a gale tried to tear them from the mountainside. They waited out the next day, as the storm dispersed, then, with little food or water left, stretched their sortie into a third day as they headed up. Starting at 6:30 a.m., they passed the high point of Mallory, Norton, and Somervell and added 500 feet to the world altitude record. Oxygen *had* made the difference, for, thanks to the storm, Finch and Bruce were far more worn out as they launched their summit attempt than their four teammates had been on their own thrust on May 20.

The choice to turn around was agonizing for Finch, but it was as canny a decision as Mallory's had been. As Finch wrote in the expedition book, "I knew that if we were to persist in climbing on, even if only for another 500 feet, we should not both get back alive." In the end, Bruce's feet were so badly frostbitten that he had to be sledged part of the way down from the North Col.

Finch and Bruce's gutsy push not only set the new altitude record, to a certain extent it eclipsed the luster of Norton, Somervell, and Mallory's brave attempt four days before. And it convinced Mallory for the first time that bottled oxygen, far from a "damnable heresy," might be the key to climbing Everest.

By June 1, the 1922 expedition had accomplished extraordinary things, reaching 26,500 feet and making known for the first time the secrets of the upper north face. The team had exercised such hubris at the cost of nothing worse than some cases of frostbite (Morshead, the worst afflicted, would lose one toe and six fingertips). Had the expedition now packed up and gone home, as most of its members were inclined to do, the venture would have been hailed in England as a grand success.

But fate was not to let the 1922 party off so easily. As May turned to June, and still the monsoon delayed its arrival, Mallory's obsession turned his thoughts upward once more. He talked his teammates into a third, last-ditch attempt.

As it was, most of them were too worn down even to make another stab. Finch gamely set out, but, unrecovered from his ordeal of May 24–26, tossed in the towel at Camp I.

On June 7, Mallory, Somervell, and teammate Colin Crawford led fourteen porters up toward the North Col. An abundance of new snow had blanketed the slope, but Mallory found the conditions ideal for step-kicking. As the party neared the crest, Somervell led up a gentle corridor. Wrote Mallory, "We were startled by an ominous sound, sharp, arresting, violent, and yet somehow soft like an explosion of untamped gunpowder. I had never before on a mountain-side heard such a sound; but all of us, I imagine, knew instinctively what it meant."

From a hundred feet above the party, an avalanche had broken loose. The three Englishmen, highest on the slope, and the porters nearest them were swept off their feet and knocked a short distance down the slope, but came to rest and dug themselves out. The porters lower on the slope were caught in the avalanche and hurled over a forty- to sixty-foot ice cliff. Their teammates scrambled down the slope and frantically dug in the avalanche debris below the cliff. Six porters were found dead, more likely from the impact of the fall than by smothering under the snow. The body of a seventh was never found.

Overcome with sorrow, the ten survivors stumbled down to Camp III. Mallory was struck by the Sherpas' forbearance in this tragedy:

> The surviving porters who had lost their friends or brothers behaved with dignity, making no noisy parade of the grief they felt. We asked them whether they wished to go up and bring down the bodies for orderly burial. They preferred to leave them where they were.

As the team trudged out from the mountain, Howard Somervell agonized, "Why, oh, why could not one of us Britishers have shared their fate?" The blame for the accident was loaded onto Mallory's shoulders, not only for pushing the late attempt, but because he had approached the North Col in dubious snow conditions. Tom Longstaff, who had already left Base Camp for home when the accident occurred, was unsparing. "To attempt such a passage in the Himalaya after new snow is idiotic," he wrote a colleague two months later.

In the expedition narrative, Mallory painfully retraced his party's steps toward the disaster, wondering out loud whether he ought to have recognized the danger. "More experience, more knowledge might perhaps have warned us not to go there," he wrote, bewildered. "One never can know enough about snow."

Mallory did nothing, however, to shirk his responsibility, writing Geoffrey Winthrop Young, "And I'm to blame. . . . Do you know that sickening feeling that one can't go back and have it undone . . . ?" For the rest of his shortened life, he harbored a black pool of guilt about the catastrophe. Clare Millikan believes that the chief reason Mallory went back to Everest in 1924 was the idea that success might somehow mitigate the tragedy he had brought upon the seven faithful porters.

Mallory's eternal friend and mentor, Geoffrey Winthrop Young, tried to gentle his return, insisting the blame for the accident could not be laid on any man, but on "that shadow of huge, dangerous 'chance,'" and reminding him, "You took your full share, a leading share, in the risk. In the war we had to do worse: we had to *order* men into danger at times when we could not share it."

All this gave Mallory faint comfort. At home, he brooded about the expedition, even as he cast about looking for a new job. In the interim, he undertook a three-month tour of America, lecturing on Everest. The tour was a financial failure, Mallory disliked most of what he saw in the United States, and he was homesick for Ruth and his children. Clare was now seven, Beridge six, John only two. Since Clare had been born, thanks to the war and Everest, Mallory had been home less than half her days.

In the spring of 1923, Mallory landed a job teaching history to working men and women in Cambridge University's extension school. He plunged into this new profession with enthusiasm, commuting between Cambridge and the family home in Holt. During these months, his relationship with Ruth was strained. As evidence, we have only certain ambiguous phrases in the letters. Yet the bedrock loyalty of each for the other was not seriously shaken. In October 1923, he moved his family to Cambridge; there, in Herschel House, he and Ruth set out with a will to furnish and beautify the ideal domicile.

Everest was never far from Mallory's thoughts. Once again, he had been writing chapters for the official expedition book. And the very lectures he gave in America were predicated on explaining to the uninitiated the appeal of trying to reach the highest point on earth, from the famous "Because it is there" quip to more extended—if equally gnomic—rationales, such as these lines from one of his American speeches:

> I suppose we go to Mount Everest, granted the opportunity, because—in a word—we can't help it. Or, to state the matter rather differently, because we are mountaineers. . . . To refuse the adventure is to run the risk of drying up like a pea in its shell.

In a thoughtful unpublished essay he wrote about this time, called "Men and Mountains: The Gambler," Mallory faced squarely the question of danger and risk in the mountains. Once more, his words seem eerily to foreshadow the future:

> It is clear that the stake [the mountaineer] risks to lose is a great one with him: it is a matter of life and death. . . . To win the game he has first to reach the mountain's summit—but, further, he has to descend in safety. The more difficult the way and the more numerous the dangers, the greater is his victory.

In closing, Mallory grappled with the inevitability of disasters such as the one that had befallen him below the North Col: "But when I say that our sport is a hazardous one, I do not mean that when we climb mountains there is a large chance that we shall be killed, but that we are surrounded by dangers which will kill us if we let them."

That British mountaineers would return to Everest, if not in 1923, then in the spring of 1924, had become a foregone conclusion. And for all his ambivalence, it seems in retrospect inevitable that Mallory would join the expedition. The mountain had become his destiny.

Only months after he had taken his university extension job, he asked Cambridge to give him half a year's leave on half pay; his alma mater was only too glad to comply. Yet as Mallory faced Mount Everest for the third time, it was not with the joyous anticipation of 1921 or '22, but rather with a dark fatalism. To his Cambridge and Bloomsbury friend Geoffrey Keynes, he confided what he dared not tell Ruth: "This is going to be more like war than mountaineering. I don't expect to come back."

from Mountain Men

by Mick Conefrey
and Tim Jordan

*The story of Maurice Wilson's 1934 attempt to climb
Everest has been told as farce and as tragedy. Mick Conefrey and Tim Jordan included their version of the tale in a
recent (2001) collection of profiles of mountaineers.*

The first thing he saw was a boot. A little further on was another,
then a heap of dark fabric partly covered by snow, which he
guessed was a tent. He turned and shouted that he had found the
supply dump from the last expedition, and his companion, who
had been resting on a stone, rose wearily to his feet and began trudging
up the slope behind him.

The dark shape was only a few yards away and the first man didn't
wait for the other to catch up. He was almost standing over it before
he realized what it was, and for a moment he struggled to contain his
shock. The body was frozen solid. Lying on its left side, the knees were
drawn up to the chest and one hand reached out towards a stone, to
which a guy-rope was tied. It trailed off into the snow and no doubt to
the remains of a tent ripped off him by the wind. A mauve pullover,

grey flannel trousers, long woollen underwear and bare feet, but no sign of a sleeping bag: why, then, had he removed his boots?

As a doctor, Charles Warren thought that he was used to the sight of the dead, but this was closer to home. After all, the man had died trying to do exactly what *he* was there to do: climb Mount Everest or at least part of it. He had known immediately whose body it was; it couldn't be anyone else. They had all read about him in the papers, first in 1933, when he had set off for the mountain—something of a comic figure then, larger than life—and again the next year, when he was reported missing. It was Maurice Wilson, the eccentric.

'I say!' Warren shouted down the slope. 'It's that fellow Wilson!' and soon the other members of the party were gathering around. Warren wondered if they ought to hide their discovery from the porters, but it was too late. They had already come to see what the sahibs were looking at. One of them backed swiftly away and vomited, but the rest, to the Englishmen's relief, seemed to accept the matter casually. Before disturbing the body they searched the snow around it. The guy-rope was indeed attached to the shreds of a tent. A small rucksack lay nearby, a Union Jack apparently signed by girlfriends, a gold pen and pencil, film canisters, a ring made of elephant hair—a lucky charm, perhaps—and at last, what they hoped most of all to find: a diary. His sleeping bag turned up almost 100 yards away. It was extraordinary that the wind had somehow stripped it from him.

The men agreed that if they buried him where he lay the movement of the glacier would soon undo their work. After some discussion they decided to wrap Wilson in the remains of his tent and carry him over to a crevasse. Having cut away the lip of a suitable one, they mumbled a prayer and, like a burial at sea, slid the shrouded body into the depths. 'We all raised our hats,' Warren wrote in his journal, 'and I think that everyone was rather upset over the business.'

Only a short distance up the slope they came to the food dump left by the last great Everest expedition two years earlier, which had clearly travelled in some style. As they helped themselves to jam and sweet-meats, cakes and Carlsbad plums from Fortnum and Mason, the men took it in turns to read out Wilson's diary. They knew something of his background, but the little notebook conveyed something altogether different from what they had imagined. It proved to be, in Warren's words, 'a most extraordinary revelation of monomania and determination of purpose.'

Maurice Wilson was born in Bradford in 1898, the third son of a manager at a woollens mill, but the true beginning of his story was the First World War. Aged sixteen when it started, he enlisted in a local infantry regiment on his eighteenth birthday and was soon selected for officer training. A portrait photograph of Wilson in uniform shows a burly youth with a strong jaw and large features; he looks into the camera with an open, expectant expression. Commissioned as a second lieutenant, he had been in France for only a few weeks when his regiment was thrust forward to defend the line at the fourth battle of Ypres. A ferocious German assault almost engulfed the machine-gun unit he commanded and, by the time it was driven back, every man around him was either dead or wounded. Wilson, however, had not received a scratch. He was awarded the Military Cross for conspicuous gallantry and mentioned by name in the newspapers.

A short time later the positions were reversed. In almost exactly the same location on the battlefield Wilson led a charge against an enemy machine-gun and was seriously wounded. Hit in the chest and arm, he was near death when a stretcher party retrieved him. His brief experience of the trenches was over. Evacuated to England, it took him a year to recover from his injuries, though his left arm was to give sudden bouts of pain for the rest of his life.

For that reason alone he was unable to forget the war. How it influenced his personality is impossible to know for certain, but two things were to shape his later life: an interest in the human body's mysterious powers of recuperation and a conviction that God had spared him for a purpose—if he could only discover it.

Like many of his generation, Wilson was unable to settle back into civilian life. After working briefly in his father's office, he moved to the brighter lights of London, but it only increased his restlessness and he began to take bolder steps. He emigrated to New York, grew impatient when he could find nothing there that he wanted to do and, after only a few months, crossed the continent to San Francisco, with the same result. It was only when he had travelled as far from home as any Englishman could—to New Zealand—that he decided to remain and make the best of it. A series of peculiar jobs followed. He took to the road as a salesman of weighing scales, then as the purveyor of a unique restorative medicine. He prepared and bottled it himself, but the recipe was the invention of another man—or so he told his customers. The scheme was a failure and his next job was more conventional. He bought a small farm, where his energy, pragmatism and eagerness to learn served him well, until he grew tired of the isolation. After eighteen months in the country he moved into Wellington and used the money from the sale of his farm to buy a women's dress shop.

After all, he had some background in the trade. The shop flourished and at last Wilson seemed to be blending into the local community as a successful independent businessman. He married twice and separated twice; without a wife or family to support, he saved a small fortune, but was beginning to realize that this kind of success did not make him happy. It only proved what he knew already: he was capable of succeeding in whatever he turned his hand to. A *driving purpose* in life was what he wanted, and selling dresses to the women of Wellington was not it. He had run the shop for several years when he abruptly sold up and took a boat for England. He was both dropping out and returning home.

The long voyage via India and the Suez Canal completed his circumnavigation of the globe. His fellow passengers, it seemed to Wilson, presented a transitory microcosm of humanity: rich and poor, purposeful and itinerant, ordinary and exotic. A party of Indian yogis joined the ship in Bombay and Wilson engaged them in conversation; he was curious about their beliefs. Quiet and reserved, the yogis responded politely to the expansive Englishman's persistent questions and, the more he listened, the more he wanted to learn. Wilson was no theologian, but he believed earnestly in the transcending power of faith. He liked what he heard about the purification of mind and body, concentration on a single object and the generation of supernatural powers. Where all this belonged in the yogis' philosophical system he soon forgot, but the fragments, a series of resonant phrases, stayed with him.

Wilson had been away for a decade. His father was dead, his mother an invalid and his brothers had become strangers. Life in Bradford had passed him by. While he was casting around for something to do in London, Wilson began to realize that he was not well. He had lost weight and was plagued by a persistent cough that seemed to be getting worse. Aimless, disorientated and now ill, he felt that his life was approaching a crisis. But everything was about to change.

When Wilson arrived in London he had tried to buy a second-hand car. He struck up a friendship with the dealer and eventually his wife. Leonard and Enid Evans became used to regular visits from the garrulous, opinionated, yet rather lonely Yorkshireman. They knew that he was ill, most probably from consumption, and that he would not see a doctor; it was typical of him to reject advice. Suddenly his visits stopped and they heard nothing. Several months passed before he called again and when he did, a very different man breezed into the house. There was no trace of the cough and his eyes were shining. He was utterly revitalized. He had important news for them, he said, but it could wait a little longer. They celebrated at a restaurant, continued to a nightclub and finally, in the small hours, Wilson told them the following story.

He had been not to a doctor, but a faith healer. The man lived in a Mayfair flat and had once suffered from a disease that his doctors diagnosed as terminal; they had given him three months to live. That was seventeen years ago, Wilson said, and the man was now in perfect health. He had discovered a means of curing himself and had been sharing the knowledge ever since with a succession of visitors to his home. More than a hundred people had been cured by his method and Wilson was now one of them. He had followed it to the letter and the result was nothing short of miraculous. It was simple: he had fasted for thirty-five days, drinking only small quantities of water. His bodily and spiritual maladies had drained away. Once purged, he had prayed to God to be born again.

Wilson would repeat the story many times, but he never named the man and there seems to be no evidence of his existence other than Wilson's word. In New Zealand, as a travelling salesman of a restorative medicine, he had claimed the recipe was the invention of another man; it may have been, but it is equally plausible that Wilson invented him and repeated the strategy in his story of the mysterious faith healer of Mayfair. He had learned about purgation from the yogis, but, whatever its provenance, the treatment had worked for Wilson and he believed in it. He had fasted and prayed and it had made him well.

But this was not the most important part of the news that he was bursting to tell his friends. What had happened to him, he said, could happen to others, if only they knew what faith could achieve. He realized now what he wanted to do with the rest of his life: to tell the world about his discovery. And he knew just how to do it: 'I believe that if a man has sufficient faith he can accomplish *anything*. I haven't gone mad and I haven't got religious mania. But I've got a theory to prove and I intend to try and prove it. I'll show the world what faith can do! I'll perform some task so hard and so exacting that it could only be carried out by someone aided with Divine help. *I'll climb Mountain Everest alone!*'

It is not difficult to see where the idea came from: Wilson had been reading the newspapers. It was towards the end of 1932 and Everest, after a long absence, was back on the front pages. Eight years earlier, the first serious attempt to climb the mountain ended in mystery and disaster when George Mallory and Andrew Irvine disappeared close to the summit. Since then, the Dalai Lama had refused to give permission for climbers to approach the mountain through Tibet, but in 1932 he was persuaded to change his mind and preparations were under way for an expedition the following summer. The party included many of Britain's outstanding mountaineers and the nation's hopes were high.

A second Everest project aroused even greater interest: the Nepalese government had granted permission for an expedition to attempt the world's first *flight* over Everest. The brainchild of a committee of British aristocrats and high-ranking military officers, it was financed by Lady Houston and would be piloted, among others, by the Marquess of Douglas and Clydesdale. The project was undertaken not 'to perform a sensational feat,' the committee insisted, 'but for the most sober purposes.' There was 'much to learn about the down-draughts and up-currents caused by the deflection of the wind on the highest peaks.' Nevertheless, the Gaumont-British Picture Corporation was planning a film about the expedition for general cinema release. It was an age of aviation heroics, when papers reported the latest feats and records set on an almost daily basis. In spite of the committee's pious statements of intent, the proposed flight over the highest mountain in the world promised to be the most sensational yet and it made headlines everywhere.

Wilson knew that Everest commanded public attention and he selected his 'task' for no other reason. He had no mountaineering experience and had taken no interest in the subject until then; if he had, he might have preferred to try swimming the Channel or walking to Cape Town instead. But his mind was made up. Influenced no doubt by reports of the Lady Houston expedition, he told the Evanses that the best way to reach the mountain was in an aeroplane. It was simply a matter of crash-landing on the lower slopes and then walking to the summit.

Leonard and Enid listened patiently. Interviewed in the 1950s by Wilson's biographer, Dennis Roberts, they said that they were immediately sceptical about his story of a faith healer in Mayfair and yet moved by the account of his own recovery. It was miraculous. But when he began to talk about Everest, they were appalled. They pointed out to Wilson the two gigantic flaws in his plan: he wasn't a mountaineer and he certainly didn't know how to fly an aeroplane. 'I know,' he replied with a confident grin, 'but I can learn.'

It seemed to Roberts a positive measure of their friendship with Wilson that the couple did *not* try to talk him out of it. Leonard, in fact, was to become the manager of Wilson's affairs. According to him, Wilson toyed with the idea of approaching members of Lady Houston's team to ask if he might parachute on to Everest from the wing of one of their planes. He doubted, however, that they would agree to it and decided that his first idea was a far better one: he would fly himself to the mountain.

Within a short time Wilson had bought a two-year-old Gypsy Moth biplane and an impressive pilot's outfit of the kind he might have seen in the movies, including leather jacket, breeches, gaiters and improbably large boots. He moved to lodgings near the London Aero Club at Stag Lane and promptly enrolled on a course of flying lessons. The instructor's first impression of the new pupil striding towards him was of a large man with an eager grin and a glint in his eye, apparently dressed for horse riding.

He soon discovered that Wilson liked to handle the controls vigorously. Wildly enthusiastic and in a hurry to learn, he had to be tamed as much as taught and needed twice as many lessons as a typical pupil before his instructor considered him safe, or safe enough, to take to the skies alone. Meanwhile he became a well-known character around the aerodrome. The name 'Ever Wrest' was painted on the nose of his plane and he made no secret of his plans. All attempts at dissuasion were dismissed with the same theatrical bravado, as Wilson declared that he would fly to India or die in the attempt. When he was not in the air he was to be seen marching around the field's perimeter in pursuit of physical fitness. He was known to be on a peculiar diet and stayed away from the clubhouse bar. 'I don't need a drink,' he told his instructor, 'I'm an apple and nuts man!'

By now the Wilson story was beginning to appear in the newspapers. He was delighted, of course, to co-operate with journalists and to pose for photographs in front of 'Ever Wrest.' With goggles on his forehead, he would tilt his head to one side and look directly at the camera, his large, animated features presenting a study in thoughtful determination. He had already devised a system of wires for photographing himself on the summit of Mount Everest.

Up to a point, he was realistic about the equipment he needed. 'Ever Wrest' was refitted with strengthened undercarriage and extra fuel tanks. He bought a tent and sleeping bag of the kind specially designed for the official Everest expedition, an altimeter, ice-axe and a selection of maps. With his preparations already at an advanced stage, he took five weeks off from flying practice in order to learn how to climb. If lessons in mountaineering were available at that time, he didn't bother to find a teacher, preferring instead to go alone to the Lake District and roam across the hills. Wilson had proved, and would prove further, that he was a practical and adaptable man. The plans for his journey, as far as it extended to India, were reasonably well thought-out. Great risks were involved in flying alone in a frail aircraft over vast tracts of ocean and desert and he understood them. But he took a quite different attitude to Everest. He made no serious attempt to learn about the environment. He might have approached veterans of previous expeditions but chose not to. His 'training' in the Lake District was irrelevant to high-altitude mountaineering; he didn't *try* to learn how to cut steps in ice or use crampons. None of this mattered to Wilson. The mountain was simply part of an equation: if he had sufficient faith, he would climb it.

As the date of departure neared, press interest increased and when he met two reporters by chance at Piccadilly Circus, he took the opportunity of stealing a headline by telling them how he had spent the afternoon: making a parachute jump over central London. With affected nonchalance he said that he had done it on impulse, to test his nerve for the adventure ahead. The story may have been an invention, but the newspaper took it at face value and within a few days a letter from the Air Ministry arrived at Wilson's lodgings to remind him that the stunt was illegal. He was rather proud of the letter and decided that irritating the authorities could add a new string to his bow.

On 23 April 1933, the eve of his departure, he decided to fly to Bradford and say goodbye to his mother. A couple of hours later, he was hanging upside-down in his cockpit having crash-landed his plane in a field outside the city. He had stalled the engine in mid air.

Attempting to glide on to a large field, he had missed it by a considerable distance, flown through a hedge, spun on to a country lane and flipped over. Within minutes press photographers were at the scene and Wilson, having released his harness, clattered to the ground and dusted himself down, was assuming a familiar pose for the camera: thoughtful determination. But the aircraft behind him was a wreck and would take weeks to repair.

A new departure date was set: 21 May. Meanwhile the Air Ministry, responding to the stories in the press, wrote another letter to Wilson. The Deputy Director wanted to know if the reports of his intention to fly to Mount Everest had any foundation; if they did, Wilson was to understand that previous permission from the Nepalese government was required—and he was most unlikely to get it. Wilson responded by pointing out that the Houston expedition was at that moment making flights over Nepal; why, then, shouldn't he? The reply came very quickly. Wilson, it was clear to the Ministry, had 'completely misunderstood the position.' Permission for the Houston expedition had been obtained by long and elaborate negotiations, and was subject to many conditions. *His* case was quite different. The flight would not be allowed.

He was keen to tell reporters of this development, announcing that he would defy any attempt to stop him. When the day of departure came, he brought a telegram with him to Stag Lane airfield: it was a final message from the Air Ministry, forbidding any flight into Nepal. He tore it up in front of the press and strode purposefully towards his aircraft. A small crowd had gathered, most of them newspapermen and photographers. Leonard and Enid Evans signed Wilson's 'flag of friendship'—a small Union Jack—and he started the engine. As he taxied away, his instructor watched with his head in his hands: Wilson was aligning his plane with the wind *behind* him. A nervous moment followed, when it seemed to onlookers that the accelerating aircraft would never leave the ground, but at the last moment it lifted, avoiding a hedge at the end of the runway by a very small margin. And that was the last any of them saw of Wilson.

One of the newspaper reports of the event carried a short interview with Wilson's mother. He had left without saying goodbye. She had no doubt that he was afraid of upsetting her. 'I have one great fear,' she told them. 'His left arm is practically useless. I keep asking myself, can it stand the strain? He can't carry anything heavy with it.' When a reporter pressed her on whether she believed that her son could climb Mount Everest alone, she wouldn't answer directly: 'My son,' she said, 'is a very brave man.'

The press regarded Wilson as an accident waiting to happen and, when he did not appear along the route he had advertised, they reported him missing. In fact he had simply changed his mind. Rather than crossing the Alps, he had decided to skirt around them via Lake Geneva and was approaching Italy by way of Marseilles and the Côte d'Azur. Navigation was proving easier than he had expected and he was in high spirits. Four days into his journey he wrote to the Evanses from Rome: 'So far this trip is a piece of cake. I'm now able to keep the plane on course without constantly looking at the compass. Funny how it comes to you.'

Crossing the Mediterranean from Sicily, he made his way in stages along the featureless coastal deserts of North Africa. The newspapers reported his arrival at Tripoli and then Cairo, just as they reported the progress of several other remarkable flights in the spring of 1933. Departing at almost the same time as Wilson were pilots attempting the first non-stop flight from London to Darwin and the first from New York to Baghdad, while a third was aiming to set a new record time for London to the Cape. But these were experienced aviators who knew what they were doing; the special appeal of Wilson was that he did not. The spotlight of the press was trained on his solitary plane.

By reaching Cairo, Wilson had already exceeded expectations. It may have been for that reason that he began to find himself restrained by the long arm of the British Establishment. His permit for flying across Persia—which he had previously arranged to collect in Egypt— was now mysteriously unavailable. Delayed but undeterred, he flew as far as Baghdad before diverting south east to avoid Persia. From Basra he followed the Gulf as far as the British Protectorate of Bahrain. Here the authorities tried a little harder to block his onward journey. On the orders of the British Consul, he was refused permission to refuel. An official at the consulate explained that as all easterly landing strips within range of his aircraft were in Persian territory, he could not be allowed to continue without a permit. It was suggested that he should fly to the nearby Persian town of Bushire and apply for a permit on landing—a sly proposition that infuriated Wilson as he knew that his aircraft would immediately be impounded. Agreeing instead to retrace his route to Basra, he was accompanied to the airstrip by the official and allowed to refuel. Once in the air, however, he turned his plane towards India.

The airstrip at Gwadar, the westernmost in India, was not *within* the range of his aircraft but almost precisely at its estimated limit. It was a reckless gamble, but Wilson was lucky: when he touched down, after more than nine hours in the air, darkness was only minutes away and his fuel gauge read zero. In spite of further attempts to deny him fuel, Wilson now made his way in a series of steps across India until he reached Purnea, the base used by the Houston expedition.

His arrival in India seems to have surprised everyone except Wilson himself. By any standards it was an unlikely achievement for a novice pilot, not least because he had outwitted a devious bureaucracy. Touching down in Karachi, Hyderabad and Jodhpur, he received a celebrity's welcome. Journalists were keener than ever to interview him; the quotable crank from Stag Lane was providing a far better story than any of them had hoped and it promised to run on. He was said to have challenged Gandhi to a fast; reports wired from India to the *Daily Express* looked forward to the next instalment:

> Maurice Wilson, the young Bradford airman and rock climber who has undertaken the amazing adventure of a combined aerial and foot climb of Everest, gave some remarkable details of his plans when he landed here after flying from England. 'Enough rice and dates to last fifty

days will be in my rucksack when I begin to climb Everest after landing on the mountain some 14,000 feet up. One trained man can succeed where a large group has failed. For ten months I have trained, testing foods and special types of fasts until I have found that the best procedure is to take one meal a day; this will enable me to breathe deep down in my stomach, taking in a vastly increased supply of oxygen.' His ten months of training and experimenting have given him the utmost confidence. He considers his optimism fully justified, as he has read every known book and studied every known map of Everest in that period. 'There is no stunt about it,' Mr Wilson reiterated. 'Mine is a carefully planned expedition.'

He emphasized the point by displaying his specialist equipment:

Mr Wilson produced various warm garments made specially to order for him; all were of the lightest woollen material. His whole kit weighs only forty pounds, including the tent, sleeping bag, outer suit of warm light material lined with silk and made to resist wind, sun and water, and a series of woollen cardigans. The unique feature of his climbing outfit is his boots, made with insulated cork, running from toe to heel.

In spite of the Air Ministry's warnings Wilson believed that he would obtain a permit to fly over Nepal, if he were tenacious enough in applying for it. But he was wrong. For three weeks he tried by every means to win a sympathetic hearing from either the British or Nepalese authorities—and failed. Nor could he make the flight illegally: the police had impounded his plane on arrival in Purnea and were keeping it under surveillance, its fuel tanks empty. The monsoon was coming and Wilson knew that he was checkmated. He would have to find another way.

He decided to sell his aircraft and forget about Nepal. He would travel to Darjeeling and approach the mountain on foot by the route of previous expeditions, through Sikkim and Tibet. He had missed his chance to make the climb that year, but would be ready by the spring. With £500 in his pocket from the sale of 'Ever Wrest' to a tea planter, he set off from Purnea and drifted out of the news.

Arriving in Darjeeling by its famous twisting railway, Wilson was relieved to be away from the heat and frustration of Purnea. It was cool and misty and he was making a fresh start. The news that the official British expedition had narrowly failed to reach the summit delighted him. With the whole winter before him, there was time to fast and pray, get fit and make plans. When the authorities informed him that he would not be given a permit to enter Sikkim and Tibet on foot, he was not unduly worried, nor did it bother him that the police were clearly keeping tabs on his whereabouts. He was confident of giving them the slip in due course, if he had to. For the time being he resumed his physical training by taking long daily walks through the hills and embarked on a diet of porridge and vegetables. In the three weeks leading up to Christmas it became a total fast.

To reach the mountain Wilson needed an ally, and for a while it seemed that Karma Paul, the interpreter who had served on each of the last three Everest expeditions, might help him. He was a well-known and respected figure among both British climbers and the local authorities and Wilson hoped to use his influence to secure permission for his journey—by a direct appeal to the Dalai Lama himself. Karma Paul was eager, at first, to help, but the more time he spent with Wilson the less he liked him. According to his biographer, drawing on information from the Evanses, Wilson was 'a difficult man to get on with,' but he does not elaborate and perhaps did not need to. He was an obsessive and a loner. Although he won many admirers for his courage and perseverance, he formed few friendships. No doubt Karma Paul discovered that he could be stubborn and manipulative, and at some point he must also have realized that the Englishman knew little of mountaineering. Wiser not to be involved, he decided.

The loss of Karma Paul was a setback, but Wilson was used to impediments by now and each new one seemed only to provoke his determination. Dismissing any chance of making his journey legally, he considered another plan. Priests, he had learned, were allowed to travel freely between Tibet and India. He was a good deal larger than the average Tibetan, but, if he could obtain the right costume and travelled only at night, he believed he had a good chance of getting away with it. Fortunately, he was able to find three Sherpa porters from the recent Everest expedition who were willing, if he paid them well enough, to go along with his scheme. They had even agreed to help him procure an elaborate disguise. He described it in a letter to the Evanses:

> Did I look sweet? Chinese brocaded waistcoat in gold, with golden buttons at the side. Slacks of cheap dark blue cotton. The worst of it is I have to hide the lovely waistcoat under a huge mantle, about six inches longer than a nightdress. Next come about four yards of bright red silk girdle. They showed me how to walk with one arm outside the mantle, disclosing the brilliant plumage of the waistcoat underneath. Then came the hat, furnished with large earflaps; dark glasses to hide my honest blue eyes. Then I had to spoil the 'I'm Jackie' feeling with a pair of oversized hobnail boots.

The final touch was an attractive rice-paper umbrella. He bought a small pony and put word around that he was joining a tiger hunt and would be away from his lodgings for a couple of weeks. Knowing the police would be suspicious, he paid six months' advance rent; by the time they discovered his subterfuge, he intended to be well out of their reach. 'It would just be too humorous,' he wrote, 'to be returned to Darjeeling under police escort.'

On the night of 21 March he packed his climbing gear, dressed up and slipped out into the back streets. The Sherpas Tsering, Rinzing and Tewang were waiting for him in the woods.

They had been walking for only a few hours when they encountered their first policeman. It was too late to take evasive action. Wilson positioned the umbrella in front of his face and bent his knees as they passed, hoping to reduce his height; he wondered if the policeman was staring at him but he didn't dare look back and a moment later was breathing a heavy sigh of relief. Wilson knew that they would have to be more cautious and when another uniform loomed suddenly in the moonlight he leapt off the road and lay face down in the bushes, emerging a few minutes later badly stung by nettles.

They camped at dawn. After a second night's travelling they found themselves within a mile of a small village. As they rested by the road-side, the inquisitive villagers gathered around. Wilson hid his face in his elbow and hoped no one would notice his unusual boots. Tsering explained that he was a priest, and not only a priest but deaf and dumb too. He was also feeling unwell and wanted to be left alone. The villagers wandered away disappointed, but Wilson realized that he would have to spend the daylight hours confined to his tent.

He had plenty of time for his diary. Dedicated to Enid Evans, addressing her sometimes as 'girlie', its entries read more like a letter than a journal:

> *March 26th.*
> Quite interesting to estimate nearness of dawn by the many sounds of the jungle—the birdcalls are so pretty and I use one when wanting anything inside tent. The Tibetans we pass sleeping on the road at night are as black as the Ace of Spades and it is only by their dirty rags that we can recognize them. Been a bit upset with water. Just had wholewheat bread—that stuff will play no small part in success. Pity the chappie is keeping it so near his socks in his rucksack.

> *March 27th.*
> Am roasting in the sun in this heavy mantle. Beautiful cascade playing right ahead of me. Wish I had a zip on my

pants. It's quite a business doing a job for myself as I must first take off my hat and shed all my little treasures from my pouch before undressing. Then Tsering comes and screws me into this damned waistband again. Feel a bit like a cross between the Prince of Wales and Santa Claus. I'm hiding off the road while the boys have a meal.

March 28th.
Overcame latrine difficulty by digging hole inside tent. Had lovely bath in a washbowl today, and needed it. Done a bit of darning. Pity mother never showed me how, though I'm improving.

Wilson was looking forward to a 'good nag.' The Sherpas spoke only a little English and the language barrier was causing a few misunder-standings. In one entry Wilson complains that Tsering is going off to a pony race and will probably come back drunk, only to realize the next day that the Sherpa had gone to a village merely to get food for their pony: pony *rice.* Generally, he was full of praise for his companions, saying that he 'couldn't wish for better.'

On 30 March they crossed the frontier into Tibet. It was an impor-tant moment for Wilson, who felt like sending a wire to the British government: 'Told you so.' Out of reach of the Raj, he could now dis-pense with his costume and travel by day. They had been climbing steadily and quickly from the lush valleys of Sikkim and were now at 15,600 feet (4755 metres), on the edge of the Tibetan plateau. Wilson had liked 'jungle life,' but a far bleaker environment lay ahead, a place of burning sun, loose sand and almost constant, freezing winds. In spite of the altitude, he pressed on at up to 30 miles a day, but was soon suffering from headaches and sleeplessness; much of the playful-ness now vanishes from his diary. Attempting to observe his special diet, he wrote monotonously and sometimes guiltily about food. Eggs, rice, dried fruit and Quaker Oats seem to have been his staple; on 8 April, after drinking nothing throughout the day, he says that he is 'going off the rails with a pot of tea.' Food begins to seep into other areas of his diary: he described the sky as 'duck egg blue,' while one of the Sherpas looks like 'a couple of sacks of wheat' and another, burned by the sun, has 'a face like a dried apricot.' It reads like the journal of a very hungry man.

Three weeks after leaving Darjeeling, Wilson was rewarded with his first view of Everest: 'Saw Everest today. Looked magnificent. One half in snow plume. Two nights from now I shall be at Rongbuk where I hope to fast for a couple of days and get my system ready for the big event. *I must win.* Looking forward to getting back—what a time we'll have over tea . . . '

Sixteen miles from Everest and in full sight of it, the famous Rongbuk monastery was the final staging post for expeditions. It had become a tradition for the head lama to meet incoming climbers and bless them as they departed for the mountain. Wilson was uncertain about the kind of reception he would receive, but in hoping the lama would welcome him he had an ulterior motive: the previous year's party had left behind a quantity of supplies and he wanted to be able to help himself. He decided to pretend that he was a member of the official expedition, returning on reconnaissance duty: 'Shall tell the Lama I am one of the expedition if anything wanted from stores—bar of chocolate or anything like that. Tsering says there is plenty of meat. What a game: maybe in less than five weeks the world will be on fire.'

Wilson dressed for the meeting in his best flying shirt and white helmet. It seems unlikely that the lama believed his ruse and in the end it didn't matter: he liked the Englishman and was touched by his courage. 'Made a hit by all accounts,' Wilson wrote in his diary. Invited to rummage freely in the stores, he selected a new tent, boots and a collapsible lantern and was relieved to find no chocolate or other food: he was spared from temptation.

News of Wilson's 'escape' from Darjeeling had reached the British newspapers. While many reported the impending climax of the story with an open mind and a sense of romance, those that drew on expert opinion were more judgemental: 'While one cannot but admire the pluck of Maurice Wilson in attempting to climb Mount Everest alone, his whole project and his training methods in particular seem to have been ill judged. It is said that he has been fasting for five months and accustoming himself to a diet of figs, dates and cereals. This will be just about as useful to him in his present venture as it would be if he were intending to swim the Atlantic.'

The article warned of intense cold, frequent blizzards and of rarefied air producing feelings of depression and hopelessness that can be assuaged only by human companionship and proper food. Quite apart from this, the climbing of Everest presented many technical difficulties and Wilson was not qualified to deal with them.

Wilson would never read the reports, but he had heard it all before. As he looked towards Everest he felt confident and serene. Of course there would be cliffs and glaciers in the days ahead, but he was now more certain than ever that Divine Providence had brought him to the mountain and would lead him, in due course, to its summit. He had seen the optimism on the Sherpas' faces; the head lama had not expressed a word of doubt—he had smiled and laughed throughout their meeting. It was as if they all *knew* that he was going to succeed.

Now he just wanted to get it over with and return home. Telling the Sherpas that he would be away for six or seven days, Wilson set out in the early morning of 16 April. On the back of his rucksack he tied a shaving mirror, hoping that the sun would catch it and that the lamas, keeping a lookout from the walls of the monastery, would see a distant glinting signal rising slowly up the mountain.

But they didn't, and nine days later the head lama became concerned that Wilson had not returned. He asked one of the Sherpas to go and wait for him at the site of the previous expedition's Camp I, but almost immediately they saw a figure stumbling towards them from the direction of the mountain. His limbs were emaciated and his face horribly swollen—the man was barely recognizable as Wilson.

According to his diary Wilson had made good progress on the first day. As if God were already helping him, the sun was bright and the air almost perfectly still; the enormous rucksack seemed astonishingly easy to manage. From what he had read he knew the 'real climbing' started at Camp III and expected to reach it within a couple of days. By the next morning everything had changed. Having assumed that he would find a track to follow along the glacier, he could find no trace of one and within a few hours he was hopelessly lost. Wherever he tried to walk he found yawning crevasses. Strange ice pinnacles towered above him and he could not see the way. His eyes burned and his head spun. He had wandered into a labyrinth and it was, as he wrote in his diary, 'a *hell* of a day.'

It took him three days just to reach Camp II and by then he was exhausted. The thin air was hard to breathe and seemed to burn his throat: 'got hell of a thirst on this damned glacier, don't know why. Am eating snow and ice.' All he was eating apart from that—indeed all he had brought with him—was bread and Quaker Oats and it gave him little strength. On the fourth day he made only three-quarters of a mile before a blizzard forced him to pitch camp; by the end of the next he was still nearly three miles from Camp III, a steep glacier ahead of him. It was not as he had imagined. That evening he confessed to his diary that he should have brought crampons. He understood now what they were for and wondered if he would find a pair in the supply dump near Camp III. If he did not, he intended to improvise with tin cans and a length of rope. He concluded tersely: 'Think I shall have to take a bit more to eat and see if that will solve the lassitude business. Don't think anyone would undertake this job for sheer bravado. Think the climbers had it cushy with servants and porters.'

The next day was his birthday, which he had hoped to celebrate on the summit. All he wrote was: 'Many happy returns to myself. Over-taken by snowstorm and parked early.' In the morning he decided that he had had enough: 'No use going on. Eyes terrible and throat dry. Thought because lack of water but have been keeping mouth open. Discretion better part of valour and with even Herculean effort could not make Camp III in time. Weather bad.'

During the long trek back to the monastery Wilson suffered acute pain in his left arm and his eyes swelled until he was nearly blind. In his distress, he found that he was thinking about his mother. Having spent the whole of his adult life away from Bradford, he suddenly wanted to be with her and to revisit the places of his childhood. He drew a line around the entry in his diary and may have intended to delete it; he wrote earlier that he would 'clean up' his writing before setting out for the mountain, no doubt with posterity in mind.

'Spent all day in bed and ATE,' Wilson wrote of his first day back at the monastery. He did not get up for three days and it would take him three weeks to recover from his ordeal, but there was no question of his giving up. 'Faith,' he wrote, 'is not faith that wavers when its prayers remain unanswered.' The diary of his convalescence dwells on his diet; he was delighted that he could find no trace of fat on his body. Eating biscuits, eggs and dates, he was occasionally disappointed with the standard of his Sherpas' cooking, but, when he tried to make them a Yorkshire pudding, it was a disaster. He was slowly 'thawing to normal,' his cheerfulness returning. It was time to think of fasting again. 'Don't suppose an evening goes by,' he wrote to Enid, 'but you and Len speculate as to where I am and what I'm doing. Good to think that I shall be with you again in less than a couple of months.'

On 12 May he set out from the monastery for the last time. He would not risk losing his way on the glacier again. Rinzing and Tewang were to accompany him as far as Camp III; from there, in the first fine weather, Wilson intended to strike out alone.

With expert guides, the climb to Camp III was 'like a spring walk' and they reached it in three days. If Wilson was breaking his bargain with God by taking the Sherpas with him, he was also about to depart from his diet in spectacular fashion. Close by was the supply dump abandoned by the official expedition. It contained an extraordinary delicatessen: plum jam, butter, Bourneville chocolate, Fortnum and Mason's anchovy paste, sugar, Ovaltine, Nestlé's milk and, Wilson wrote, 'other treasures from heaven. Talk about a Santa Claus party outside my tent.'

The next evening Wilson continued: 'Eaten everything about the place today. Soup, Ovaltine, and heaven knows what. Rinzing went for another box of food and brought a greater variety including maple sugar, cake and a vegetable ration. Guess what I'm wallowing in as I write? A one pound box of King George chocolates!'

A blizzard had confined them to camp and it lasted several days. At more than 21,000 feet (6401 metres), the altitude was giving all the men painful headaches and Wilson seemed to be suffering more than the others. He was unable to sleep: 'Terrible when you can't put your head down for aching nerves.'

They had been at Camp III for a week when Wilson set out towards the steep slopes of Everest's famous North Col. Rinzing agreed to show him the route taken by the last expedition. In spite of the passage of time, wind and snow, Wilson expected to find intact a staircase of cut steps and a guiding rope, but there was nothing: the vast escarpment was blank. Any mountaineer could have warned him, but Wilson, of course, had never sought their advice. As the sun descended Rinzing made his way back to the camp, and Wilson, alone once more, turned to the slope.

For two days he struggled to ascend the North Col. He had made some progress when the slope suddenly rose ahead of him into a vertical wall of ice more than 40 feet high. However hard and however many times he tried, he could not master it. It drained the last reserves of his strength and, on the third day, he was too exhausted to get out of his sleeping bag: 'Had a terrible job yesterday and whoever selected that route ought to be pole axed. Am parked at an angle of 35 degrees but have shaped the snow to my carcass. Had five dry biscuits yesterday morning and nothing since, as there is nothing to have. Funny, but I feel all these stick ups I get have a reason.'

The pencil felt like a shard of ice in his hand and his writing was beginning to trail wildly across the page. The next morning he roused himself: 'Only one thing to do—no food, no water—get back. Did two sheer drop rolls down the face of the ice, but fortunately without any effect. Ribs sore but not much.'

At Camp III the Sherpas pleaded with him to return to the monastery. Wilson refused and merely lay in his bag for the next three days. He did not want to speak and wrote nothing in his diary. On 29 May he began to climb again: 'This will be the last effort and I feel successful. Have pulled out my flag of friendship and it feels quite cheering. Strange, but I feel there is someone with me in the tent all the time.' He walked only half a mile before pitching camp. He lay there for a further thirty-six hours and again wrote nothing. The next entry in his diary were the last words of Maurice Wilson: 'May 31st, Thursday. Off again. Gorgeous day.'

from Quest for Adventure
by Chris Bonington

Chris Bonington (born 1934) has been to Everest four times and climbed it once—in 1985, at age 51. He led 1972 and 1975 expeditions to the Southwest Face (the second was successful), as well as a 1982 attempt on the Northeast Ridge. Here he offers an authoritative and even-handed account of events that led to the mountain's first ascent.

From the south Mount Everest (8848 metres/29,028 feet) resembles a mediaeval fortress—its triangular summit, the keep, guarded by the turreted walls of the outer bailey; Lhotse, fourth highest mountain in the world, is a massive corner tower linking the high curtain wall of Nuptse. The gateway to this fortress is the Khumbu Icefall, portcullised with séracs, moated with crevasses. Few mountain peaks are better guarded or have resisted so many assaults. There was no doubt concerning the whereabouts of the mountain or even of how to approach it from the south, as there had been in the case of Annapurna and Dhaulagiri, but there was a great deal of doubt as to whether it could be climbed from this direction.

British climbers had reached the Lho La before the war and had seen the entrance to the Khumbu Icefall, but the way to the peak itself was barred by the outlying spurs of the West Ridge and the South-West Face.

The first westerners to approach Everest from the south were Bill Tilman and Charles Houston, who had attempted Everest and K2, respectively, in 1938. As members of a small trekking party, for them it must have been like venturing into an incredible Aladdin's cave of treasures, of unknown, unclimbed peaks, of unspoilt villages that were the homes of the Sherpa people, or turbulent glacier torrents, lush vegetation, high pastures, *mani* walls and prayer flags. It is hardly surprising that they took little more than a cursory glance at the approach to Everest, walking a short way up the Khumbu Glacier to peer round the shoulder of Nuptse into the Icefall and Western Cwm. They could only see the steep buttresses of the South-West Face of Everest, which appeared to reach the South Col; as a result, their report was discouraging.

But even as they made their reconnaissance, a young, unknown climber of the post-war generation was also thinking of Everest. Mike Ward had started climbing in North Wales during the war, while still at school, had gone to Cambridge in 1943 to study medicine and climbed at every possible opportunity. With the end of the war, he was able to go out to the Alps. He had already shown himself to be a brilliant natural rock climber, and the thoroughness and persistence with which he researched and then pushed through his plans for a further Everest reconnaissance, despite Tilman's unfavourable report, displayed his capacity as an organiser as well as a climber. Yet he was in the traditional mould of pre-war climbers, essentially amateur, knowing that however great his enthusiasm for climbing his career in medicine would always take priority.

He realised he was short on big mountain experience and therefore invited Bill Murray, a Scot who had led an expedition to the Garhwal Himalaya the previous year, and had climbed extensively in Scotland both before and after the war. Murray's books *Mountaineering in Scotland* and *Undiscovered Scotland* have become climbing classics. The other member of the team was to be Tom Bourdillon, one of the most outstanding of all the post-war young climbers.

Pre-war expeditions to Everest had been sponsored through an organisation called the Everest Committee, formed from members of both the Royal Geographical Society and the Alpine Club. It was coming into existence once again, under the name of the Himalayan Committee, and was to play a very important role in the Everest expedition, but for the time being Mike Ward simply wanted its approval and blessing which, after some hesitation because of Tilman's unfavourable reaction, was finally given.

Only a short time before they were ready to depart, Eric Shipton came onto the scene. Undoubtedly Britain's most eminent mountaineer at this time, he had established himself, with Tilman, as an outstanding mountain explorer, surveying and exploring the Himalaya with small, lightweight expeditions. Shipton was more mountain explorer than technical climber for whom reaching the top of a mountain was just part of the experience as a whole and not an end in itself. Of average height and build, with bushy eyebrows shielding piercing blue eyes, he seemed to gaze straight through you to some distant mountain range. There was also a slightly absent-minded distance in his manner, not cold or aloof, for he was essentially a kind man, but a distance born, perhaps, of shyness, a certain inhibition of emotion. He did not enjoy the hurly-burly of big expeditions, their politics and ponderous slow movement, but he had been unable to resist the lure of Everest and had taken part in four pre-war Everest expeditions, while his books were an inspiration to countless youngsters, including myself, who were just starting to climb. During the war he was British Consul-General in Kashgar, in Sinkiang, and had gone on to Kunming in China, but this had ended with the victory of the Communist forces and he arrived back in Britain, not at all sure what to do next. He was promptly invited to lead the Reconnaissance expedition.

Mike Ward and Bill Murray had already set out by sea when Shipton received a telegram from the President of the New Zealand Alpine Club, saying that four of his countrymen were climbing in the Garhwal Himalaya and asking if two of them could join the Everest Reconnaissance. Up to this point Shipton, who always favoured the smallest possible numbers, had resisted several applications to join the expedition, but on impulse, mainly because of good memories of climbing with

New Zealander, Dan Bryant, on Everest in 1935, he accepted the proposal—even though it meant taking on two climbers whom none of them knew.

This also gave the four New Zealanders a very real problem—which two of the four should accept this opportunity? Ed Hillary, a big, raw-boned bee-keeper, was an obvious candidate. Although having only started climbing at the comparatively late age of twenty-six, his physique was superb and, on the expedition in the Garhwal, he had been outstandingly the strongest. The second place in the team was open to question, however. The leader of the party, Earle Riddiford, was determined to go, even though George Lowe, a primary school teacher who combined a rich sense of humour with a great deal of climbing ability and determination, felt that not only was he stronger, but also that he and Hillary made a particularly good team. Nonetheless, it was Riddiford and Hillary who joined Shipton.

And so there were six climbers on the Everest Reconnaissance. They had a tough approach through the height of the monsoon from Jogbani in the south to reach the Upper Khumbu Valley on the 29th September 1951. Bourdillon, Riddiford and Ward ventured into the Icefall, while Shipton and Hillary climbed a spur of Pumori to look into the Western Cwm. The view they got showed that Everest was undoubtedly climbable from the south, for they could now see right up the Cwm, the long easy slope of the Lhotse Face and the comparatively easy angle of the South-East Ridge leading down to the South Col. The way into the Western Cwm, however, lay through the daunting obstacle of the Khumbu Icefall.

This Icefall descends about 800 metres, a maze of tottering ice towers and blocks, of crevasses and huge holes, all of it shifting under the relentless pressure from the glacier above, and threatened by avalanche from the steep slopes on either side. It has always been one of Everest's major hazards. It was a particularly formidable barrier for the first men to set foot upon it, being considerably larger and more complex than any icefall they had experienced, though the two New Zealanders were at some advantage, since they had been climbing all summer and the icefalls of the New Zealand Alps are both bigger and more difficult than anything in Europe.

Their progress must be judged against this background. On their first attempt they got about three-quarters of the way up when they were hit by an avalanche and were lucky to escape without serious injury; they decided to leave the Icefall for a fortnight, in the hope of letting the snow settle. This also gave Shipton an opportunity to explore the mountains to the south of Everest, which I suspect he found much more intriguing than the challenge of the Icefall.

Returning to the fray, on the 19th October, they were undoubtedly shaken when a complete section, that had seemed fairly stable, collapsed during the night, leaving behind an area of chaotic debris. When, at last, they reached the top of the Icefall they found that the way into the Western Cwm was barred by a huge crevasse that stretched from wall to wall. This was the place where Camp 1 is usually situated. Now a long way above their last camp, they were tired, stretched to the limit by the very level of the unknown, but the younger members of the team were keen to press on, while the older and more experienced decided that the risks were too high and that they had seen enough. In retrospect, Shipton regretted this decision but, at the time, it seemed sensible. They had proved that Everest was feasible by this route.

Unfortunately, however, the British had lost the opportunity to confirm it. The Himalayan Committee, perhaps over-confident that Everest was a 'British' mountain, had not applied for permission for 1952 in time. A Swiss expedition had got in first. There was some discussion about making it a Swiss-British effort under joint leadership, but this came to nothing. The Swiss were given first chance and they nearly made it, with what was really a very small expedition. Although the team numbered twelve, only six of them were hard climbers; the rest were scientists or had a support role such as doctor or camera man.

The Sherpa force numbered twenty, led by Tenzing Norkay, who had already gained a considerable reputation not only as a sirdar, or foreman, of the Sherpas, but as a climber in his own right. He was thirty-eight years old, tall and heavy by Sherpa standards, weighing over ten stone. With his swept-back hair, strong, square-cut chin and broad smile, he had an almost European look which was reflected in his attitude to the mountains. Most of the Sherpas still regarded mountaineering purely as a job; Angtharkay, Herzog's sirdar on Anna-purna, whose experience was even greater than Tenzing's, declined an invitation to go to the summit of Annapurna. His job was to super-vise the efforts of the high-altitude porters and he saw no point in the struggle and risk to reach the top. Tenzing, on the other hand, had the same driving ambition as a European climber to reach the summit. Already he had been to the top of Nanda Devi East with the French in 1951; he wanted to reach the summit of Everest in 1952. With the Swiss, Raymond Lambert, he got within 250 metres, high up on the South-East Ridge, just 165 metres below the South Summit.

The Swiss had shown the way to the top; almost all the route was known. Their failure to finish was partly the result of the comparative lightness of their assault, in the face of the huge gulf of the unknown that they had to penetrate, through the mysteries of the Western Cwm, the Lhotse Face and the final Summit Ridge; but, most of all, it was because the oxygen sets used by Lambert and Tenzing were ineffective, feeding them insufficient oxygen to compensate for the weight of the cylinders they were carrying. The sets were so primitive, they could only use them while resting, which meant having to carry the extra load of the oxygen bottles without getting any benefit from them whilst actually climbing. The Swiss did not give up; they made another attempt in the autumn, after the heavy snows of the monsoon, but the savage cold and high winds of the winter overtook them and they got no higher than the South Col.

Meanwhile, the British had to sit it out, praying secretly that the Swiss would not succeed. This did at least give them more time to work on some of the specialised equipment, particularly oxygen systems which seemed a vital ingredient for success, and a rather abortive expe-dition to Cho Oyu (8153 metres/26,750 feet) under Shipton's leader-ship gave further altitude experience to some potential members of the next British attempt on Everest, which was now scheduled for 1953.

It was generally assumed that Shipton would lead this attempt, but he himself had some doubts about the suitability of his temperament for such a role, as he confessed in his autobiography, *That Untravelled World:*

> It was clear that the Committee assumed that I would lead the expedition. I had, however, given a good deal of thought to the matter, and felt it right to voice certain possible objections. Having been to Everest five times, I undoubtedly had a great deal more experience of the mountain and of climbing at extreme altitude than anyone else; also, in the past year I had been closely connected, practically and emotionally, with the new aspect of the venture. On the other hand, long involvement with an unsolved problem can easily produce rigidity of outlook, a slow response to new ideas, and it is often the case that a man with fewer inhibitions is better equipped to tackle it than one with greater experience. I had more reason than most to take a realistic view of the big element of luck involved, and this was not conducive to bounding optimism. Was it not time, perhaps, to hand over to a younger man with fresh outlook? Moreover, Everest had become the focus of greatly inflated publicity and of keen international competition, and there were many who regarded success in the coming attempt to be of high national importance. My well-known dislike of large expeditions and my abhorrence of a competitive element in mountaineering might well seem out of place in the present situation.
>
> I asked the Committee to consider these points very carefully before deciding the question of leadership and then left them while they did so.

The Chairman, Claude Elliott, and several members of the Committee already had doubts about Shipton's leadership, particularly in the light of his failure to push through into the Western Cwm and his seeming lack of determination on Cho Oyu, but they could not bring themselves to dispense with him altogether—the main problem being that there was no other obvious candidate. It was felt, however, that a more forceful climbing leader was needed for the final push on the mountain, together with a good organiser to co-ordinate preparations in Britain, so that Shipton could remain a figurehead for the expedition whilst the two most vital executive functions of leadership were hived off. It was a compromise decision with all the weaknesses that this involved.

The Committee liked the idea of a military man with a proven ability in organisation and management. Two soldiers were particularly discussed—Major Jimmy Roberts, a Gurkha officer who had climbed extensively in the Himalaya, and Colonel John Hunt, who had also served in India, and had had both Alpine and Himalayan expedition experience, but was almost completely unknown in British climbing circles. The previous summer, however, Hunt had climbed in the Alps with Basil Goodfellow, who was secretary at this time of both the Alpine Club and the Himalayan Committee. Impressed by Hunt's ability as a mountaineer, combined with his obvious drive and capability as an organiser, Goodfellow pushed Hunt's case very strongly and it was decided that he was the ideal choice as assault leader and organiser.

On being told of the Committee's suggestion that there should be an assault leader, Eric Shipton concurred but suggested that 'deputy leader' would be a better title and that Charles Evans who had been on Cho Oyu with him could best fill this role. There was no question of Evans, a busy brain surgeon, being able to take on the job of full-time organiser, however, so this left an opening for Hunt.

But Elliott and Goodfellow were determined to go much further than this and, the day after the Committee meeting, without consulting Shipton, Elliott wrote to Hunt asking whether he would be available for the expedition as assault or deputy leader, and also to act as full-time organiser. A few days later Goodfellow telegrammed Hunt, inviting him to come over to England to discuss his role with Shipton.

It must have been downright embarrassing for all concerned. Shipton was under the impression that he was interviewing Hunt for the job of expedition organiser, while Hunt had been given the impression that he was to be deputy leader—a role that Shipton considered was already held by Charles Evans. The meeting was a failure and Hunt returned to Germany where he was serving at the time. Charles Wylie, another Army officer, was made full-time organiser and set up an office in the Royal Geographical Society building.

But Goodfellow, convinced that Hunt was essential to the success of the expedition, was not prepared to let the matter drop. At the next Committee meeting on the 11th September, the question of deputy leadership was at the top of the agenda. Shipton was asked to leave the room—an extraordinary slight to the leader of the expedition— while the Committee discussed it. When Shipton was asked back in, he was told that the Committee had decided to make John Hunt, not deputy leader, but co-leader, something that they must have realised would have been unacceptable to Shipton who felt he had no choice but to resign.

Inevitably there was uproar throughout the mountaineering world and within the team. Eric Shipton was by far the best-known and most popular mountaineer in Britain at that time. Nobody had ever heard of John Hunt. Bourdillon, loyal as always, said he was going to withdraw from the expedition and it was Shipton who persuaded him to stay on. Evans was very distressed though, ironically, received the title deputy leader. Hillary, first hearing about it in a newspaper report, was indignant, saying that Everest just wouldn't be the same without Shipton, but he never thought of withdrawing from the expedition.

Were the Committee right? Would Everest have been climbed under Shipton's leadership? Certainly several members of his team thought so, arguing that Charles Evans and Charles Wylie would have ensured that the organisation was sound and that the determination of the climbers out in front, men like Hillary and Lowe, would have carried the expedition with its own momentum, even if Shipton had left it to look after itself. I experienced something like this when I went to

Nuptse, the third peak of Everest; the leader of the expedition believed in letting the climbers out in front make their own decisions, without actually appointing anyone in authority. We had no radios, but left each other little notes at the various camps with the plans that each member had made. We climbed the mountain in a storm of acrimony, that might have had a certain dynamic force of its own. But in the case of Everest, I suspect that the problem was so huge and complex, the need for careful co-ordination so great, that it required a firm and positive overall leadership. This can only come from one person who has this responsibility vested in him, is prepared to use it, and at the same time has the acceptance and respect of his fellow team members. From this point of view, the expedition almost certainly had a higher chance of success under John Hunt's leadership than it would have done under Shipton who, apart from anything else, never seemed totally committed to the enterprise or happy directing a single-minded thrust up a mountain. It was very unfortunate, however, that the decision was made in such a messy, indecisive way.

Shipton was cruelly hurt by this rejection. It is one thing to be allowed to stand down from an expedition, quite another to be manoeuvred into an impossible position. It triggered off a series of personal crises that had a traumatic effect over the next five years and it was only in 1957, through an invitation by a group of university students to lead their expedition to the Karakoram, that he returned to the mountains and then, in his fifties, had a renaissance, which he described as the happiest years of his life, exploring the wild, unmapped glaciers and mountains of Patagonia in the southern tip of South America. This was the style of mountaineering in which he excelled and in which he could find complete commitment and happiness.

In the meantime, John Hunt had been given the opportunity of his life. Shipton and Hunt, who were so very different in personality, had very similar backgrounds. Both were born in India, Shipton in Ceylon in 1907, the son of a tea planter, Hunt in Simla in 1910, the son of a regular Army officer; both lost their fathers at around the age of four; both were sent to prep schools in England, but here the similarity ended. Shipton was a slow learner, perhaps suffered from dyslexia, for he was a very late reader. As a result, he failed the common entrance examination to public school, and after a sketchy schooling took up tea planting in Kenya; for him, this led naturally to a life of individual adventure.

The young Hunt, on the other hand, was brought up from a very early age to the idea of a life of serious and dedicated public service. He went to Marlborough, then followed family tradition by going to Sandhurst where he distinguished himself, becoming a senior under-officer and winning both the Sword of Honour and the Gold Medal for Top Academic Attainment. He was commissioned into the fashionable Rifle Brigade and posted to India. But here he ceased to be the stereotyped young subaltern; he was not happy in the claustrophobic pre-war Army officers life of polo, cocktail parties and mess gossip. He preferred playing football with his soldiers, and already had a sense of social responsibility combined with a strong Christian belief that made him much more progressive in his political and social attitudes than the average Army officer. Tiring of the fairly aimless routine of garrison life, he applied for a temporary transfer to the Indian Police to work in intelligence and counter-terrorism. Already he was addicted to mountaineering, having had several Alpine seasons before going out to India. With the Himalaya on his doorstep, he took every opportunity to escape to the mountains with adventurous ski tours in Kashmir and more ambitious climbs on Saltoro Kangri and in the Kangchenjunga region. Hunt was considered for the 1936 Everest expedition but, ironically, failed the medical test because of a slight flutter in his heart-beat. He saw active service during the war, commanding a battalion in Italy, where he was awarded the Distinguished Service Order, and then getting command of a brigade in Greece at the end of the war. He went to Staff College and served on Field-Marshal Montgomery's staff at the end of the 'forties, at Fontainebleau, getting to know French climbers and being invited to join the Groupe de Haute Montagne. He married Joy, who was a Wimbledon tennis player, in 1935. Theirs is a very close relationship and between an exacting career and raising a family, they have done much of their mountain adventuring together.

Hunt certainly looked the part of the professional soldier, but he was no martinet. He plunged into the job of organising the expedition, but in doing so fully involved everyone around him, overcoming any initial resentment. One commentator, Ingrid Cranfield, summed up what has become a popular interpretation of Hunt's approach, writing: 'To Hunt an "assault" merely meant a concerted, military-style operation; whereas to Shipton "assault" sounded more like a criminal offence.' In fact, this was hardly fair, for Hunt's approach to climbing was essentially romantic, with an almost spiritual undertone. Wilfrid Noyce remembered Hunt commenting how mountains made him want to pray. Hunt undoubtedly saw Everest as a romantic, perhaps even spiritual, challenge, but used his military training to approach a task that needed careful planning. He could see the basic principles of ensuring success on a mountain are very similar to those of success in war and one finds oneself using similar terminology.

Dr. Griffith Pugh, the physiologist who had accompanied the Cho Oyu expedition, played a very important part in the preparations. The way the human body adapted to altitude was still a mystery and it was largely Griff Pugh's work that determined the need for acclimatisation to altitude and, perhaps even more important, the need to drink a lot to avoid dehydration. The diet of the expedition was carefully worked out and the equipment, with specially-designed high-altitude boots, tentage and clothing, was better than anything that had been used before.

There were plenty of strong incentives demanding success; the fact that the French had permission for 1954, the Swiss for 1955, so that if the British failed this time they were most unlikely to have another chance; the fact that it was the year of the Queen's Coronation; the amount of money and effort involved; the controversy over the change in leadership; but, most important of all, Hunt—and for that matter most of his team—wanted success for its own sake. If you set out on a climb, there is a tremendous drive to succeed in what you are attempting. On Everest, certainly in 1953 when six serious attempts had failed (five on the north side and one on the south), the chances of success seemed slim, however large and well-equipped the expedition might be.

Hunt settled on a slightly larger team than perhaps Shipton would have taken, making it up to a total of twelve climbers, plus thirty-six high-altitude porters. Evans, Bourdillon, Gregory, Hillary and Lowe had been in the Cho Oyu party, Michael Ward, who had been on the 1951 Reconnaissance as doctor, and George Band, Wilfrid Noyce, Charles Wylie and Mike Westmacott were newcomers. Even the Cho Oyu men were thin on real high-altitude experience; Charles Evans had reached 7300 metres on Annapurna IV in 1950, while Hillary and Lowe had collected a fine crop of peaks around 6400 metres and had been to about 6850 metres on both Mukut Parbat and Cho Oyu, but they had not climbed any really high mountains. In this respect John Hunt was the most experienced, for he had been to 7470 metres on Saltoro Kangri and had made a bold solo ascent of the South West Summit of Nepal Peak (7107 metres/23,350 feet) in East Nepal. It was Tenzing Norkay, however, who had more high-altitude experience and knew Everest better than any of the other members of the party and, because of this, he was made a full team member as well as being sirdar of the porters.

The British part of the expedition came from traditional Oxbridge or military backgrounds, the only exception being Alf Gregory, who was a northerner, running a travel agency in Blackpool. The selection, however, was a natural one, for the climbing explosion that hit Britain in the early 'fifties, spearheaded by the tough Mancunians of the Rock and Ice Climbing Club, had only just got under way. In completing the selection of the team, Hunt had looked for compatibility as much as a record for hard climbing. This certainly worked out, for the team functioned well together under Hunt's firm, but tactful direction.

Preparations were complicated by the fact that the Swiss were having their second try for the mountain that autumn, which meant that Hunt and his team could not let go at full bore until the end of

November, when the Swiss finally admitted defeat. The British had just three months to put the expedition together, much of the equipment had to be specially designed and manufactured and, although some work had already been started, they had not been able to place any firm orders until they knew the outcome of the Swiss attempt. It is unlikely that they would have been able to raise the financial support for a second ascent of the mountain.

All the gear and food was ready to leave by sea on the 12th February 1953. The team reached Thyangboche, the Buddhist monastery a few miles south of the Everest massif, on the 27th March. This was early in the season, but Hunt was determined to allow an acclimatisation period before the start of the serious climbing. This was a concept fashionable in pre-war expeditions and in those of the early 'fifties, though later expeditions tended to concentrate all their efforts on the climb itself, acclimatising by working on the lower slopes of the mountain.

The story of the Everest expedition, like that of all siege-type expeditions, is a complex yet stereotyped one, of establishment of camps and different parties moving up and down the mountain, as the route is slowly pushed towards the summit.

The first barrier is the now famous Khumbu Icefall; the route then relents through the Western Cwm; it is a long walk, skirting crevasses which tend to force the climber into the sides, and the consequent threat of avalanche from the steep, crenellated walls of Nuptse. At the head of the Cwm is the Lhotse Glacier, a giant series of steps, steep ice walls alternating with broad platforms, leading up towards the summit rocks of Lhotse. From near the top of the glacier, a long traverse across snow slopes leads to the South Col of Everest, the springboard for a summit bid up the South-East Ridge, soaring for 860 metres past the South Summit which, deceptively, looks like the top from the South Col, and then beyond it to the summit itself.

Throughout, John Hunt pressed himself to the limit, determined to be seen to be working as hard, if not harder, than anyone else on the expedition, either in carrying a load whilst escorting porters, making a reconnaissance in the Western Cwm or on the Lhotse Face, as well as coping with the detailed planning and day-to-day administration needed for the expedition. On several occasions he pushed himself too hard, as he struggled, grey-faced, to complete the day's task. There was a strong competitive element in his make-up, noticed by Hillary on the approach march and recorded in his autobiography:

> I learned to respect John even if I found it difficult to understand him. He drove himself with incredible determination and I always felt he was out to prove himself the physical equal of any member—even though most of us were a good deal younger than himself. I can remember on the third day's march pounding up the long steep hill from Dologhat and catching up with John and the way he shot ahead, absolutely determined not to be passed—the sort of challenge I could not then resist. I surged past with a burst of speed, cheerfully revelling in the contest, and was astonished to see John's face, white and drawn, as he threw every bit of strength into the effort. There was an impression of desperation because he wasn't quite fast enough. What was he trying to prove, I wondered? He was the leader and cracked the whip—surely that was enough? I now know that sometimes it isn't enough—that we can be reluctant to accept that our physical powers have their limits or are declining, even though our best executive years may still be ahead of us.

Mike Ward had an uncomfortable feeling in his presence, noting, 'My first impression of John was of some disturbing quality that I sensed but could not define. Later, I understood this to be the intense emotional background to his character, by no means obvious, and yet an undercurrent came through.' George Lowe commented, 'He greeted me most warmly and said how much he was depending on *me*—his assault on personal susceptibilities was impossible to resist.'

This was an experience that everyone I have talked to remembered.

At the same time, however, both through his own personality and also from his position as leader, he kept a certain distance from his fellow members and had an air of authority, very similar to that Thor Heyerdahl inspired in his crew on *Kon-Tiki*. Even when members of the team disagreed with him they always ended up complying with his wishes.

From the very start Hunt had thought Hillary and Tenzing potentially his strongest pair, though they had never met before the expedition, and climbed together for the first time in the lower part of the Western Cwm. Hillary was immediately impressed by Tenzing's energy, competence, enthusiasm and, above all, his determination. He wrote later:

> If you accept the modern philosophy that there must be a ruthless and selfish motivation to succeed in sport, then it could be justly claimed that Tenzing and I were the closest approximation we had on our expedition to the climbing prima donnas of today. We wanted for the expedition to succeed—and nobody worked any harder to ensure that it did—but in both our minds success was always equated with us being somewhere around the summit when it happened.

Another strong pairing was that of Charles Evans and Tom Bourdillon. Although Bourdillon was younger than Evans and had climbed at a much higher standard in the Alps, they had much in common. Both had a scientific background and Evans, though initially sceptical, became deeply involved in Bourdillon's brainchild, the closed-circuit oxygen system, which his father had specially developed for the 1953 expedition in the hope of avoiding the wastage of the conventional open-circuit set. In theory it should have been the best system, but in practice it proved to be less reliable than the open-circuit system and the other members of the team were not impressed. Privately, Hunt felt the same way, but gave his support to the closed-circuit trials all the same. Bourdillon and Evans had been the two members of the team closest to Eric Shipton, Bourdillon having actually resigned from the expedition, and only brought back in after a great deal of persuasion. Hunt had been very touched on the walk in, when Bourdillon had told him how happy the expedition seemed to be. He wanted to keep it that way.

Hillary, down-to-earth and practical, preferred the look of the open-circuit oxygen system and felt that too much time was being expended in trying to prove the closed-circuit equipment. At 6.30 a.m. on the 2nd May, Hillary and Tenzing set out from Base Camp, using the open-circuit set, carrying a load that totalled forty pounds. They reached Camp 4, the Advanced Base in the Western Cwm, 1525 metres of climbing with about four miles in lateral distance, breaking trail most of the way through soft snow. It was as much an affirmation of their fitness and suitability for the summit as a vindication of the open-circuit system. Hunt was already thinking of them as his main summit hope, and this confirmed his choice.

By modern standards, Hunt's approach to the assault was slow if methodical, not so much a blitzkrieg as a steady siege. But there was a great deal more that was unknown in 1953 than there is today. Only one mountain of over 8000 metres had been climbed and Hunt had no desire to repeat the desperate, ill-supported summit bid, followed by the near disastrous retreat from Annapurna experienced by Herzog's expedition, nor the failure through an inadequate oxygen system and cumulative exhaustion of the Swiss. It was believed climbers deteriorated physically, even while resting, at heights of over 6400 metres, and it was not known how long anyone could survive and function effectively above this height. Hunt, therefore, was determined to nurse his team, particularly the climbers he was considering for the summit.

It was on the 7th May, with most of the team down at Base Camp, that he laid before them his final plan of assault. He felt that he had only the resources, both in materials and man-power, to mount one strong attempt on the summit. If this failed they would all have to come back down, rest and think again. But his thinking for the summit bid was consistent with his policy up to that point; it was one of reconnaissance, build-up of supplies and then the thrust forward. To do this, he first had to reach the South Col and he gave this job to George Lowe who, with Hillary, probably had the greatest all-round snow and ice experience of the expedition. With him were to be George Band and Mike Westmacott, two of the young newcomers to the Himalaya, and a group of Sherpas. Once the route was made to the South Col, Hunt planned a big carry to the Col, supervised by Noyce and Wylie, after which Charles Evans and Tom Bourdillon would move into position and make a bid for the South Summit, using the closed-circuit sets. Since, in theory, these sets were more effective and had greater endurance than open-circuit sets, they should be able at least to reach the South Summit from the South Col, a height of around 780 metres, and it was just conceivable that they could reach the top. In this way Hunt could satisfy the two exponents of the closed circuit system as well as making what he felt was a vital reconnaissance, opening the way for the main summit bid. In this respect one must remember just how huge a barrier that last 250 metres on Everest appeared to be in 1953. Just one day behind them would be Hillary and Tenzing, with a strong support party consisting of Hunt, Gregory and two Sherpas. They would establish a camp as high as possible above the South Col on the South-East Ridge, and then Hillary and Tenzing, using open-circuit sets, would make their bid for the summit—hoping to benefit from the first party's tracks and with that indefinable barrier of the unknown pushed still higher up the mountain.

Subsequently Hunt modified his plan so that he, with two Sherpas, would move up with Evans and Bourdillon to give them direct support just in case anything went wrong and, at the same time, to make a dump for the high camp. Hunt hoped to stay up on the South Col throughout the period of the summit attempts, since this was obviously the place of decision and the only place from which he could effectively influence events.

It must have been a tense moment for the entire team when they assembled for the meeting that was to give them their roles in the final phase of the expedition. Up to this point, Hunt had used a low-key approach to leadership, consulting with people as far as possible, often sowing the germ of an idea in others' heads so that they could almost believe that it was their own; but now he had to lay down a series of roles for the team, knowing all too well that some members would be bitterly disappointed.

Ward came out very strongly against Hunt's plan on two counts. He could not understand the logic of making an initial bid from the South Col, when only a slightly greater porter effort would be needed to establish a high camp for Evans and Bourdillon's attempt which, of course, could also be used by Hillary and Tenzing. He also challenged Hunt's plan to take charge of the carry to the top camp himself on the grounds that he was not physically fit for it—a heavy charge, coming from the expedition medical officer. But John Hunt weathered both attacks, which were delivered with great vehemence, and stuck to his guns.

I myself have always wondered at the thinking behind John Hunt's decision to allow Bourdillon and Evans to make their attempt from the South Col which meant, in effect, that there would be only one strong attempt on the summit itself. Had Bourdillon and Evans been granted that top camp, in all probability they would have been the first men on top of Everest. It is easy, however, to be wise after the event. Hunt was probably the only member of the team fully aware of just how thin was the ferrying capability of his Sherpas, particularly once they were above the South Col. Had Hillary and Tenzing failed in their summit bid, and the British team not climbed Everest in 1953, then no doubt the post-mortems would have been long and furious—but no-one is too interested in a post-mortem after success.

Whatever reservations some members of the team might have had, they all settled into their roles and worked themselves to the limit in the next three weeks. But things began going wrong almost from the start. It needs ruthless determination to keep the momentum of a climb under way. At altitude time seems to be slowed up by the very lethargy of the climber himself; the chores of struggling with a recalcitrant Primus, washing up dirty dishes in cold snow water, fighting with frozen crampon straps, can eat into a day and somehow dominate it so that the real aim of the climber, in this case to reach the South Col, becomes obscured. This is what happened now.

At Camp 6 on the night of the 15th, Lowe took a sleeping tablet for the first time. It had a disastrous effect. The next morning he just couldn't wake up. Noyce pleaded with him, cursed him, pummelled him, but it was not until 10.30 that Lowe staggered out of the tent and they were able to start up the tracks he had made the previous day. They didn't get far; he was falling asleep while he walked; they had no choice but to return, a precious day wasted. On the 17th, fully recovered and now well-rested, Lowe went like a rocket and at last they established their seventh camp, about half-way up the Lhotse Face at a height of 7315 metres. They still had 670 metres to go to the South Col. Noyce now dropped back, for he was going to be responsible for supervising the first big carry up to the South Col. Mike Ward went up to join Lowe that day, but he had a struggle just reaching the camp. Next day an icy wind blasted across the slope; Ward felt the cold bite through him. He went more and more slowly before being forced to turn back after less than a hundred metres' progress. They stayed in the tent on the 19th and barely reached their previous high point on the 20th. The forward drive of the expedition seemed to have come to a grinding halt.

Hunt now made a bold decision, pressured no doubt by desperation. Even though they were still far short of the South Col, he resolved to send Wilfrid Noyce up to Camp 7 with the Sherpa carrying party to try to push the route out and make the carry at the same time. In Hillary's view, Wilf Noyce was the best and most determined mountaineer of all the British contingent. A schoolmaster and a poet, he had a diffident manner, but once on the mountain was a very different person, with a single-minded drive and the immense determination of a man who had been one of Britain's most outstanding young rock climbers before the war.

Hunt, still desperately worried, uncharacteristically snapped at Lowe when he came down after his marathon ten days out in front on the Lhotse Face. In Mike Ward's words 'he was excessively rude'—an outburst caused by strain, and very quickly rectified. Hunt now realised, though, that he had to reinforce the push for the South Col; but who to send without weakening his summit assault? That night he resolved to send two more climbers up to Camp 7 the following day.

On the morning of the 21st things looked bad at the top camp. The Sherpas with Noyce had eaten something that disagreed with them and were all sick. There seemed little chance of getting up to the South Col, particularly on a route that was still unclimbed. Noyce, therefore, decided to set out with Anullu, a powerfully-built young Sherpa who chain smoked and enjoyed his *chang*, the local beer, brewed from fermented rice, maize or barley.

Back at Advanced Base, Hunt watched the slow progress of the two tiny dots and decided that Hillary and Tenzing would have to go up to the front and lend a hand. Hillary had come to the same conclusion already. Tenzing, more than anyone, would be able to encourage the Sherpas and Hillary had a huge vested interest in getting the camp on the South Col established. In addition, he was confident that he had the fitness to make this lightning push up to the Col, come back down, rest a day or so, and then make his summit bid. So Hillary and Tenzing set out from Advanced Base that afternoon and surged straight through to Camp 7.

Meanwhile, Wilf Noyce and Anullu had passed the high point reached by Lowe and Ward and were now working their way across the steep snow slope that swept down in a single span to the floor of the Western Cwm 900 metres below. They reached a crevasse that stretched its barrier right across the slope, and cast in either direction to find a snow bridge; but there was none:

> I looked at Anullu, and Anullu, behind his mask, looked back at me. He was pointing. Where he pointed, the crevasse, some eight feet wide, had narrowed to perhaps three. The cause of narrowing was the two lips, which had pushed forward as if to kiss over the bottle-green depths below. The lips were composed, apparently, of unsupported

snow, and seemed to suspend themselves above this 'plea-sure-dome of ice', into whose cool chasms, widening to utter blackness, it would at other times have been a delight to peer. I walked right once more, then left. Nothing. I signed to Anullu that he should drive his axe well in and be ready for me. Then I advanced to the first unsupported ledge. I stood upon this first ledge and prodded. Anullu would have held me, had one ledge given way, but he could not have pulled me up. As the walls of the crevasse were undercut to widen the gap, I would have been held dan-gling and could not have helped myself out. It would be silly to face such a problem in the Alps without a party of three. But I cannot remember more than a passing qualm. Altitude, even through oxygen, dulled fears as well as hopes. One thing at a time. Everest must be climbed. Therefore this step must be passed. I prodded my ice axe across at the other ledge, but I could not quite reach deep enough to tell. I took the quick stride and jump, trying not to look down, plunged the axe hard in and gasped. The lip was firm. This time the Lhotse Face really was climbed.

Slowly, they plodded on towards the wide gully that led to the crest of the Geneva Spur, which in turn would lead them easily to the South Col:

Strange, how breathless I could feel, even on four litres a minute. Anticipation was breathless too as the crest drew near, backed by the shadow of Everest's last pyramid, now a floating right-handed curve from which snow mist blew. I was leading again, and hacked the last steps on to the crest. Still no view, and no easy traverse; we must go on up to the widening top. First boulders, up which we stumbled easily, then more snow, the broad forehead of the Geneva Spur, and then suddenly nothing was immediately above us any more. We were on a summit, overlooking in this whole scene only Lhotse and Everest. And this was the scene long dreamed, long hoped.

To the right and above, the crenellations of Lhotse cut a blue sky fringed with snow cloudlets. To the left, snow mist still held Everest mysteriously. But the eye wandered hungry and fascinated over the plateau between; a space of boulders and bare ice perhaps four hundred yards square, absurdly solid and comfortable at first glance in contrast with the sweeping ridges around, or the blank mist that masked the Tibetan hills beyond. But across it a noisy little wind moaned its warning that the South Col, goal of so many days' ambition, was not comfortable at all. And in among the glinting ice and dirty grey boulders there lay some yellow tatters—all that remained of the Swiss expeditions of last year.

Wilf Noyce had achieved his own personal summit; he knew that for him the expedition was probably over. He had fulfilled his role in John Hunt's master plan, had established one vital stepping-stone for others to achieve the final goal, but that goal was denied him, as it is to the vast majority of members of a large expedition. Some are better than others at suppressing ambition and envy; in his book, *South Col*, Wilf Noyce only allowed: 'Yet when I looked up and saw John's trio setting out for the Face, a demon of suppressed envy pricked me, now that my job was done.'

On the 22nd May, Ed Hillary and Tenzing helped cajole and encourage Charles Wylie's carrying party to the South Col; Charles Evans and Tom Bourdillon with John Hunt in support, were on their way up to the Lhotse Face to put in the first tentative assault or reconnaissance of the South Summit, though I am quite sure that as Bourdillon and Evans plodded up the long slopes, enclosed in the claustrophobic embrace of their chosen oxygen sets, they were dreaming and hoping for the summit. In theory, the closed-circuit system should give them the speed and have the endurance to get them to the top, but what if it failed or ran out near the summit? They had talked endlessly about this eventuality. The sudden withdrawal of a flow of almost pure oxygen could have disastrous effects. Would it be like running out of oxygen in a high-flying aircraft? Could they adjust to the complete loss of oxygen in time to get back down the mountain? There was no way of knowing for certain.

Until now, Wilf Noyce, George Lowe and all the others had been pursuing a series of limited adventures, limited not so much by their own strength, determination and acceptance of risk, as by the roles imposed upon them by the leader of the expedition. Bourdillon, however, had been given the opportunity of seeking out adventure in its fullest sense, for not only had he an outside chance of getting to the top, but also he was putting on trial his own oxygen system.

It is often argued that the use of artificial aids reduces the level of adventure; it certainly does with the indiscriminate use of expansion bolts, drilled and hammered into a rock wall to aid an ascent, for this dramatically reduces the level of uncertainty experienced by the climbers. In this respect, perhaps, had the closed-circuit oxygen system been perfect in every respect, lightweight and reliable, reducing Everest's summit to the height of Snowdon or Scafell, the feeling of adventure would have been lessened, though no doubt the satisfaction to Bourdillon the scientist would have been enormous. As it was, the system was by no means perfect. With fully-charged bottles and spare soda lime canisters (which absorbed the carbon dioxide), it weighed fifty pounds: it was temperamental in the extreme and uncomfortable to use. Charles Evans went along with Bourdillon out of friendship, coupled with his own scientific interest in the outcome of the experiment. It was a loyalty and enthusiasm that was to be severely tried.

Initially, their route went up a snow gully on the side of the ridge. They reached the crest, at a height of around 8290 metres, just after nine o'clock, having taken only an hour and a half to climb 400 metres. At that rate they had a good chance of not only reaching the South Summit, but getting to the top; but the going now became much more difficult. Fresh snow covered the rocks of the ridge; the clouds rolled in and soon it began to snow; their pace slowed down and it took two hours to cover the next 245 metres. They had now reached the high point achieved by Lambert and Tenzing the previous year and were confronted by a difficult decision. The soda lime canisters had a life of around three and a half hours; they were slightly awkward to charge and there was always a risk of valves freezing up immediately after the change. At this point the angle had eased and it would be safe and easy to make the change. On the other hand, they could probably get another half hour or so out of the canisters that were in place—something that could make a big difference later on. They had a muffled conversation through the masks clamped around their faces. They decided to make the change.

Once again, they set out, now on new ground. The cloud swirled around them, the angle steepened and the snow was unstable, a fragile crust overlying loose deep snow beneath. There was a serious risk of avalanche. Even more serious, Evans' set now developed a fault which caused laboured, rapid breathing. Slowly, they forced their way upwards and, at last, reached the crest of the South Summit. The cloud was milling around them, clinging to the eastern side of the ridge like a great banner, but the crest of the ridge was clear.

Now higher than any man had ever been before, for the first time they were able to examine the final ridge to the summit of Everest. It did not look encouraging. Looking at it head-on made it appear much steeper and more difficult than it actually was; it also looked very much longer, a phenomenon noticed by Doug Scott when he arrived just below the South Summit in 1975. It was one o'clock in the afternoon; they had already been going for five and a half hours; they were tired and were now well into their second canister. To go on or not? The summit was within their grasp; they could almost certainly reach it, but could they get back? They would undoubtedly run out of oxygen, might well be benighted. Bourdillon was prepared to risk all; he had that kind of temperament, had made a whole series of very bold and committing climbs in the Alps. Evans, however, whom John Hunt had put in charge of the pair and who was that little bit older, resolved that the risk was too great. They had a furious argument, muted no doubt by their oxygen masks, but Evans stuck to his point and Bourdillon, reluctantly, agreed to retreat. They only just got back, falling in their exhaustion on several occasions and tumbling, almost out of control, down the final gully leading back to the South Col, only saved by Bourdillon taking braking action with the pick of his axe. Had they pushed on to the summit, it seems most unlikely that they would have managed to get back alive.

Back on the South Col, there had been a moment when the onlookers, who now included Hillary and Tenzing, thought that Bourdillon and Evans were going to be successful. It was something that Hillary and Tenzing must have watched with mixed emotions. Whatever he felt, Hillary was able to muster a show of Anglo-Saxon team spirit. Tenzing, however, was both visibly and vocally agitated as he saw his chances of being the first man on top of the world starting to vanish.

Bourdillon and Evans, lying exhausted in their tents, had done a magnificent job; had they started from a higher camp they would almost certainly have reached the summit of Everest. As it was, they had opened the way for Hillary and Tenzing, though the story they brought back, understandably, was not encouraging.

John Hunt, who was also exhausted after his carry, felt a deep sense of satisfaction. His oxygen set had given trouble and, as a result, he had received a flow rate of only two litres per minute—half of what he really needed to make up for the weight of the oxygen cylinders and then to give him real help. Even so, he had struggled on to a height of around 8336 metres before dumping his load. For the leader of an expedition it is very important psychologically to make this carry to the top camp; in doing so he can feel that everything possible has been done to make the ascent viable and in some measure, I suspect, have a stronger sense of vicarious involvement in the final summit bid. The expedition as a whole becomes an extension of the leader's personality and ego and, because of this, it is not a huge sacrifice to forego the summit bid, for the success of the expedition overall is very much his handiwork, bringing a satisfaction that is as much intellectual as purely egotistical.

On the other hand, the other expedition members inevitably experience frustration on many occasions because they are being held back, or given humdrum tasks, or are denied the chance of going to the summit. On a large expedition, some can lose the sense of personal adventure they would have experienced on a smaller venture.

Not so the irrepressible George Lowe who, as Hunt returned to the Western Cwm, had bobbed back up to the South Col, after the very minimum of rest from his herculean efforts on the Lhotse Face. He had no thought and little chance of making a summit bid himself; he just wanted to get as high up the mountain as he could, and was all too happy to do this in a support role.

After a day of storm the 28th dawned fine, though bitterly cold at $-25°C$, and still very windy; but they had no choice, they had to start the final push for the summit. Of their two Sherpas, only Ang Nyma, another hard-drinking, chain-smoking young man, was fit, so Gregory, Lowe and Ang Nyma had to take on heavy loads, but the heaviest of all were those carried by Hillary and Tenzing, who each took around fifty pounds. They reached the place where John Hunt and Da Namgyl had dumped their loads, but decided that this was too low and therefore picked up everything, sharing it out amongst themselves. Hillary was carrying the heaviest load—over sixty pounds.

Slowly, they clambered on up the ridge to a height of around 8494 metres, before finally stopping. Hillary and Tenzing started digging out a platform for their tent, while the others dropped back down towards the South Col. Both Hillary and Tenzing were in superb condition, finding they could work at the platform and put up the tent without using oxygen. That evening they dined well off endless cups of hot, sweet lemon water, soup and coffee, which washed down sardines on biscuits, a tin of apricots, biscuits and jam.

They woke up at 4 a.m. on the morning of the 29th May. It was a brilliant, clear dawn and, even more important, the wind had almost vanished. Tenzing was able to point out the Thyangboche Monastery, 5180 metres lower and twelve miles away. It took them two and a half hours to get ready for their bid for the summit; melting snow for a drink, struggling with frozen boots and fiddling with the oxygen sets. At 6.30 they set out. In the event, they got little benefit from the previous party's tracks. They did not like the look of the route taken and therefore waded up through steep, insubstantial snow that felt as if it could slip away with them any minute. It was only nine in the morning when they reached the South Summit, and the view from it was magnificent. Makalu in the foreground, Kangchenjunga behind, were almost dwarfed from their airy viewpoint; little puffballs of cloud clung to the valleys, but above them the sky was that intense blue of high altitude, while to the east it was traced with no more than light streamers of high cloud. Hillary looked with some foreboding at the final ridge, about which Evans and Bourdillon had made such a gloomy forecast.

> At first glance it was an exceedingly impressive and indeed frightening sight. In the narrow crest of this ridge, the basic rock of the mountain had a thin capping of snow and ice— ice that reached out over the East Face in enormous cornices, overhanging and treacherous, and only waiting for the careless foot of the mountaineer to break off and crash ten thousand feet to the Kangshung Glacier. And from the cornices the snow dropped steeply to the left to merge with the enormous rock bluffs which towered eight thousand feet above the Western Cwm. It was impressive all right! But as I looked my fears started to lift a little. Surely I could see a route there? For this snow slope on the left, although very steep and exposed, was practically continuous for the first half of the ridge, although in places the great cornices reached hungrily across. If we could make a route along that snow slope, we could go quite a distance at least.

They had a short rest and Hillary changed both his and Tenzing's oxygen bottles for full ones. Then they set out, Hillary out in front cutting big steps for their ungainly, cramponned high-altitude boots, down a slope of good firm snow leading to the col between the Main and South Summits. Tenzing kept him on a tight rope, and then followed down. From the col they followed the heavily corniced ridge, moving carefully, one at a time. Hillary noticed that Tenzing had slowed down badly and was panting hard; he checked Tenzing's oxygen mask and saw that one of the valves was iced up so that he was getting hardly any oxygen. Quickly, he cleared it and they carved on, cutting steps, edging their way round ledges, ever-conscious of the dizzy drop down into the Western Cwm, 2438 metres below.

The most serious barrier was a vertical rock step in the ridge. At first glance it looked smooth and unclimbable, but then Hillary noticed a gap between the cornice that was peeling away from the rock on the right of the ridge and the wall of rock itself.

> In front of me was the rock wall, vertical, but with a few promising holds. Behind me was the ice wall of the cornice, glittering and hard but cracked here and there. I took a hold on the rock in front and then jammed one of my crampons hard into the ice behind. Leaning back with my oxygen set on the ice, I slowly levered myself upwards. Searching feverishly with my spare boot, I found a tiny ledge on the rock and took some of the weight off with my other leg. Leaning back on the cornice, I fought to regain my breath. Constantly at the back of my mind was the fear that the cornice might break off, and my nerves were taut with suspense. But slowly, I forced my way up—wriggling and jamming and using every little hold. In one place I managed to force my ice axe into a crack in the ice, and this gave me the necessary purchase to get over a holdless stretch. And then I found a solid foothold in a hollow in the ice, and next moment I was reaching over the top of the rock and pulling myself to safety. The rope came tight—its forty feet had been barely enough.

Tenzing then followed.

• • •

As I heaved hard on the rope Tenzing wriggled his way up the crack and finally collapsed exhausted at the top like a giant fish when it has just been hauled from the sea after a terrible struggle.

I checked both our oxygen sets and roughly calculated our flow rates. Everything seemed to be going well. Probably owing to the strain imposed on him by the trouble with his oxygen set, Tenzing had been moving rather slowly but he was climbing safely and this was the major consideration. His only comment on my enquiring of his condition was to smile and wave along the ridge.

They had now overcome the last real barrier and at last, at 11.30 in the morning, Hillary, with Tenzing just behind him, reached the highest point on earth. Suddenly everything dropped away around them. They could gaze down the North Ridge of Everest, across the endless, arid brown hills of Tibet, across to Kangchenjunga in the east and the serried peaks of the Himalaya to the west. They shook hands, embraced, flew their flags in those few moments of untrammelled delight, of complete unity in what they had achieved. Then they started the long and hazardous way down.

The first ascent of Everest caught the imagination of the entire world to a degree as great, if not greater than, any other venture before or since. Only the arrival of the first man on the moon, a victory of supreme technology, perhaps surpassed man's reaching the highest point on earth. But the very scale of the interest and adulation brought its accompanying problems the moment the expedition reached the Kathmandu valley. Nepalese nationalists wanted to adopt Tenzing as a standard-bearer for their own cause; the adulating crowds pounced upon him, shouting, *'Tenzing zindabad'*, long live Tenzing! They ignored Hillary and waved placards which depicted Tenzing arriving at the summit of Everest hauling behind him a fat and helpless white man. Hunt and Hillary were awarded knighthoods, Tenzing the George Medal. The fact that, as an Indian or Nepalese citizen, he was not allowed to accept a foreign title was ignored and, inevitably, the Indian and Nepalese press tried to exploit what they described as a racist slight to Tenzing. Hillary, perhaps extra-sensitive to the implications that he was hauled to the summit by Tenzing, wrote a frank description of what he thought happened on the day of the summit bid. Tenzing was affronted by the suggestion, which I suspect was true, that Hillary took the initiative on the push to the summit, particularly from the South Summit onwards. In his autobiography, *Man of Everest*, compiled by the American novelist, James Ramsay Ullman, Tenzing stated:

> I must be honest and say that I do not feel his account, as told in *The Ascent of Everest*, is wholly accurate. For one thing, he has written that this gap up the rock wall was about forty feet high, but in my judgement it was little more than fifteen. Also, he gives the impression that it was only he who really climbed it on his own, and that he then practically pulled me, so that I 'finally collapsed exhausted at the top, like a giant fish when it has just been hauled from the sea after a terrible struggle'. Since then I have heard plenty about that 'fish' and I admit I do not like it. For it is the plain truth that no one pulled or hauled me up the gap, I climbed it myself, just as Hillary had done; and if he was protecting me with the rope while I was doing it, this was no more than I had done for him.

In their own ways both accounts are probably true, but it is noticeable that Hillary toned down his account of how Tenzing climbed the step, both in his own personal story of the expedition, *High Adventure*, and in his autobiography, *Nothing Venture, Nothing Win*.

The other members of the expedition, who had helped Hillary and Tenzing reach the top, got only a fraction of the acclaim. The public needs easily identifiable heroes and is little interested in whole teams. The team itself, however, have held together, meeting regularly for reunions and, in various combinations, joining each other for other climbs or expeditions. Perhaps this is the ultimate tribute to John Hunt's leadership.

Charles Evans avoided the fanfares of the return journey, going off trekking to the south of Everest. Two years later he led a small, low-key expedition to Kangchenjunga, third highest mountain of the world, and George Band, the youngest of the Everest team, who had had difficulty in acclimatising, reached the summit with Joe Brown, the Manchester plumber who was the representative of a new driving force in British climbing. Wilf Noyce, also, went on to climb other mountains in the Himalaya, until he was killed in the Pamirs in 1962 with the brilliant young Scottish climber, Robin Smith. George Lowe made the Antarctic crossing with Vivian Fuchs, meeting Ed Hillary who led the New Zealand contingent coming in the opposite direction, and ended up marrying one of John Hunt's daughters. John Hunt's career was undoubtedly helped, as in fact was that of most of the others, by his experience on Everest, but he has always remained a distinguished public servant rather than an adventurer. After retiring from the Army, he ran the Duke of Edinburgh's Award Scheme for some years, before becoming Chairman of the Parole Board. He has also taken part in several public enquiries and became a Life Peer in reward for his many and varied public services. Hillary, also, has put a great deal back. His greatest work and contribution has undoubtedly been with the Sherpas, running a Sherpa Trust which has brought them small hospitals and schools, helped them build bridges and adapt in general to a changing world.

from from South Col
by Wilfrid Noyce

Poet and teacher Wilfrid Noyce (1917–1962) was a member of the 1953 Everest expedition that made the first ascent. These poems appeared in his account of the expedition. Noyce died in an avalanche in the Pamirs nine years after returning to England from Everest.

A PRAYER FOR EVEREST
Written before the Mountain

That I may endure,
And love of friends confirm me;
That I lend my ear
Kindest to those who vex me;
That I may be strong,
My will guide the faint footsteps;
That heart and lung
May learn, rhythm is conquest;
That in the storm
My hand may stretch to help,
Not cringe in the glove to warm;

That courage of mine
Bring to friends courage too,
As I am brought by them;
That in the lottery
(My last, my worthiest prayer)
No envy bleed,
When, as I know my heart,
Others succeed.
Here be content, the thought:
I have done my part.

NEPALESE VILLAGE
Written at Bhimpedi

The beauty of evening. Curtained the valley mist,
Orange skirt frilled, at last has coolly kissed
The darkening ridges. A hushed good-bye is said
With rain libation softening the dusty tread,
Planting quick seeds of coolness underfoot,
Painting spring's colour across the emblazoned shoot.

Carriers have laid their loads; this day is done.
Miles of blind path, the scraping foot on stone,
Sweat of the cheek, plumb weight's tug at the head,
The slow step in the naked stream bed,
All for a day are done. On the far hill
A glow, then a flash, a brighter light still
Than the first stars written over a paling sky,
Like the eyes of an old man defying death to die . . .

Fire: it is food. The metallic overtone
Drops with the earth's light. The hungry day is done.

WALKING TO EVEREST

Here on the green grass lawn,—
Pine-tree and primula rare,—
Here I would rest and be done,
By my one self this one,
    But I do not dare.

Beyond, the hill climbs away
From forest to grass, from grass
White to where snow-tops sway,
Rock-tower cloud-capped grey
    By mists that pass.

Man made to suffer, to stray,
Why must you go beyond?
Fountains your thirst allay,
Torrents their sweetest play
    Here, the still pond.

Sadly the answering heart:
World, you were never mine.
Tiger and snake have art,
Gorged, to sleep out their part
    Of Time's tortured line.

Lost among these comes one
Who cannot once be still.
Sleeping he dreams with moan,
Waking he will not be done
    Until done his will.

Wandering he must know
The first grey peak and the last;

Sunset and polar snow,
Tropic to desert glow,
   Present with past.

And if he suffer for these,
That is his voyage too:
Dim-wrapped in doubts that tease,
Half-lord of doubtful ease,
   He must pass through.

Knowing death is his end,
Death he weighs in his hand.
Where the ice ridges bend,
Where the feat's pride is his friend,
   Straight let him stand.

EVEREST FROM THE WEST
Camp Below Pointed Peak

Everest: terror and love:
No veil is upon you, no cloud
Doubts the huge hump, mighty monument set on earth,
Harp of the wind, snow-song and avalanche tears,
And tinier tale of men. But men are so proud,
Their mole-story is hill-high. Glorious their one wish
   absurd
To stand on that cone, one moment enough. Aloud
They recite the story: Changtse, North Col, the tilt
Of slab swinging sky-bound; yellow band thrust in black
And the wicked steps; here, perhaps here they fell,
Those two. And the others went on, gasped and loathed.
The cone still taunts them; storm and the years fret on,

Terror and love remain. Again the men come
Drawn from soft home, comfort and ease, to endure
One spell and be done: suffer, and win a crown,
Memory's store for life. Look then, the south,
An easier slant, one tiny point, and between
Our glasses grip in hot fingers of hope; there, there,
That is our ridge; down still to South Col, joy gone
In the sting of wind on a cheek. Now it is calm,
Now beckons to hope in the afternoon's serene.
The heart-break breath, dim of the eyes, the swing
Of axe upon ice are hard to disravel from beauty's dream,
Dream of a summit, ten thousand feet up, all seen,
And not known.

Everest: terror and love.
We fear and are drawn, love your infinite sides
And loathe our Lilliput crawling. Men we descend,
Conquerors never. So soon has the ant-marked trace
Of our step disappeared. Again quiet reigns,
And the choughs wheel in a world dead once again.
Terror and love are done.

THE CHOUGH
Base Camp in April

Beautifully black, with frilly ruff,
Pecking at the snow is the immortal chough.
Solitude's inhabitant, over the dead
Glacier he wings to lonely bed;
Yet sociable by nature, a friendly bird,
Gracing our company with cries absurd,
Foraging the scum of tea-leaves, abased

To fatten on muck no other will taste.
Are the worms scarce? Or do you prefer
Company of humans as a higher sphere?
Unasked you encourage us; mocking our pain
Fly to twenty thousand and back again
Before we are started; and higher as we climb
You laugh from Pumori at our laggard time,
And again are back—just right for tea,
Cheerful, untired, still fancy-free,
Ready for a bite of whatever may clatter
Down from our tent-site: gobble, gobble, chatter!
You accompanied Norton to heights hard won;
Mallory, perhaps, you saw dragged down,
And Herzog dropping the fateful glove.
But here you are, back, as if we were your love!
No story for us of the immortal dead,
Only one vast, oceanic greed.
Such is the chough . . .

ICEFALL
Written at Camp II

Silent stream:
Once a god took note of you,
Struck with his rod, ordered you guardian of treasuries.
Then your voices were stilled, your babble, your slithering
Cool between walls' primeval dream of the valley bed.
Slowly your level rush broke, the great pits
Yawned as your deep waves toppled to motionless,
Yawned as the waters crunched to icy, to cavernous,
Yawned as your lower rush foamy, cascading,
Halted and tangled and stayed. The little waves creamed up

Frothed to a fall. But so slow! Silence and night's shade,
Only these mark the change.
                              Wavelets are pinnacles
Pressed by the silent stream from above to oblivion.
Built for a day, a week, they fall, and confusion
Gapes in the spray of blocks that have once been
Reared with the hugeness of marble, ghost city ruined
At the day's shaft.
                              Still the river creeps onward,
Still in each fringed crevasse the wind of silence
Echoes the trump that once froze. Mortal man pressing
Sees astonished the rift; as once, land-faring,
The Israelites stared, dumb at the parting of waters.

AT CAMP IV, 24,000 FEET

One two three four
Five six seven eight
Steps and my head
Falls a plumb weight.
One breath and two, the picture again
Is a silvered back-cloth
To release from pain.
As breath to the legs,
So ease to the mind,
So joy in the scene
For a cause undefined.
Below, the white table
Of glacier plain,
The toy dot of tents
A human stain.
Above, the steel curve

Of greyest ice,
The blue and black gulf
Of hungry crevasse.
And leaning over
One rocky spire
Bending to watch me—
The world's highest spire.

BREATHLESS
Written at 21,200 feet on May 23rd

Heart aches,
Lungs pant
The dry air
Sorry, scant.
Legs lift
And why at all?
Loose drift,
Heavy fall.
Prod the snow
Its easiest way;
A flat step
Is holiday.
Look up,
The far stone
Is many miles
Far and alone.
Grind the breath
Once more and on;
Don't look up
Till journey's done.
Must look up,

Glasses are dim.
Wrench of hand
Is breathless limb.
Pause one step,
Breath swings back;
Swallow once,
Dry throat is slack.
Then on
To the far stone;
Don't look up,
Count the steps done.
One step,
One heart-beat,
Stone no nearer
Dragging feet.
Heart aches,
Lungs pant
The dry air
Sorry, scant.

THE SOUTH COL
In Retrospect from the Plains

Great hill above
And cloud below;
Reckless of love
The fast winds blow.
But all between
Is space beyond dead;
Spirits unseen
Here make their bed
In blackened rock-rift

And ice rubbed bare,
Crusted snow-drift
That blizzards tear.
Long ago
These were the same,
Never small, never slow,
Never soft, never tame.

What are men here?
What have they done?
A heap of rags here,
Yellow and brown.

from # Ascent
by Laurence Leamer

The climbers who made the first American ascent of Everest on May 1, 1963 followed the established South Col route. Twenty-one days later, Americans Willi Unsoeld and Tom Hornbein set out to finish a new and far more difficult route on the mountain's West Ridge—and soon climbed past the point of no return.

For years Willi had been waiting for this morning. Yet May 22, 1963, began as any ordinary climbing day began, in that drowsy, half-conscious state where habit is the only sovereign. At about 4:00 a.m. the oxygen ran out and Willi and Tom woke up. They got the bouillon brewing on the tiny stove and started dressing. They already wore layers of clothing. They topped it with relatively lightweight wind parkas and stuffed their heavy down parkas into their packs along with the extra oxygen cylinders. They pulled on their felt-lined reindeer boots over two pairs of wool socks, strapped on their crampons, and put on oxygen helmets, wool balaclavas, and parka hoods. With down parkas, lemonade, oxygen bottles, cameras, and a radio their loads came to about forty pounds a piece.

Outside in the gray dawn Willi fiddled with his oxygen regulator.

"Even with the regulator turned off it hisses," Willi said, relieved that Hornbein was the expedition's oxygen expert.

"It's always the regulator," Hornbein said, knowing what had gone wrong before. "I've got a spare."

For twenty minutes Hornbein fiddled with the regulator. He double-checked the valves for ice, but the bottle kept hissing away.

"It doesn't sound too bad," Hornbein shrugged. "Let's just keep an eye on the pressure."

If that didn't work out, Hornbein figured, they could share as they did when they slept, using one bottle, the T valve, and long tubing. It was a measure of the toll the mountain had already taken on their judgments that the two of them thought climbing to the summit tied to each other like Siamese twins made perfect sense. They couldn't bring themselves to walk back even the forty feet to the tent to pick up the extra oxygen cylinder. Instead they decided to set the oxygen regulators at half the regular rate, only two liters a minute, turning them off entirely while belaying and resting.

Willi looked down. Below for a thousand feet lay the steps Corbet had cut. Above, the gully was only about ten to twelve feet wide, rising at a 45-degree angle, covered with loose, unstable snow. Willi led up the couloir, driving his toes into the snow, cutting steps with his ice axe. Below, Hornbein belayed his partner, bracing himself if Willi should fall. When Willi had moved up the hundred feet of rope, he belayed his partner up to join him and started out again.

Willi and Hornbein were in Tibet. Below to the east between the Rongbuk and East Rongbuk glaciers lay Everest's 23,000-foot North Col, the route the early British climbers had used. Above that, not far from where Willi was climbing now, and almost exactly parallel but hidden by protruding walls, was the place where Mallory and Irvine had been last seen, two black specks moving upward.

Four hours had gone by already. Willi had climbed only about five hundred feet. The couloir had begun to narrow. It became so thin that they had to climb sideways. It looked like a crack pointing up toward the summit. They were at the Yellow Band that girds Everest. Facing them lay the most technically difficult climbing anyone had yet done on Everest. For sixty feet they would have to climb a sheer cliff. It was not even solid rock, but a crumbling tawny slab rock surface covered with unstable snow. Tom saw that "the rock sloped malevolently outward like shingles—rotten shingles on a roof." It was a roof in which the last ten feet rose absolutely vertically, without a trace of a handhold.

"You want to lead this one?" Willi asked.

"Sure, I'll try," Hornbein said, not thinking.

While Hornbein waited, Willi drove a pin into the wall as a belay point and tied the rope through. Belaying was an almost automatic reaction for Willi. He switched off the oxygen. While Hornbein worked overhead Willi dozed. After a while Willi heard Hornbein hammering a piton into rock far above him. If his partner had to use pitons, then the pitch was really a bear. There was nothing he could do. Willi fell half asleep again. After close to an hour, he realized the rope was moving through his hands. Hornbein was right above him moving down through the air on the rope like a great spider.

"I couldn't do it," Hornbein said as he landed in the snow beside Willi. "You'll have to finish it. "

First the two men sought an alternative route. They traversed onto the North Face itself, seeking some other way up. That looked even worse. It was the couloir or nothing.

"Tom, if you didn't do it, what chance do I have?" Willi believed that of the two, Tom was the better rock climber.

"No, you won't have any trouble," Hornbein said reassuringly. "Turn your regulator clear up."

Willi moved the oxygen gauge up to the full five liters a minute, feeling the rush of adrenaline. Then, wearing his forty-pound pack, Willi moved back up the unfinished pitch. Tom had gotten most of the way up the limestone, pounding a piton into the crumbling, rotten surface. It was the last ten feet that had stopped him.

Snapping the rope into the high piton, Willi surveyed what lay above. He would have to gut it. Taking off his mittens, he clawed his way up, using his frozen hands as if they were crude instruments. His fingers touched the edge. He felt for some kind of hold on the rotten rock. Then he thrust himself upward. His crampons scraped for a momentary hold, rock splintering and falling downward. He hurled his body upward, grasping a toehold, pulling himself over the top. He had made it.

Willi belayed Hornbein up the pitch. "Good lead," Hornbein gasped as he reached his partner. "That wasn't easy."

"Thanks. Let's roll."

From here the couloir widened and was not so vertical. After six hours of climbing they found a place to sit down. Willi discarded his empty oxygen cylinder, glad to be rid of the ten pounds. The rotten rock had about ended. Above lay gray rock, firm rock, *real* rock, and snow into which they could dig their crampons. The altimeter read about 27,000 feet, still 1,100 feet from the summit. It was one o'clock. A great bulk of mountain rose above with no hint of the summit or a route up.

Willi took the radio out of his pack.

"West Ridge to Base," Willi yelled into the walkie-talkie.

"This is Base here, Willi," Whittaker replied, his voice surging with excitement. "How are you? How are things going?"

"Man, this is a real bearcat!" Willi said. "It's too damned tough to try to go back. It would be too dangerous."

"I'm sure you're considering all exits," Whittaker replied. He knew what that altitude did to a person's brain. He knew how gung-ho the two climbers were. He was worried about how much judgment Willi and Tom had left. He felt they simply weren't being rational. "Why don't you leave yourself an opening? If it's not going to pan out, you can always start working your way down. I think there is always a way to come back."

"Roger, Jim. God damn it, if we can't start moving together, we'll have to move back down."

"Don't work yourself up into a bottleneck, Willi. How about rappelling?" Willi could tell that Whittaker was upset at this talk of being past the point of no return.

"There are no rappel points, Jim. Absolutely no rappel points," Willi said. "There's nothing to secure a rope to. So it's up and over for us today and we'll probably be getting in pretty late, maybe as late as seven or eight o'clock tonight."

The rock was so rotten that if they tried to rappel back down the pitons would probably tear out, sending Willi and Hornbein smashing down the mountain. If they had wanted to, however, they could have found a way back down the West Ridge. "It was not reasoning but desire that moved us," Willi said. "We had committed ourselves." How many times before had Willi thought that there was no turning back? It had not been true though. Out of the corner of one eye Willi had always looked back. Now all hesitancy, self-doubt, conjecture, reflection were gone, left below the Yellow Band. The only direction was up.

By three o'clock there was still no news of Lute and Barrel coming up the South Col. That meant that when Willi and Tom reached the summit they would probably have to find their way down the South Col route by themselves. Willi pushed onward, reaching the snowfield at the bottom of Everest's summit pyramid. They were at about 28,400 feet. From here they had been thinking about going up the northeast ridge. The West Ridge looked easier.

At 4:30 they stopped for a belated lunch. Out of his pack Willi pulled slushy lemonade wrapped in his down jacket and some frozen kipper snacks to share with Tom. After eating, Willi led onward again, moving diagonally upward, first on cruddy slate, then on snow. Though the wind was blowing close to sixty miles an hour, Willi was feeling the joy of climbing up here, alone with his partner and the mountain. For Hornbein it was fine too, like a day climbing in the Rockies.

They were at the crest of the West Ridge. A hundred and fifty feet above, Willi saw the south summit of Everest ablaze in the late afternoon sunlight. The main summit itself lay only 400 feet above. All that stood between Willi and his one great dream was a rocky spine.

Willi looked at the stretch of pure rock with anticipation. He and Tom took off their crampons and overboots. Willi headed up, the Vibram soles clasping onto the rock.

How Willi loved the feel and touch of rocks. Close to 29,000 feet in the sky, Willi moved joyfully up, choosing the tiniest footholds, feeling the rock through his down mittens, sensing the texture of the stone each time he grasped a new hold. He moved further and further out onto the face, into more danger, into more risk, further out than he had any right or reason to take them, further and further out, and it was pleasure, pure pleasure. Five thousand feet below to one side lay the Rongbuk Glacier that Mallory had ventured up so many years before. Below to the other side stood Lhotse and Nuptse. Eight thousand feet down lay the South Col and Advanced Base Camp. Willi did not have to be climbing out here so exposed, but he was beyond reason, and it was good and beautiful and fine. He was far beyond where he had ever been, and he moved upward and upward and upward.

Willi regretted when the rock ended in a snow belt. Willi and Tom stopped to strap on their crampons, taking twenty minutes. Willi headed up again. This was good snow, firm snow, the spikes digging in.

Willi stopped. He waved Hornbein ahead, coiling the rope as his partner moved forward. Hornbein drew up beside Willi. Forty feet ahead on a pure spire of snow was the tattered American flag that Whittaker had planted three weeks before. As the evening sun cast its last rays of light across the mountain, the two men embraced. Tears ran out of their eyes and down their faces. Holding onto each other they walked onto the summit of Everest, Chomo-lungma, the Goddess-mother of the World. Everest cast its massive shadows down across the bulk of Makalu, the mountain Willi had attempted so many years before.

It was 6:15, nearly dusk. No mountain cast shadows down on Everest's summit. The sun shone bright and pure, the sky so clear that it was as if they had risen beyond time itself, beyond dawn and dusk and darkness. The wind blew fiercely across Willi's face. Northward stretching for hundreds of miles, he saw the brown hills of Tibet, rolling on and on. Southward lay the gentle valleys of Nepal covered by a wispy white blanket of cloud.

Willi and Tom did not try to talk. They were full of an understanding beyond understanding. They turned off the oxygen and stood looking down on the world. Within the beauty of the moment they felt loneliness. Within the roar of the wind they felt silence. Within the glory they felt fear, not for their lives, but for the unknowns that weighed down on them. Within the triumph, they felt disappointment that this, only this, was Everest, the summit of their dreams. They knew that there were higher summits still if they could only see them.

The two men took pictures, including a shot of Willi holding the Oregon State Mountain Club flag. Then Willi took a crucifix, given him by The Reverend Andrew Bakewell, a member of the 1951 Everest reconnaissance expedition; and two Buddhist prayer flags, a gift of the Sherpa Ang Dorje. He put them at the base of the flagpole tucked into a *kata*, a Buddhist ceremonial scarf that Gombu had left three weeks before.

"Buddhist prayer flags and ceremonial scarf, the American flag, and the cross of Christ all perched together on the top of the world—supported by an aluminum rappel picket painted 'Survival Orange'. The symbolic possibilities rendered my summit prayer more than a trifle incoherent. Feelings and thoughts melted and merged in our moment of climax. My thoughts were heavily weighted with history—the early drive and vision of such men as Mallory, Norton, Smythe, Shipton, and Tilman. And the later generations of Everesters led by Hillary and Tenzing. . . . Following these years of effort and achievement appears our own expedition and the tremendous output on the part of the entire team—sahibs and Sherpas alike—output and sacrifice without which our own summit moment would never have materialized.

"But dominating such thoughts were the surging emotions which colored them. Control is thinned by the altitude and the tears came readily—called forth by a wave of gratitude and a burst of comradely feeling for each member of the expedition—our wives and families— eliciting their own peculiar mixture of guilt and exaltation. Twenty minutes of emotional flux such as this and the marvel is that we still had the starch even to start the descent."

It was 6:30. They could stay no longer. They headed off the summit toward the South Col, Bishop's and Jerstad's fresh footprints their only guide.

"Want to go first?" Willi asked.

"Doesn't matter, Willi, either way."

As Hornbein uncoiled the rope in the gathering gloom, he watched Willi moving out ahead. Climbing down a mountain the man who went second had the tough belaying job to do. Tom wondered if Willi was finally tiring.

Fifty feet from the summit Willi stopped. It was 6:35. As he took out the radio, Willi looked down on a sea of shadows, only the summit of Everest still bathed in light. Willi told Maynard Miller at Advanced Base Camp that they had reached the summit and were on their way down.

"Have you seen any sign of Barrel and Lute?" Maynard asked.

"We saw fresh tracks on the summit so they must have been here."

Before ending the conversation, Willi spoke a few lines derived from Robert Frost:

> . . . I have promises to keep,
> And miles to go before we sleep,
> And miles to go before we sleep.

If they could only make it down to Camp VI where Dingman and Girmi were waiting, they would be okay. Willi moved downward as if intuition and instinct were one, without fear or apprehension, feeling his way in the gathering gloom, all he had ever learned in the mountains guiding him. He didn't need his goggles any longer. It was getting too dark for that. For a moment Willi caught a glimpse of Advanced Base Camp over 8,500 feet below. Makalu was all darkness. Lhotse too. The sun was setting on the summit of Everest.

Seven-thirty. All that was left of day was what Tom called "a dream landscape of feathery vagueness." Willi took out the flashlight. He had to see. He had scarcely begun to use it when the light dimmed. He leaned over and held the flashlight just off the snow, trying to find Bishop's and Jerstad's footprints like a blindman reading Braille. He couldn't lose them. He just couldn't.

"No tracks over here," Willi called.

"Maybe we should dig in for the night," Hornbein suggested.

"I don't know. Dave and Girmi should be at Six."

No one had ever survived a bivouac nearly this high. If they stopped they could end up frozen statues left forever on the summit flanks of Everest. Down they stumbled, groping their way along the massive slopes of the mountain. Nothing stayed the same. For a few feet the snow was firm. As soon as they got used to that, they hit soft snow. For a while the snow was deep, then so shallow that their crampons struck rock. The wind ripped at them from one side. When they caught on how to lean into the bitter gusts, the wind struck them from the other side, battering them down.

If only they could make it down to Camp VI where Dave and Girmi would have food and rest, and guide them down the mountain in the morning. If only . . . *"Helloo."* Willi shouted, his shrieks picked up by the wind and cast off into the void.

"Hello! "

"Hello!" Hornbein shouted.

Willi yodeled.

"Hello."

"Hello."

The wind seemed to be answering, not an echo, but game.

"Hello."

Could it be?

"It's Dingman," Willi shouted. "He hears us."

"Then we're near Camp Six," Hornbein replied.

"But why doesn't he show a light?" Willi said irritatedly. "He could show us where the lousy camp is if he would just flash a light."

Willi moved on again, feeling his way down the mountain. Time and time again they heard the beckoning voice. It was like a warm embrace waiting below in Camp VI.

Hornbein moved cautiously following Willi's footprints, belaying his partner whenever necessary. *"Willi!"* Hornbein shot out into space. As the rope stiffened, he fell into the snow.

The wind picked up, tearing at them. The two men stopped, cut the climbing rope in two, and tied in close to one another. Even five feet away, Willi could hardly see Hornbein. Down and down they went, over hard snow and crunchy snow, firm rocks and rotten rocks, down and down, following the voices. The wind let up finally and they could hear words, sentences even, wafting up out of the blackness. If only Dave and Girmi had a flashlight to guide them. But they didn't and Willi's light gave off only a dull glow.

It was after nine o'clock. Still they continued downward. Willi ran out of oxygen. That slowed him even more. Nine-thirty. Still they kept moving.

"This way—come on," a voice sounded out of the dark. As Willi heard the voice again he fell five feet down a crevasse. "That's right— come on—you're going fine." The fall was nothing, nothing. He pulled himself up. Still they moved down the mountain, the voice appearing and disappearing, like a mirage.

"It sounds like a Sherpa," Willi said.

"Wait a minute, there it is again."

"Is that you, Dingman?" Tom shouted.

"HELLO. HELLO," Willi yelled. Then he muttered to himself, "Why doesn't he flash a light?"

A shout. A shout from below.

"Hear that?" Tom said. "They're still there."

"Come on. Let's go!"

They hurried onward with a rush of urgency, knowing that soon there would be sleeping bags, tents, and rest, and warm food.

"This way—come on."

The voices were so near.

Out of the black night two figures appeared, standing in the snow leaning on their ice axes. "Is that you, Dingman?" Tom asked, hugging the first man as if to reassure himself that he was real.

"No. It's Lute. Lute and Barrel."

Like children waking from a dream, Willi and Tom took awhile to realize just what this meant. They were not at Camp VI at all. They were 850 feet above, at the top of a knifelike snow ridge. They were not in the hands of two fresh climbers who would guide them down. They had two exhausted remnants on their hands.

That morning as Bishop and Jerstad had been preparing to leave Camp VI, their gas stove had exploded in a sheet of orange flame, burning their beards and eyebrows, devouring Bishop's sleeping mask. They had put the fire out and left two hours behind schedule, not arriving on the summit until 3:30. The two climbers had waited as long as they could, but seeing no sign of Willi and Hornbein had left the summit at 4:15. They were still moving downward when they heard the voices from above. Although they were terribly tired, the idea of continuing on down to Camp VI did not even occur to them. They believed that they had no choice but to wait and help lead Willi and Tom down.

If this would be what they called a "terminal experience," Jerstad and Bishop decided they would go out with dignity. They would not lie down. So they stood leaning on their ice axes, stomping up and down, using what energy they had left shouting up Everest. There were few things on earth below as tiring as standing waiting that high on a mountain. Bishop was not wearing the expedition boots but the lighter, more comfortable boots that the British had worn in 1953. He could feel his feet beginning to freeze, moving from discomfort, to growing numbness, to no feeling.

Willi and Hornbein thought that Bishop appeared as if he didn't care anymore, wanting only to be left alone. Jerstad's eyes were so hemorrhaged that he could hardly see, as was Bishop's left eye.

Here in these two men Willi and Tom thought they would find strength and succor. But while they were waiting so much had drained out of Bishop and Jerstad. Willi and Hornbein found weakness worse than their own. That truth became itself a gift of strength and succor. Jerstad had saved some oxygen for Bishop, but he had been too tired to change the cylinders. Hornbein took off his mittens and screwed the oxygen hose to the regulator, his fingers growing numb. Willi took the Dexedrine in Hornbein's pocket—and gave one tablet to Bishop, one to

Jerstad. Even with the oxygen and the Dexedrine, Willi had to prod, to insist to get Bishop moving again.

"Get your ass in gear," Willi yelled.

"Let's go," Hornbein said. "This is no place to spend a night."

Hornbein led, followed by Jerstad, then Willi and Bishop about sixty feet behind. The rope jerked as Bishop collapsed in the snow. Willi helped Bishop up and tried to pump him with encouragement. Off they moved again. Lute was trying to find the route but his eyes were swollen shut. As they moved downward they kept stumbling. Willi and Hornbein pushed, and prodded, cursed and threatened. When Bishop fell Willi yanked him up.

"Anybody can walk a hundred yards, anybody!" Willi shouted. "No matter how tired you are, keep going."

Bishop could barely stand, but he stumbled downward. One by one the other climbers ran out of oxygen. Jerstad tumbled down, his fall stopped when his neck caught on the climbing rope.

An outcropping of rock appeared far below.

"Now where, Lute?" Hornbein asked.

"Can't see, Tom. Can't see a damn thing. We've got to turn down a gully between some rocks."

"Which gully? There's two or three."

"Don't know, Tom."

"Think, Lute. Try to remember. We've got to get to Six."

"I don't know. I just can't see."

It was after midnight now. In three hours they had come only four hundred feet. They had reached the rocks. But which gully?

They were at about 28,000 feet. They knew that no one had ever survived overnight at such a height. If they went down the wrong gully they probably would never get back. They had no choice. It was too dangerous to go on. They set their packs on a narrow fifteen-foot sloping outcrop of rock and perched there the best they could.

Willi and Hornbein huddled together. Bishop and Jerstad sat a few feet down to the right. Jerstad was so tired, his fingers so uncoordinated, that he couldn't even zip up his down parka. He knew that if he was going to survive he had to keep his circulation going. He kept hugging himself, banging his feet together. He couldn't stop. He wouldn't stop. Bishop's feet didn't even hurt anymore. His fingers were growing numb. There was nothing he could do. Nothing. Lying with his feet propped above, he drifted into sleep.

Willi's feet were numb. But that was okay. He wasn't worried about them. Hornbein had wanted to keep warm by hugging Willi. But Hornbein was shaking uncontrollably. Hornbein reached down and took off his steel crampons. In the 18-degree-below-zero weather they were conductors of cold right up into the soles of his feet. Willi noticed what Hornbein was doing. He came out of himself a moment and offered to rub his partner's feet. Then Willi helped Hornbein remove his boots and socks, slid the chilled feet under his parka and underwear, up against his stomach, held them there, and drifted off again. When Hornbein offered to do the same for his feet, Willi said no. He was okay. He was in better shape than Tom. He drifted off again.

If the wind had blown across the high ridges of Everest as it had the last ninety-three nights in a row, they would almost certainly have died. The wind had let up, though, and the four men settled into the cold, endless night.

Willi looked up and saw stars gleaming like icy diamonds. He looked down on the world. Far out on the Indian plains bolts of heat flared up, illuminating the low, distant sky.

Lying on the cold rock the four mountaineers had the same flashes of illumination. It was as if the landscape of their souls was the same, or the landscape of all men's souls was the same. None of them thought of living or dying. They were beyond that. Tom and Willi had gone through so much together; still Willi felt so far from his climbing partner that Tom hardly existed. Tom knew that he was completely alone too. So did Lute and Barrel.

Barrel "felt a speck in the universe realizing the tremendous insignificance of man." Tom "floated in a dreamlike eternity, devoid of plans, fears, regrets. . . . Death had no meaning, nor, for that matter, did life." It came to Lute that nothing mattered, not laws, not relationships, not even his children, nothing. He disappeared into nothingness and felt free.

Willi was the philosopher. Willi was the mystic. Like the others, he too was journeying beyond the summit. He was not even trying to encapsulate what he was feeling into mere words, mere thoughts. He lay there lost in time and space, peering out into the darkness.

Were the stars dimming? Or was that his imagination? It was only four o'clock. Were the rocks not quite so black? Or did they just seem so? In the eastern skies the great bulk of Kangchenjunga loomed up before his eyes. Tom's face was clear now, as gray as the mountain. Each minute the rocks grew lighter. Yet another peak rose up out of the darkness. The night had gone from black, to gray, to purple, to a pink alpine glow. A half hour had passed. Still, there was no sun.

The peaks turned golden. Light shimmered down the white mountains. The sun rose up above the Himalayan peaks, fiery and intense and alive. It was five o'clock, a new day.

"Wake up, Lute."

Lute opened his eyes too, as best he could, and saw the great fireball. Light passed down from the South Col. As the sun moved on up into the blue sky, it seemed to cool, to grow more distant. The rich colors of dawn faded away. The day was upon them, stark and real.

Hornbein strapped on his crampons. Then the four men set off as they had begun their journey, Willi leading tied to Tom, followed by Lute and Barrel on a second rope. Lute's eyes and Barrel's left eye were blood-red slits.

Willi and Hornbein trudged down the gully that they had been unable to find at night. Though he was not feeling as strong as his partner, Willi had no trouble making his way down Everest. Turning a corner Willi saw Dingman and Girmi moving up the mountain one hundred feet below.

Dingman ran up the mountain, reaching the two summiteers too breathless even to greet them. Looking at the faces masked in beard and frost, Dingman was doubly speechless. He was amazed that this wasn't Barrel and Lute, but Willi and Tom.

"There's oxygen," Dingman said finally, preparing to get out his extra cylinder.

"We're okay. Lute and Barrel will need it more."

Dingman and Girmi could almost certainly have made it to the summit themselves this day. Instead, they hurried on up the mountain to help Bishop and Jerstad.

Willi and Tom continued down the mountain. At Camp VI, Nima Dorje, another Sherpa, greeted them. Willi took off his boots. His feet were a deadly white, as hard as metal. Willi knew that he might lose his feet. He was so thirsty. He drank coffee, tea, hot chocolate, lemonade, anything.

After the other summit team arrived and rested, the seven men headed on down Everest. The South Col was a desolate, deadly place. For Willi the South Col was all new. As tired as he was, he drank it all in. At Camp V, the climbers huddled in a tent eating lunch, then moved out into gale-force winds. Further down the mountain the winds let up.

All the Winds of Asia
by Peter Boardman

Chris Bonington's expedition to the Southwest Face of Everest put four—possibly five—men on the summit. Peter Boardman and Sherpa Pertemba were the second pair of team members to summit.

All the winds of Asia seemed to be trying to blow us from the ridge. A decision was needed. It was four in the afternoon and the skies were already darkening around the South Summit of Everest. I threw my iced and useless snow-goggles away into the whiteness and tried, clumsily mitted, to clear the ice from my eyelashes. I bowed my head into the spindrift and tried to peer along the ridge. Mick should have met us at least three-quarters of an hour before, unless something had happened to him. We had been waiting for nearly one and a half hours. There was no sign of Doug and Dougal's bivouac site. The sky and cornices and whirling snow merged together, visibility was reduced to ten feet and all tracks were obliterated. Pertemba and I huddled next to the rock of the South Summit where Mick had asked us to wait for him. Pertemba said he could not feel his toes or fingers and mine too were nailed with cold. I thought of

Mick wearing his glasses and blinded by spindrift, negotiating the fixed rope on the Hillary Step, the fragile one foot windslab on the Nepal side, and the cornices on the Tibetan side of the ridge. I thought of our own predicament, with the 800 feet of the South Summit Gully—guarded by a 60 foot rock step halfway—to descend, and then half of the 2,000 foot great traverse above the Rock Band to cross before reaching the end of the fixed ropes that extended across from Camp VI. It had taken Doug and Dougal three hours in the dawn sunshine after their bivouac to reach Camp VI—but we now had only an hour of light left. At 28,700 feet the boundary between a controlled and an uncontrolled situation is narrow and we had crossed that boundary within minutes—a strong wind and sun shining through clouds had turned into a violent blizzard of driving snow, the early afternoon had drifted into approaching night and our success was turning into tragedy.

A mountaineer when he is climbing is doing, seeing and feeling and yet on his return home from the hill he often baulks at recollection in public of these experiences because he treasures the privacy and intensity of his memories. And yet, as Hornbein remarked after being asked to write about his ascent of the West Ridge:

'I soon learned, Everest was not a private affair. It belonged to many men.'

The stories of man's adventures on Everest have almost reached the stature of myth in the popular imaginations of the 20th century. The full record of our expedition will eventually appear to add to these stories. I do not aspire here to document the planning and events of the expedition, nor to presume to evaluate its achievements, nor to predict the future of climbing on Everest. I fear that at such a cold touch the pains and charms that are my memories of Everest will fly.

My memories are of a keen apprehension that turned into a living nightmare. Even on the leech infested walk-in we dreamt about the climb to come—one morning Tut and Doug confessed, with gallows humour, 'I keep getting stranded above the Rock Band' and, 'Dougal got severe frost-bite last night'. Whilst Nick and Tut were tackling the Rock Band I wrote:

> 'Everyone is very optimistic that we'll crack it soon, but it's still early days. We've been lucky with the weather and there could easily be a storm at any time to curtail or even set back all movement.'

'Think upwards' always seems to be a good dictum for success in climbing and the Everest summit was in my mind night and day all the time I was moving up the face into position for the second attempt. Aside from the physical effort and practical judgement and worry there is a dreamlike quality in the climbing on Everest. At Camp VI wrote:

> 'The face is a strange unreal world. All dressed up in one piece oversuits and six layers on the feet, oxygen mask and goggles one seems distanced from where one is and what one is doing, like a sort of moonwalk.'

This half-glimpsed quality was preserved far back in my mind. As a child I used to daydream over a painting in a big picture book, *Adventure of the World*, which depicted the tiny bold figures of Hillary and Tenzing on the top of a summit that thrust out of a sea of clouds.

As Pertemba and I crossed the traverse above the Rock Band in the early dawn of our summit day it felt as if we were on that highest peak above the clouds, as if the sight of the endless cloud sea was joining hands with the dreamland of the past. The weather was changing and the cloud layer was up to 27,000 feet, covering Nuptse and everything beyond it. Only the top of Lhotse peeped out below us, whereas above us the sun sparkled through the snow smoking over the Summit Ridge. For three days I had been jumaring up fixed ropes, counting steps and trying to keep in front of some Sherpas coming up to Camp IV, gasping up to Camp V, and then following Nick and Tut's intricate route through the Rock Band. But now I felt free and untrammelled, and exhilarated as if I had just become committed on the start of a climb in the Alps. Pertemba and I moved, unroped, steadily away from the end of the fixed line and kicked away the spindrift from the tracks that Doug and Dougal had made two days before. Everest, the myth, with its magic and history, seemed to make me feel strong, thinking upwards. Invincible together.

The snow was only a few feet deep on top of the rocks and the route wavered around spurs and over rock steps. The South Summit gully was steep but there was a fixed line hanging over the rock step half way up it. As I reached the South Summit, Pertemba dropped behind and I waited for him. His oxygen mask had stopped working. One and a half hours and several cold fingers later we had slit open the tube and cleared the two inches of ice that were blocking the airway, and patched the mask back into working order. We changed to fresh oxygen cylinders and moved, roped now, along the ridge towards the summit of Everest. Its red ribbons were fading in the strong light and fluttering prayers from the other side of the mountain. The Chinese tripod was catching drifting snow and leaning defiantly in the wind. Its presence was strangely reassuring. Pertemba attached a Nepalese flag to it and I hung a Deadman snow anchor from it. We ate some chocolate and mint cake and I burbled into a tape-recorder. We started down.

We were amazed to see him through the mist. Mick was sitting on the snow only a few hundred yards down an easy angled snow-slope from the summit. He congratulated us and said he wanted to film us on a bump on the ridge and pretend it was the summit, but I told him about the Chinese maypole. Then he asked us to go back to the summit with him. I agreed reluctantly and he, sensing my reluctance, changed his mind and said he'd go up and film it and then come straight down after us. He borrowed Pertemba's camera to take some stills on the top and we walked back 50 feet and then walked past him whilst he filmed us. I took a couple of pictures of him. He had the Blue Peter flag and an auto-load camera with him. He asked us to wait for him by the big rock on the South Summit where Pertemba and I had dumped our first oxygen cylinders and some rope and film on the way up. I told him that Pertemba was wanting to move roped with me—so he should catch us up fairly quickly. I said, 'See you soon' and we moved back down the ridge to the South Summit. Shortly after we had left him the weather began to deteriorate.

A decision was needed. I pointed at my watch and said 'We'll wait ten more minutes'. Pertemba agreed. That helped us—it gave some responsibility to the watch. I fumbled in my sack and pulled out our stove to leave behind. The time was up. At first we went the wrong way—too far towards the South Col. About 150 feet down we girdled back until we found what we thought was the South Summit Gully. There was a momentary lessening in the blizzard, and I looked up to see the rock of the South Summit. There was still no sign of Mick and it was now about half past four. The decision had been made and now we had to fight for our own lives and think downwards.

Pertemba is not a technical climber, not used to moving away from fixed ropes or in bad conditions. At first he was slow. For three pitches I kicked down furiously, placed a Deadman and virtually pulled him down in the sliding, blowing powder snow. But Pertemba was strong and adaptable—he began to move faster and soon we were able to move together. Were we in the gully? I felt panic surge inside. Then I saw twin rocks in the snow that I recognized from the morning. We descended diagonally from there and in the dusk saw Dougal's oxygen cylinder that marked the top of the fixed rope over the rock step.

We abseiled down to the end of the rope and tied a spare rope we had to the end and descended the other 150 feet. From there we descended down and across for 1,000 feet towards the end of the fixed ropes. During our traverse we were covered by two powder snow avalanches from the summit slopes. Fortunately our oxygen cylinders were still functioning and we could breathe. It was a miracle that we found the end of the fixed ropes in the dark, marked by two oxygen cylinders sticking out of the snow. On the fixed rope Pertemba slowed down again and I pulled him mercilessly until he shouted that one of his crampons had fallen off. The rope between us snagged and in flicking it free I tumbled over a 15 foot rock step to be held on the fixed rope. At one point a section of the fixed rope had been swept away. At half past seven we stumbled into the 'summit boxes' at Camp VI. Martin was there and I burst into tears.

The storm pinned the three of us to Camp VI at 27,600 feet for 36 hours. Pertemba and I shared one of the two boxes and were completely dependent on Martin. Pertemba was snow-blinded and I was worried about my feet. Martin had a good supply of gas and he kept us supplied with tea and oxygen cylinders. Our box was becoming buried in snow every four hours and Martin kept on dragging himself out to clear them, damaging his fingers from frost-bite. It was miserable inside the box, the snow was pressing the walls and it felt like that medieval dungeon cell known as 'the little ease'—maddeningly too short to stretch out, too low to sit up. Pertemba lay back, his eyes closed and lips moving in silent incantation. I felt isolated from my friends lower down the mountain by a decision and an experience I could not share.

During the second night the wind and snow ceased but their noise was replaced by the roar of avalanches sweeping past either side of the snowy crest on which we were perched and plunging over the edge of the Rock Band. Dawn came—clear and cold, sad and silvery. We looked across the traverse and up the gully to the South Summit but there was no sign of Mick. We turned and began the long repetitive ritual of clipping and unclipping the piton brake and safety loop and abseiling, rope-length after rope-length, 6,000 feet down to the Western Cwm.

As we emerged from the foot of the gully through the Rock Band we could see tiny figures outside the three boxes of Camp V, 1,000 feet below us. It took a long time to reach them, for many of the anchors on the fixed ropes had been swept away. Ronnie, Nick, Tut and Ang Phurba were waiting for us and helped us down into the living air and warmth of the Western Cwm and the reassuring faces of Camp II.

Messner and Habeler:
Alone at the Top
by David Roberts

The climbing partnership between Reinhold Messner and Peter Habeler ended with their 1978 ascent of Everest, which made them the first men to climb the peak without supplemental oxygen. David Roberts' 1982 Outside article investigated the reasons for the break-up.

The astonished proclamation swept through the climbing world late in 1974: Messner and Habeler had done the Eiger in ten hours. *Ten hours.* The previous best time on the most dreaded wall in the Alps had been almost twice as long. At one point, high on the Eiger's North Face, the two climbers had met up with a party of Austrians, friends of Habeler's, who were on the third *day* of a climb. "What are you doing?" Habeler asked when he found the men still in their sleeping bags. "It's a perfect day, you should be climbing." "We're too tired," came the listless reply. Habeler offered to join the dispirited party; they waved him on. The two strongest mountaineers in Europe continued to stroll up the treacherous wall, reaching the top by three in the afternoon.

The extent of their celebrity was recorded that evening when they got drunk with Clint Eastwood in the Kleine Scheidegg, at the foot of the mountain. (Eastwood was on location for the filming of *The Eiger Sanction*.) A photo was later circulated in the climbing press, showing the tanned and fit climbers arm in arm with Eastwood and the beautiful actress Heidi Brühl. In the photo, Brühl and Eastwood look like admiring fans; Habeler and Messner are the stars.

The next year there was a new focus of astonishment: Messner and Habeler had done a new route on Hidden Peak. Three days, alpine style. No porters. Lots of hard climbing, and they hadn't even roped up. In one stroke, Messner and Habeler had brought an extreme lightweight alpine style, perfected in the lower ranges, to an 8000-meter Himalayan objective and pulled off the ascent without a hitch.

In 1978 Messner and Habeler astounded the climbing world again, this time by climbing Everest without oxygen. Doctors had told the pair they would die; climbers who had been to the top of the world with oxygen had sworn it was impossible without. On the summit Messner had managed to take good photographs. Habeler had glissaded most of the way down to the South Col, reaching it an hour after he had left the summit.

Messner and Habeler. In the history of mountaineering there have been a small number of perfect partnerships, pairs of men wedded by an almost extrasensory attunement to each other's gifts, whose combined accomplishments have changed the face of the sport. One thinks of those British pioneers of lightweight expeditionary assault, H. W. Tilman and Eric Shipton. Or of the great postwar French duo, Lionel Terray and Louis Lachenal, with their second ascent of the Eiger North Wall and their brilliant efforts on Annapurna. Or of the Austrian Hermann Buhl and his inseparable partner, Kuno Rainer. (After the first years Buhl did become the dominant partner, and his greatest feat—being the first to reach the summit of Nanga Parbat in 1953—was accomplished alone.)

Since 1960 no partnership in mountaineering has had anything like the impact of that between Reinhold Messner and Peter Habeler. For fifteen years the two brilliant climbers from the Tirol—Habeler an Austrian, Messner a northern Italian of Austrian descent—climbed in a transcendent cooperation. Each testified in print that he had found the ideal mountaineering complement to himself.

But the sad fact—perhaps "tragic" is not too strong a word—is that since 1978 Messner and Habeler have barely spoken to each other. An apparently irreparable breach has sundered the perfect partnership. Each man doubts that he will ever again climb with the other. Most ironic of all, the breach is the product not of any quarrels or conflicts that took place in the mountains, but rather of wrangles and jealousies that sprang out of the wilderness of print and film and television.

Peter Habeler is thirty-nine. He lives in the small Tirolean village of Mayrhofen, where he grew up, with his striking wife Regina and his two sons. Since 1972 he has made part of his living by running the Peter Habeler Alpinschule Zillertal, a climbing school with ten instructors and a perfect safety record. He doubles in the winter as a ski instructor and supplements his income with lecture fees. He has established a great reputation in his home region, becoming Austria's best-known mountain climber. But his fame, until recently, has always been in Messner's shadow; Habeler was the silent partner.

When Habeler was five, his father died; it was his grandfather, an amateur guide, who took him on his first mountain tours. By his teens he had a local climbing reputation as "the lunatic boy," earned for his solo explorations of dangerous glaciers. Not until he was seventeen did he gain any instruction from more experienced partners. In 1966, with a much weaker partner, Habeler made the third ascent of the Central Pillar of Frêney on Mont Blanc, a climb that had become famous a few years earlier when a strong party led by the great Walter Bonatti lost four of its seven members during a retreat in a blizzard. After Mont Blanc, Habeler climbed Bonatti's extreme route on the Grand Pilier d'Angle, again with the same, less-skilled partner.

His new partner, it soon became evident, would be Reinhold Messner. That same season, 1966, the two men did their first hard climb together, the Walker Spur on the Grandes Jorasses.

At thirty-seven, Reinhold Messner is two years Habeler's junior. But, with the possible exception of Sir Edmund Hillary, he has surpassed

Habeler in reputation to become the most famous mountain climber in the world. He manages to spend about two months each year near his home town of Villnöss, in the Italian Tirol, where he has built a cabin that serves as a retreat from his own celebrity. The rest of the year is divided about evenly between expeditions and what Messner calls "working"—lecture tours, lining up contracts, and writing. After each expedition Messner hastily produces a book; each is a European best seller. His entire income—a comfortable one—is derived from sharing his adventures with a vicarious public. It is not an exaggeration to say that Messner is as renowned a sport hero in Europe as Reggie Jackson or Larry Bird is in the United States. One sees his picture in shop windows and in magazine ads.

The second oldest of nine children (eight boys), Messner was first taken climbing by his parents at the age of five. Like Habeler, he showed an early penchant for soloing: at fourteen, when his father balked at seconding the first pitch during a climb in Italy's Dolomites, Reinhold dropped the rope and finished the climb alone.

In the late 1960s Messner began to acquire a reputation, first in Europe and then worldwide, for his daring and fast big-wall climbs, many of them first solo ascents. The excellence of those climbs remains obscure to climbers unfamiliar with the Alps, having been eclipsed by Messner's Himalayan exploits in the 1970s. Commenting on Messner's first solo ascent of the North Wall of Les Droites in 1969, Jon Krakauer, an outstanding American ice climber, says, "In terms of sheer boldness, I think the Droites North Face is the most impressive thing Messner's ever done. In 1969 it was the most formidable ice climb in the Alps. He had only really primitive ice tools. It was before the specially curved ice axes or the chrome-moly crampons. In America at that time people were still chopping steps up Pinnacle Gully on New Hampshire's Mount Washington."

Messner made an early splash in print with a polemic called "The Murder of the Impossible," an impassioned plea against the overuse of mechanical aids in an attempt to force *direttissimas*, or unnaturally straight lines up mountain walls. "Put on your boots and get going," the article exhorted. "If you've got a companion, take a rope with you and a couple of pitons for your belays, but nothing else. I'm already on my way, ready for anything—even for retreat, if I meet the impossible." The article struck a sympathetic chord among climbers the world over.

In 1969 Messner and Habeler first joined on an expedition—to Yerupaja in the Peruvian Andes. There they pulled off a difficult route on the mountain's east face. The next year both were slated for an expedition to the Himalaya to climb the Rupal Face on Nanga Parbat, arguably the largest wall in the world. During the planning stages, however, Habeler got a job offer at Jackson Hole and had to back out; his place on the expedition was taken by Messner's brother Günther. It was a fateful substitution. After a long struggle the Messner brothers made the summit, but Günther was so exhausted he doubted that he could descend the face unaided. A conversation shouted over a storm, between Reinhold and two other team members, produced a misunderstanding; earlier there had been confusion over flare signals shot off from a lower camp by expedition leader Karl Herrligkoffer. In desperation, Reinhold and Günther traversed *over* Nanga Parbat and descended the easier Diamir Face. Near its base, Reinhold briefly left his debilitated brother to scout the route; upon his return he found no trace of Günther and had to conclude that an avalanche had obliterated all trace of him. Reinhold virtually crawled out to the lowlands, where some hill people came to his rescue.

Back in Europe the expedition stirred a controversy. There were accusations that Messner had sacrificed his brother to his own ambition, that he had secretly planned the traverse to redound to his own glory.

Messner's toes had been so severely frostbitten on the Nanga Parbat climb that one big toe and parts of seven others had to be amputated. After such surgery, few climbers are ready for further ordeals in the cold, but Messner plunged right back into mountaineering. Two years later, in 1972, he was again involved in a major controversy. On the first ascent of the South Face of Manaslu, like Nanga Parbat a Himalayan 8000-meter peak, Messner left a weaker partner to go to the summit alone. A blizzard trapped that man along with three others near their highest camp; in their efforts to save each other, two of the team members perished in the storm. Once again Messner was accused of sacrificing partners to his ambition—even though his comrade had insisted, as he turned back, that Messner go on to the summit alone.

Messner continued his quest for 8000-meter summits at the pace of at least one a year. There were failures on Lhotse, Makalu, Annapurna, Nanga Parbat, and Dhaulagiri (the last with Habeler), but there were the stunning successes on Hidden Peak and Everest. Along with these achievements, Messner's books began to create a sharply etched public persona. It was clear that modesty was not Messner's forte. The first of his books translated into English was called *The Seventh Grade* (1973). Its title implied that the conventional six grades of climbing difficulty were all but obsolete in the face of routes being done in the Alps. Of his own climbs, Messner wrote, "I would venture to ascribe Grade VI or VI+," adding with some coyness, "I would be fascinated to see who would be the first to climb a seventh-grade route."

In *The Big Walls* (1977) Messner updated a famous 1949 article by Anderl Heckmair that identified the "three last problems of the Alps" as the north faces of the Matterhorn, the Eiger, and the Grandes Jorasses. The "three great faces of the world," Messner declared, were the Eiger, the south face of Aconcagua in Argentina (which he mistakenly claimed was the biggest face in the Western Hemisphere), and the Rupal Face on Nanga Parbat. After the Rupal Face, he declared, "a significant advance is no longer possible." Messner emerged as the only man to have climbed all five of the great faces.

An avid nonclimbing public seemed to buy Messner's self-congratulation. In his *Everest: Expedition to the Ultimate* (1978), he ventured the opinion that an attempt on the world's highest mountain without oxygen was so radical an idea that "in the Middle Ages we would have been burned as heretics." About his next Himalayan scheme, an unsupported solo ascent of Nanga Parbat, he asserted, "This is my last great alpine dream. Indeed it is the last great alpine idea."

With each successive book, Messner also became more confessional about his private life. Along with the external struggle against rock and ice, readers were offered the details of his inner struggle with self-doubt, fear, and loneliness. An integral part of his stories was the anguish of his five-year marriage to Uschi, who had left her first husband, a Nanga Parbat teammate, for Messner. But in the next few years she had grown increasingly vexed with his mountain obsessions.

Perhaps partly in reaction to Messner's flair for self-publicizing, some climbers began to gossip that Habeler was really the tougher climber of the two. During his four-year stint in Jackson Hole, Wyoming, Habeler had climbed with a few top American mountaineers, including Yvon Chouinard and George Lowe. (He had also teamed with Englishman Doug Scott to make the first non-American ascent of the Salathé Wall route on El Capitan in Yosemite.) The Americans were impressed. Galen Rowell recorded a story about Habeler and Lowe in the Tetons:

> Lowe invited Habeler to join him on a new route he had been eyeing up the direct north face of nearby Mount Moran. Hiking at high altitude in the backcountry almost every day, Lowe thought he was in excellent condition—until he tried to keep up with Habeler, who consistently outdistanced him on the steep approach to the climb. When they reached the cliff, Habeler began climbing unroped with a rucksack. Lowe, breathing heavily, tried to keep up. At one point he came to an overhang and saw Habeler waiting for him above it. Lowe tried it, backed down, and asked Habeler for a rope from above. "Are you sure? It's not that hard." Lowe said that he was sure, and without further discussion Habeler passed down the rope. Lowe tried it again and fell off—held, of course, by Habeler's belay.

It was undeniable, however, that when Messner and Habeler got together, extraordinary deeds were done in the mountains. In *The Big*

Walls, Messner wrote: "In all my climbing career I have not known a better partner than Peter Habeler, and although we have made relatively few climbs together, we have always come out of them in perfect harmony." With prophetic irony, he added: "That we have a sympathetic partnership is also demonstrated by the fact that neither of us has felt the need to criticize the other, or underplay his role, after any of our climbs. How often one gets the impression from climbing reminiscences and attendant gossip that years after a major Alpine enterprise one of the participants is seeking to take more than his share of credit, as if to eclipse his former partner."

Whence, then, the feud? Looking back, Habeler thinks the conflict had begun to emerge by 1978, on Everest. "We never had problems," he says, "as long as I was not making anything out of myself. He was happy, and I was happy. But we were not as close friends on Everest as we were in 1976 or 1977. For some reason, something had started already. And I am not sure, but I think it could be connected with my work as a lecturer. I was giving many lectures, I had the opportunity to tell many people [about our climbs]. It seems to me that Reinhold simply wants to be number one, and he doesn't want anybody to be beside him. As long as you told him, 'Well, you are number one,' it was just fine."

The catalyst for the rift—perhaps even its cause—was Habeler's decision to write a book of his own about Everest (*The Lonely Victory: Everest,* 1978). "In the beginning," claims Habeler, "he did not object to the things that I wrote. But the fact that a book by me was written at all, that was very, very hard for him. Furthermore, my book was first on the market. It is a simple book. It is not as psychologically deep as Messner's."

Messner's rejoinder is that Habeler's book was not written by Habeler at all, but rather by a ghost writer and journalist named Eberhard Fuchs. Fuchs's help is acknowledged in the German edition of *The Lonely Victory,* but the name does not appear in the English edition. "This Fuchs," says Messner, "knew a little bit about climbing, and he was a psychologically well-educated person. He knew exactly what other people would like to know about me. Or what they would like to have happened on the expedition. The critics, they were waiting for it. And they are still using it against me.

"On expeditions," Messner says, "everybody is free to do what they like. Afterwards [Habeler] can sell a book or not sell a book, that's not the problem. I don't know if he had a contract before or not. That's not so important. But I think that if he's discussing the other personalities, he has to pay at least as much attention to his own personality. He sells my problems, but not his own.

"And there is one sentence in the book that makes me so upset that I say, I can never understand why he let his editor write it. He says that in my books I do not speak in the right way about him, and that I more or less used him in the last years. And so I thought, 'Please don't let me use you in the next expeditions. Do your own expeditions, what you like, but please don't come on my expeditions.' "

The offending passage in Habeler's book is, apparently, the following:

> Reinhold has set this all out [the details of their climbs together] in his books, even if the reader may gain the impression that he was the leader and I was simply a passenger. However, I don't feel bitter about this—the books sell better that way. The applause of the general public is not as important to me. But Reinhold needs their recognition. He likes to appear on television; he needs the interviews. . . .
>
> There is a photograph which shows me on the summit of the 8,068-metre-high Hidden Peak. Reinhold took it, simply because I got there first. The picture was published everywhere with the caption, *"Reinhold Messner conquered the Hidden Peak."* Friends and acquaintances often ask me: "Why do you put up with this? Have you no ambition? All your common ventures simply become a one-man show for Messner!" Others might have reacted differently—I just let it pass. After all, I would not have reached the summit

without Reinhold, and he wouldn't have reached it without me. We are both equally good. . . .

What else could have provoked Messner's fury? Habeler, who seems the more regretful of the two, suggests another possibility: "Reinhold's the toughest guy you can think of, but sometimes he has a moment when he gets very, very tired. About halfway up Yerupaja in 1969, he said, 'I have a stomach problem,' and I said, 'Well, OK, let's wait a little bit and then we go on.' Until then we were always changing the lead. From that point on I was leading, naturally. Because I knew if I get sick, he will lead. There was no point making a fuss about it.

"On Hidden Peak I was much stronger, but there is also a reason. He had just come from Lhotse and he was very tired. And maybe he had problems with Uschi. At one stage he told me that maybe he would have to go back because he felt funny. I am sure it still bothers him that he arrived on the summit of Hidden Peak three-quarters of an hour later than I did. It doesn't bother me, but maybe it bothers him.

"Don't get me wrong. Reinhold was always the one who started an idea. He said, 'OK, Hidden Peak would be something we can do.' I was really difficult to get started. He had to come and fetch me. When we were on our way, I was usually a little bit stronger, which doesn't mean anything. Every day is different. It could be, just by chance, you feel a little bit better that day.

"At the South Col on Everest, he got out of the tent first, he did the first few meters, and then I passed him. I kept going, breaking the track, all the way to the South Summit." Habeler laughs. "I have pictures to prove this, but it seems not important to me." Habeler does say in *Lonely Victory* that Messner was the first on the Main Summit.

But some other incidents that took place on Everest are described differently in the two books. High on the mountain, Habeler began to draw downward-pointing arrows in the snow at regular intervals. Messner's account explains it this way: "We converse in sign language. Every time Peter scratches a downward-pointing arrow in the snow, meaning 'We should turn back,' I reply with another pointing upwards—a discussion without words." Habeler rejects this interpretation. The arrows were markers for the descent—like the willow wands climbers sometimes leave to indicate their trail. To anyone with expedition experience, Habeler's explanation makes more sense.

Messner describes his snow blindness at the South Col after reaching the summit, mentioning the agony he felt and that "the tears help to soothe the pain and Peter comforts me as if I were a small child." But according to Habeler, the two had made a pact that if one got in trouble, the other would think only of rescuing himself. Now, snow-blind, "Throughout the night Reinhold screamed with pain, sobbing and crying. He implored me again and again, 'Don't leave me alone, Peter. Please, you must stay with me. Don't go; don't climb down alone without me!'" The next day Habeler led Messner down the Lhotse Face.

Obviously, this is no superficial spat. It has been magnified and scrutinized in the European press, with the probable effect of exacerbating the bad feelings. Both men allude to attempts at reconciliation, but they still have little to say to each other.

Habeler has not climbed in the Himalaya since 1978, although he is planning a small expedition to some peaks in China on the north side of Everest for fall 1982. In 1980 he went to Mount McKinley, in Alaska, to climb the relatively easy West Buttress route. At 19,300 feet he came upon the bodies of two Germans who had frozen to death. He then found two Czechs blundering about, unable to help themselves. (It was later determined that they were suffering from cerebral edema.) Habeler gave up the summit, and after failing to talk the incoherent Czechs into descending under their own power, he made one of his characteristic descents—from 19,000 to 14,000 feet in a forty-five minute glissade—to reach a radio set above Windy Corner. The radio was out of order, but a rescue effort managed to save the Czechs.

Habeler remains impressed by McKinley. "It's colder than all the peaks I have attempted in the Himalaya," he says, "and quite serious as well."

At thirty-nine, Habeler looks wonderfully fit. His handsome, clean-shaven, weather-beaten face is deeply lined, but it glows with energy. He is short—perhaps five feet eight or nine—with a slender build. But he does have a worry about his health—a worry that dates back to the 1978 Everest expedition. One reason that Habeler decided to make his hour-long glissade from the summit to the South Col was that he was terrified about a lack of oxygen—that he might inflict brain damage upon himself. Four years later, he is not sure that damage did not occur. "I know that I now forget many things," he says. "And my concentration is not as sharp. I am sure that attempting 8000-meter peaks without oxygen is really doing some damage. I also think Reinhold has changed. He is not willing to take any criticism, for example."

Habeler says fame has changed little in his life. "Maybe my time has become a little more limited," he says. "I am proud to say that I am still together with the same friends as I was before all this." Almost inevitably, his thoughts come back to Messner. "Reinhold has changed all his friends; he has replaced them with people who are more important to him now."

As he approaches forty, Habeler seems—if his own testimony can be trusted—to be making just the kind of adjustment to middle age that so many top climbers fail at. "I still find it challenging," he says, "to do something easy, to go on a ski tour. And I *love* guiding, I really do. I don't consider it below myself to guide, and quite often people are amazed at that.

"Last year I lost two very good friends, good climbers, who fell into crevasses here in the Alps. One was married, with three children. That makes you feel so rotten. I do not want to die too early in the mountains. I want to prolong it as long as I can. I still want to do hard routes on nice peaks, but the will to risk my neck is not as strong as it used to be. If I fall off a mountain, to me it does not mean a thing. I come off, maybe five more seconds, and then I am dead. It's my wife, it's my two boys that are left behind. . . .

"I think I know now what I want to get out of my life. I find it very, very nice to combine my job with my hobby. I love to teach climbing and ski touring and to make it possible for people to survive. Life is too valuable to throw it away. I find that I'm happier than ever now being back home in Mayrhofen. The circle will finish again here."

In contrast with Habeler, Messner has in the last four years pursued an expedition pace of extreme intensity, and he has added two more astounding "firsts" to his already impressive record. Only weeks after climbing Everest in 1978, he made a solo ascent of Nanga Parbat via a new route on the Diamir Face—down which he and Günther had made their desperate retreat eight years earlier. Rather than stage a traditional expedition, with a team of climbers building a pyramid of camps and supplies, Messner went to Nanga Parbat with only two others—a Pakistani liaison officer and a nonclimbing woman friend, Ursula Grether. Above base camp he was utterly on his own.

Two years later he pulled off the same kind of solo expedition on the north side of Everest. This time his only companion was his girl friend, Nena Holguin. He had no climbing partner, no competent Austrian expedition in support. He made the whole ascent alone—and again without oxygen.

Messner spends much of the year on the road, either giving lecture tours or pursuing expeditions. Insofar as he lives anywhere, it is in Bolzano, Italy, near his home town of Villnöss. He and Nena Holguin share an apartment there. Despite his divorce, he and Uschi are still on good terms, and he sometimes stays with her in Munich. He speaks quite openly about his feelings for one woman in front of the other.

Like Habeler, Messner is short (about five feet nine) and slender. He no longer has time to train the way he used to, and he claims that rock climbing would in any event be detrimental to his high-altitude mountaineering, because it would unnecessarily build up chest and arm muscles.

Messner interrupts a question to deny its premise, that he is the world's foremost solo mountaineer. He will deny even that he is its leading high-altitude expert. "If we are speaking about mountaineering, not just rock climbing, I think at the moment [the American] John Roskelley is the strongest one. He's stronger right now than I. At the moment I don't feel so strong," Messner says, breaking into a smile. "I work too much."

Work, at the moment, includes lecture tours of Great Britain, Italy, and Germany, as well as "a big book" on Everest. Because Messner has chosen to turn his expedition accounts into almost compulsively confessional tracts, he invites scrutiny of the obscure personal wellsprings of his drive. A theme that runs through all his writing is fear of loneliness—curious, one would think, in a mountaineer who deliberately inflicts upon himself solo expeditions to the world's biggest mountains. His English biographer, Ronald Faux, reveals that in his early days in the Alps Messner feared lonely bivouacs so much that he would start climbs in late morning and force himself to finish before dark. "It is true," Messner says. "It was too difficult for me to start in the dark."

Before he succeeded on Nanga Parbat in 1978, Messner had twice set out to climb the mountain solo. Both attempts failed—not because of Messner's physical condition, which was excellent, but because of his mental state. The second attempt came in 1977, the year Uschi was to divorce him; he gave up while he was still on the hike to base camp, later writing, "Suddenly . . . I am overwhelmed by such bleak despair that we have to turn back. Soloing an eight-thousander has become in an instant a matter of no import; Uschi, I now know, has left me for good, and the passion I felt for this project has dissolved in a wave of indescribable loneliness."

It is no accident that Nena was waiting on Everest in 1980, that Ursula Grether was waiting on Nanga Parbat and K2. Messner is ensuring himself far more than a base-camp companion; the waiting woman is a deep source of confidence. "In my first expeditions," he says, "I suffered because I had no girlfriend at base camp. I don't think it is so important that I am suffering, but it is important that my whole person have an inner quietness. And I reach it much easier if I have a person that can stay with me."

In the maze of Messner's inner feelings, supportive women are inextricably connected with overcoming loneliness. In his first Everest book, he wrote, "The only person on whose account I could give up climbing is my mother. . . . She is one of the very few people who really understands me." Messner reveals in *The Challenge* (1976) that before the Hidden Peak climb Uschi leveled a kind of ultimatum: " 'If you had to choose,' Uschi asked me at length, after we had been sitting silently side by side, 'choose between the mountains or me—which would it be?' " Messner's evasiveness made the answer clear to her.

Faux, the biographer, sees significance in a childhood experience of Messner's—as described by Messner's mother. It seems that Reinhold, after being teased by a schoolmate, beat the boy up so badly that he was sent to a doctor. Reinhold's father wanted to punish his son, but the mother interceded; she claimed that Reinhold had dispensed the proper justice. Messner himself tells another childhood story: "A few days ago, my mother gave me a small book. She wrote about all of us when we were children. There is one line where she describes how each child acted. She says that when we were all playing, I always had to be the shepherd; my brothers were the sheep. I think this sentence is still very important for my own understanding of myself."

It makes a provocative psychological constellation: an angry, aggressive boy who channels his rage into ambition; his deep love for his mother, and a corresponding fear of loneliness; the attempt to find a haven from loneliness in adulthood through heroically supportive women; the death of his brother, for which much of the world blames him. It is tempting to see those early concerns, so candidly laid forth in his books, as the source of the distrust Messner now displays toward critical journalists and suspect teammates. But those concerns also account for much of the drive that has made him his generation's outstanding mountaineer.

Discussing his future, Messner sounds restless and ambivalent. "I am killing myself with working too hard," he says. "When I give away a date [for a lecture engagement], I feel like a prisoner, because I know I have to wait, I have to be there. I have to climb more in the future if I hope to be able to have the same impact that I had in the last years. But in the last half-year I worked so hard that I am losing quite all my energy."

On the horizon stands Messner's own vision of a personal mellowing: "Just now I am not so interested in doing the highest peaks alpine style. I am at least as interested in going to Tibet to see what's happening there, to Bhutan to live with the Bhutanese, just to see the country. That's at least as interesting for me as climbing the mountains."

It is hard to escape the conclusion that, of the two men, Habeler is the happier, the closer to resolving his own paradoxes of achievement and contentment. But one emerges from an acquaintance with both men with a deep admiration for their singular excellence. It is easy to point a finger at Messner; in a sense he sets himself up for it. Beneath the oversensitive skin, however, there is a powerful psyche animating the man to an exquisitely accurate calculation of what he can get away with in the mountains. It is worth remembering that he climbed Everest twice without oxygen, Nanga Parbat solo, Hidden Peak and K2 alpine style, with most of his toes lost to frostbite.

One emerges, also, with a strong sense of how much both men have lost in the rupture between them. Both cite as personal heroes Shipton and Tilman, those inseparable friends who, as Habeler says, "did exactly the same thing that we wanted to do later on—they started it." Shipton and Tilman lived long and explored distant ranges and oceans right up to the end. Today no one cares which man reached the summit of Mount Kenya first in 1929, which one broke the trail up the Aghil Pass in 1937. We care about their shared vision and the sunny example it set for future mountaineers.

One wishes Peter Habeler and Reinhold Messner an evening together, say around 1995, when they might sit before a fireplace somewhere in a snowbound Tirol and drink to the days twenty years before, when nothing mattered more in life than finding the line on the next hundred meters of the Northwest Face of Hidden Peak—when they labored in the bliss of their craft, at the heart of the mystery that is precocious brilliance, alone in the Karakoram.

from Blind Corners
by Geoff Tabin

Geoff Tabin was a first-year student at Harvard Medical School when he was asked to join a 1981 expedition to climb the largely unknown East Face of Mount Everest.

Mount Everest is a three-sided pyramid lying on the border between Nepal and Tibet, rising to a height of 29,028 feet above sea level. The first reconnaissance of Mount Everest with a view to climbing the peak was the British expedition of 1921 with George Leigh Mallory as one of the principal explorer-climbers. Mallory made an excellent topographical map of the mountain and was the first Westerner to walk up the Kangshung glacier and gaze upon Mount Everest's largest and steepest face. His report was not encouraging. He wrote:

> We had already by this hour taken the time to observe the great Eastern Face of Mount Everest, and more particularly the lower edge of the hanging glacier: it required but little further gazing to be convinced, to know, that almost everywhere the rocks below must be exposed to ice falling from the glacier;

that if, elsewhere, it might prove possible to climb up, the performance would be too arduous, would take too much time, and lead to no convenient platform; that, in short, other men, less wise, might attempt this way if they would, but, emphatically, it was not for us.

Mallory then moved around to the north where he discovered what he felt to be a feasible route. He returned in 1923 to attempt the northern approach to Mount Everest. After a failed first attempt he made plans to return the next year. When a reporter asked him why he was attempting to climb Mount Everest, Mallory replied, "Because it's there!" In 1924, with Andrew C. Irvine (for whom the A. C. Irvine Grant is endowed), Mallory disappeared high on the slopes of Mount Everest. The mountain remained virginal until May 29, 1953, when Sir Edmund Hillary and Tenzing Norgay Sherpa reached the summit via the mountain's south side from Nepal. In 1960, Wang Fu Chow and his Chinese compatriots, climbing in a large national expedition, made the first ascent of Mallory's route on the north side of Everest. In 1963 the first Americans reached the summit of Mount Everest with Tom Hornbein and Willy Unsoeld climbing the technically challenging West Ridge, which delineates the border between Nepal and Tibet. In 1975 Chris Bonington's British expedition achieved a breakthrough in climbing difficulty on Everest when they scaled the imposing and sustained Southwest Face. Three years later Peter Habeler and Reinhold Messner succeeded in making the first climb of Mount Everest without supplemental oxygen, and a Polish expedition climbed the mountain in winter. By 1979 every face and ridge on two thirds of the mountain had been climbed. The mountain had also been climbed solo and during the monsoon. But the largest and steepest side of Mount Everest, the massive Kangshung, or East Face, had still not been approached.

Meanwhile, the Chinese government was changing its policy toward outsiders. China had annexed Tibet in 1950. The Dalai Lama, the theocratic ruler of the country, fled into exile in India. China kept Tibet a completely restricted area. In 1979 the Chinese gave a permit for a Japanese expedition to enter Tibet to attempt Mount Everest from the north. Rumor was that they were soon to open Tibet to Western climbers. Dick Blum, the husband of Senator Dianne Feinstein (then-mayor of San Francisco), was a keen trekker who had walked in the Nepal Himalayas on several occasions. He was about to depart for a friendship trip to China with his wife when American climber Eric Perlman suggested that he request a permit for Americans to attempt the Chinese approaches to Mount Everest. The timing was perfect. Blum was in the right place at the right time. The Chinese government granted the first permit for an American expedition to climb in Tibet.

Blum asked Lou Reichardt, a well-known Himalayan climber from San Francisco, to help plan the climb. The permit would allow an assault on the mountain from any side. Reichardt had seen a photo-graph taken from the top of neighboring Makalu, the world's fifth highest peak. From the photo he thought there might be a feasible route up Everest's East Face. Perlman argued that the object was to climb the mountain and that the best chance of success lay in the north. Meanwhile Blum had enlisted the help of Sir Edmund Hillary whom he knew from his charitable work with Hillary's Himalayan Foundation. Hillary stated that, "if the Americans climb Mount Everest from the north it will just be another ascent of the mountain, but a climb from the east will be history." With this in mind Andrew Harvard, an experienced expedition mountaineer who was already in China, was dispatched to do a reconnaissance of the East Face of Everest. Traveling with a Chinese interpreter and liaison officer, he journeyed to Tibet and trekked to Mount Everest. Andy became the second outsider to view the face. Based on improvements in equipment and techniques he felt it would be difficult, "probably the hardest climb ever attempted," but possible, to scale the East Face of Mount Everest.

With the objective established, the next tasks were fund-raising and team selection. Blum, a professional financier by trade, remained expedition leader while Reichardt was named climbing leader on the mountain. Sir Edmund Hillary joined the effort as a special expedition advisor who would accompany the team to base camp. The team that was selected was a who's who of the best American climbers in 1980. In addition to Eric Perlman, Andy Harvard, and Lou Reichardt, the group included the current hot Himalayan superstar, John Roskelley; the tandem responsible for the hardest alpine ascents in North America, George Lowe and Chris Jones; a top Alaskan guide in Gary Bocarde; and arguably the two top rockjocks, Jim Bridwell and Henry Barber. Also on the initial team were Sue Giller, an excellent Himalayan climber; two experienced climbing doctors, Jim Morrissey and Dan Reid; and Bruce McCubbry, a solid Bay area mountaineer. The fund-raising went smoothly. Many people and organizations, including ABC television sports, were eager to be involved in the historic ascent.

A few months before departure Jim Bridwell decided that he could not go on the expedition. The team began looking for a replacement. Because most of the expedition members were in their thirties or forties it was suggested that they might choose a strong rock climber under twenty-five. This happened at the same time that Sam Moses' two-part article appeared in *Sports Illustrated*. When I first heard Sam's account of our trip to Irian Jaya was going to be published I had some trepidation. I had no idea how he perceived me. We had become friends during the trip and I had led our team up the climb. However, Sam never seemed comfortable with my painted toenails. I also had donned a *kebowak* for part of our approach march, ate insects when the Dani did, carried three penis gourds to the top of Carstensz Pyramid, and insisted Sam and Bob strip naked for a *kebowak* summit photo despite a raging blizzard. In addition, Sam found out that he had been deceived about the *Surat Jalan* when we were arrested upon our return from the mountain.

Although he did describe me as "cheerfully oblivious to society's norms," Sam's articles made me out to be incredibly energetic and enthusiastic: "Geoff was up there on the leading end of the rope, the 'sharp end,' as climbers call it, often unprotected, 800 feet off the ground, standing on tiny edges and clinging to a wall of rock while icy water dribbled down his sleeves to his armpits." Moreover, he mentioned that a Kowloon fortune teller had said that I was the "luckiest sonofabitch" he had ever seen, which is a good attribute to have on an expedition. Sam's article got me noticed, and no one on the team knew me well enough to say anything negative. Finally, Bruce McCubbry was a friend of my father's and actively supported my candidacy.

I had enrolled in Harvard Medical School in the fall of 1980. My focus was on becoming a doctor, and I had no plans for big climbing adventures in the near future. This idea was further enforced six weeks later when I was bouldering without a rope at a small outcrop just outside of Boston called Hammond Pond. A rock broke off while I was climbing an overhanging route. I was only fifteen feet off the ground, but I had my foot hooked up above my head so that when my handhold pulled loose I torpedoed straight down, breaking my left arm and knocking myself unconscious. Fortunately, I was with a medical school classmate named Hansel Stedman who saved my life when I stopped breathing. Hansel gave me mouth to nose resuscitation and kept me breathing while carrying me a few hundred yards to the road, where he flagged down a motorist who took me to Newton-Wellesley Hospital. I remained in a coma for thirty-six hours and spent a week in the hospital. I struggled to catch up with my medical studies while having continued problems with short-term memory and concentration. By second semester I was back to doing some rock climbing on the weekends. With the help of the medical school I had nearly caught up with my classes.

In the spring of 1981 I was studying for a pharmacology exam when Lou Reichardt called to ask if I would be interested in joining the team that was going to attempt the last unclimbed face on Mount Everest. Lou would be in Boston the following week and wanted to know if I could meet him for lunch. I was bouncing off the walls with excitement. I would have been overjoyed just to have lunch with Lou Reichardt. The people on the team were the heroes whom I had been reading about. Reichardt was America's best high-altitude mountaineer.

I knew of the tragedy on Dhaulagiri when he had been the only person to survive an avalanche that killed six of his teammates, and of his successful ascent of the mountain two years later. I had read of his exploits on Nanda Devi and how he made the first ascent of K2 without supplemental oxygen. And now he wanted to talk to me about joining him to climb Mount Everest. It would probably ruin my medical career. I knew that I was not experienced enough for that kind of climb: the biggest mountain I had been on was 17,000-Foot Mount Kenya. I was also in the worst shape of my life. I instantly replied, "YES!"

I put on my faded pile jacket, my Peruvian herder's cap, and painter's pants, trying to look like the kind of experienced climber he would want for his expedition, and went to meet Lou Reichardt on the steps of Harvard Medical School. I arrived early and waited. The only other person on the steps was a long, gangly man with checked polyester pants, a striped polyester shirt that was a size too small, and thick glasses that were fogged, filthy, and sitting askew on his nose. With large, open-mouthed bites he was eating a tuna fish submarine sandwich. I was looking desperately for the great mountaineer when, with a big tuna fish smile, Lou Reichardt warmly extended his hand and said, "Geoff?"

Lou went back to California telling me that I would be considered for the team. A few weeks later I was told that they had chosen Kim Momb, a top young climber from Spokane, Washington. I was selected as an alternate. The week before the team departed I called Lou and Jim Morrissey, wished them good luck, and thanked them for considering me. Then, several days after the team was supposed to have left, I received a phone call from a man who introduced himself as Scott MacBeth, the team's base camp manager. Scott explained that he was delayed in his departure because of a blood infection and hadn't left with the rest of the group. He said one of the other climbers, Henry Barber, had not gone at the last minute because of personal reasons. "Do you still want to go to Everest?" he asked.

"What?! YES!!!" I answered. I was soaring ten feet off the ground. I made a quick phone call to the dean of students and told him that I had just been invited to go to attempt the last unclimbed face of Mount Everest. I'd be leaving medical school, and would be returning in December. Inexplicably, the dean was not as excited as my climbing friends. He said that it was impossible for me to go. I tried to explain that this was Everest. He replied, "Yes, and other students like to go to the beach on their vacations. What's the difference?"

Now a full two and a half weeks behind the rest of the team, Scott and I flew from San Francisco to Beijing. Scott turned out to be an ideal traveling companion, and our Chinese hosts most hospitable. Unfortunately, the transportation into Tibet was not regular at that time. Moreover, Scott was as interested in seeing the sights of China as in getting to the mountain. The days in Beijing rolled on. We were guests at wonderful banquet after wonderful banquet. The meals lasted for hours with dozens of courses and toasts of Mao Tai liquor between each dish. We took trips out to the Ming tombs and the Great Wall of China, and explored the Forbidden City and other tourist sites of Beijing. We wandered the streets early in the morning watching the city awaken with Tai Chi, felt the bustle of the days, and rode bicycles through the town in the late afternoon, absorbing the sounds and smells before our evening banquet. It was fun, but my mind was on Everest. I was concerned about my role on the team, nervous about meeting my teammates, anxious about climbing in the Himalayas, worried about my own acclimatization, and a bit more impatient than Scott. Finally, after six days, we boarded a plane to Chengdu in the Szechuan Province. We encountered similar delays in Chengdu before finally being shuttled out to an old Russian turboprop. The flight took us over a seemingly endless array of immense, shimmering rock and ice peaks. I kept my face pressed to the window throughout the spectacular four-hour trip, over hundreds of miles of uncharted Himalayan mountains, to land in Lhasa, Tibet.

Lhasa was a place of contrasts in 1981. Physically, it was beautiful. Softly colored, hills rose on all sides of the city and golden statues glistened from the rooftops of the temples and monasteries. On a hill above town, the traditional home of the Dalai Lama, the Potala Palace, dominated the architecture of the city and projected a feeling of grandeur to everything below. Traditionally clad Tibetans chanted mantras and spun prayer wheels as they went about their business. Yet, the tension between the Tibetans and their Chinese conquerors was palpable. All of the main religious buildings were completely shut down with only Chinese guards outside. The smiles vanished from Tibetan faces as they passed Chinese soldiers. There were no tourist hotels in Lhasa at the time, so we were housed in an army barracks on the edge of town. We spent several days wandering through the city. It felt awkward to be allowed access to the monasteries and temples that the faithful were denied. We visited the deserted Jokang temple which had previously been the main shrine for the people of Tibet. In the Potala Palace the artwork and ornate golden statues were beautiful beyond my imagination, yet there was an eerie feeling walking alone through the vast 999 rooms with only the occasional glowering Han Chinese soldier sharing the sacred building.

We were delayed another week in Lhasa waiting for transportation. By this time I was fully enjoying Scott's company, his knowledge of the region, and his explanations of Tibetan Buddhism. I learned that Siddhartha believed that there are four essential truths: "Man suffers; suffering comes from unfulfilled desires; one can eliminate suffering by overcoming desire; and to overcome desire one must follow the eightfold path to wisdom." I finally began to adopt a Buddhist attitude of acceptance. Things were the way they were and I couldn't rush the trip. I became absorbed in David Snellgrove and Hugh Richardson's wonderful text, *A Cultural History of Tibet,* in reading about Mahayana Buddhism, and in trying to understand the changes in Tibet since the Chinese invaded.

After a week in Lhasa, Scott and I were given a jeep and a driver and set out along the arid Tibetan plateau. Our first stop was Xigatse, the second city of Tibet, with its impressive Drepung monastery. From there we drove on a heavily rutted dirt road to Xegar, the site of the Xegar Dzong, a hillside fortress that was the last outpost of Tibetan resistance to the Chinese invasion in 1953. The Tibetan landscape unfolded before us with a long, arid, richly textured plateau stretching to the horizon in one direction and the spine of the Himalayan range on the other side of our jeep. Unfortunately, the mountains were socked in with monsoon clouds, and we had no views of the highest peaks. The monsoons sweep north from India and hit the high Himalayan peaks where they drop their precipitation, leaving the Tibetan plateau a harsh thirteen-thousand-foot desert.

From Xegar, Scott and I followed a winding single track that wove into the mountains with precipitous drops at every curve until we finally arrived at the small yak-herding village of Kharta. We were given three yaks and a yak driver to help us with our seven-day trek to Mount Everest, which proved to be one of the greatest hikes of my life. Glimmering twenty-thousand-foot peaks rose up on all sides. I was mesmerized. I was overwhelmed by the scale. The jagged summits floated a vertical mile and a half above us. At every turn in the trail the views changed, becoming even more dramatic. We walked over a high pass adorned with prayer flags and dropped into the lush Kama Valley. We descended to a small wooded camp with beautiful rhododendrons in full bloom from the monsoon storms. The trail then wove back upward into the world of rock, snow, and ice to join the Kangshung Glacier at sixteen thousand feet. Nothing I had ever seen prepared me for the grandeur of the highest Himalayan peaks. The icy walls of Chomolonzo glistened in the morning sun and Makalu rose twelve thousand feet vertically above us as we came out onto the glacier. We followed the side of the glacier for one day on our way toward base camp before we were able to see the East Face of Mount Everest and the North Face of Lhotse in the distance. Both rise over two vertical miles. The sheer mass and beauty would have taken my breath away, had I not already been gasping from the altitude.

Looking up the glacier we were surprised to see people coming down. It turned out to be Dick Blum and an entourage of porters. Dick had decided he didn't enjoy life in base camp and was leaving the expedition. I thought it was strange that the expedition leader was leaving. I was also a bit worried as Dick seemed to have no knowledge that Scott had invited me along.

We walked only a few more hours before we ran into the next group of people descending the trail. I instantly recognized Sir Edmund Hillary from his photographs. He was staggering along the path with a bloody bandage wrapped around his head. The man with Hillary warmly greeted Scott and, after being introduced, I too was enthusiastically welcomed by Dr. Jim Morrissey. Sir Edmund Hillary then turned to me and asked, "Are you driving the bus?"

Morrissey explained that Hillary had developed a slight case of cerebral edema, had fallen and struck his head, and then rolled over, contaminating the open wound in fresh yak dung. The gash in his scalp had become infected. Morrissey was terrified that our expedition would only be remembered for killing Sir Edmund Hillary. He was rushing Hillary down to lower altitude, expecting to take him to Beijing where he would receive additional medical care. Despite a dirty rag wrapped around his head and an altered mental state, Hillary had the carriage of a great man. I had read many books by and about him. Beyond making the first ascent of Everest and his impressive climbing resume, Hillary had traversed Antarctica, been to both the North and South Poles, built schools and hospitals for the Sherpa people, started his own foundation to help the indigenous populations of the Himalayas, and served as New Zealand High Commissioner to India and Nepal. He was one of my heroes. Yet, despite his illness, I was even more impressed than I expected to be by Hillary, the man. He had a quiet warmth that emanated from his dazed eyes. I asked him to pose for a picture. He smiled gamely and wished me luck on the climb before stumbling on down the trail.

Two days later we walked into base camp. It was obviously not a happy place. I tented my first night with John Roskelley. Roskelley had distinguished himself with the hardest climbs of any American over the past several years and had recently been hailed by the media and the top European climber, Reinhold Messner, as the greatest mountaineer in the world. I knew of his bold climbs in the Himalayas, including the first ascents of several technically difficult peaks as well as the first American climb of K2, and I was eager to learn from him. As I crawled into our tent, slightly in awe, John Roskelley's only words to me were, "This face is suicide. If you climb on this route, Geoff, you are going to die," before he rolled over and went to sleep.

I lay awake all night. This was not turning out like I had expected. The expedition leader had left, Sir Edmund Hillary had high-altitude sickness, and our route was too dangerous for John Roskelley. Before morning I was aware of what a great adventure I had already had and how privileged I was to be in Tibet and seeing these mountains. I attempted to push my preconceptions out of my conscious thoughts, keep an open mind, and flow with the adventure.

The East Face of Everest is enormous. There was no consensus over what was a feasible or safe route. One faction, spearheaded by Chris Jones, wanted to follow the ridge that makes up the north side of the buttress. Jones felt that this would be much easier climbing and afford a feasible route to the upper snow slopes. A second group felt that Jones' line was suicidal because of avalanche danger. This team, led by George Lowe, was trying to push a very difficult direct route up the sheer initial five-thousand-vertical-foot rock and ice buttress. Roskelley felt that Lowe's route was impossibly hard. The vertical mile of technical difficulties was insurmountable. And, even if it proved possible to climb the buttress, he was certain the slopes above were suicidal, with unreasonable avalanche danger. Roskelley argued that Jones' proposed route was ridiculous, being suicidal the entire way. He strongly advocated going around to the easier and safer north side to make a successful climb on Mount Everest. Andy Harvard told me to ignore Roskelley. He said that John, as a professional climber, needed to reach the top of the mountain for his reputation, and wanted to do what was easiest and best for himself. While the arguments raged, Lou Reichardt, our climbing leader, avoided the controversy and led by simply carrying heavy loads, often making double carries in a single day, to support whatever activity was going on up on the mountain.

I was shocked to see my heroes bickering and confused about what to do. Adding to my discomfort was a feeling that I was in over my head, even if the route were climbable. Base camp sat at an altitude of seventeen thousand feet, the same as my previous high point. I felt the pulse pounding in my temples and became short of breath with moderate exertion. I was worried that my physical skills were not in the same league as any of the superstars on the team. I rested a week before moving seven miles across the Kangshung Glacier to our advanced base camp. I decided that I should at least check things out for myself before making any decision. On the day that I moved to advanced base camp, Roskelley made an impassioned plea on the radio for Kim Momb to come down. He said, "I brought you on this trip, Kim. I owe it to your family. Don't let me down. You must come home alive. Come off the mountain at once if you want to live. I'm getting out of here tomorrow. Walk out with me. Please!" I met Kim Momb for the first time as he was retreating off of the mountain. We briefly shook hands before he, Bruce McCubbry, and Roskelley, left.

Meanwhile, the climbing team pushed along Lowe's route toward the top of the initial vertical buttress. The climbing was hard, at a level of technical difficulty never before attempted on a peak the scale of Mount Everest. There were pitches of vertical ice, arduous free climbing, and very strenuous overhanging aid climbing on crumbly schist where the only progress that could be made was by pounding pitons into the friable rock and pulling oneself up on these insecure anchors. George Lowe was doing the majority of the leading on the hardest sections. Also working on the route were Eric Perlman, Gary Bocarde, Sue Giller, Dan Reid, and ABC cameraman David Breashears. An enormous avalanche had swept over the ridge that Jones had suggested. Fortunately no one was in its path. All climbing efforts were now concentrated on the "Lowe Buttress" route.

I rested a few days at advanced base camp listening eagerly to stories of what had happened on the mountain. I was particularly fascinated by the tales of Dan Reid. He was supposed to be a team physician, but when they needed help on the route he headed right up. I heard about how he had attempted to solo climb a vertical icicle, and had taken several long falls, self-belayed on a single knife blade piton, before finally giving up on a stormy day when no one else was willing to climb. This pitch later became known as Reid's Nemesis.

When I started up the fixed ropes, I was amazed by the difficulty of the climbing that the team had accomplished. The leaders installed permanent ropes which I followed using mechanical ascenders that slide up the rope but catch and lock when weighted downward. I spent a night at Snow Camp, the first camp on the mountain, which was located below a snow ridge leading up to the ice gully where much of the debris from the upper face funneled down. Unfortunately, the gully was the only line of weakness in a series of impassable mushroomed snow ridges, and our only possible route to the upper headwall. The worst time to be on this part of the buttress was in the afternoon, when the sun warmed the upper face. The heat melted the ice into water which seeped into cracks. At night, the water froze and expanded. The next day the warming loosened adhesions, and rock eroded down the mountain into the gully. They called the chute the "Bowling Alley," as bowling-ball-sized pieces of rock and ice ricocheted through every day as soon as the upper face was touched by the sun. I left very early in the morning and then raced as quickly as possible, like a scared rabbit, up the seven-hundred-foot, sixty-degree ice chasm to reach the camp on top of the chute, aptly named Pinsetter Camp.

At Pinsetter Camp I met Dan Reid for the first time. This slightly built man projected an incredible energy. He had a wide grin, scraggly beard, and through his granny glasses his eyes focussed intensely on anyone he was speaking to. He spoke matter-of-factly, saying that he thought the Bowling Alley was overrated and that I shouldn't be scared because "when it's your time to go, it's your time to go and there's nothing you can do about it."

Meanwhile Eric Perlman and Gary Bocarde had just reached the Helmet Camp, on top of the buttress at 21,500 feet. Gary, a veteran mountain guide on Mount McKinley, observed the crevasses stretching out above and declared the upper face to be unclimbable. He and Eric then retreated off the mountain, saying they were not going to climb any more. Similarly, Sue Giller decided the risks were too great to venture higher. Chris Jones had broken some ribs with a high-altitude coughing fit and was unable to climb, Andy Harvard was sick, and the film crew had pulled back. Thus, there were only four of us still on the mountain willing to move upward. These were Lou Reichardt, George Lowe, Dan Reid, and me. We discussed our options. George, who had done most of the difficult leading to that point and had been breaking through psychological barriers in the climbing world for fifteen years, felt that we should at least give it a try. Lou argued that it was not worth the risk. He pointed out that of the four of us, he was the only one who had been above twenty-three thousand feet previously without oxygen, and that I was still poorly acclimatized. Moreover, we had no support and only twelve days of supplies. Dan Reid then said that the only thing to do was to sign a death pact. If we all agreed that we should make a headlong dash for the summit, then one of us would most likely reach the top and get down alive, and we'd succeed on the first ascent on the East Face of Mount Everest. The death pact would state that if any one of us became sick or injured we wanted our partners to leave us to die so that they could make the top. As long as we signed a death pact he felt it would be legal. The other three of us looked at each other and realized that this expedition was over.

The next morning we began rappelling down the ropes. "Death-pact" Dan said he wanted to take one last look, and remained high on the mountain. George, Lou, and I descended through the Bowling Alley in the dark and waited at Snow Camp for Dan. We began to worry when the sun crept up onto the upper face, and were relieved when we heard Dan yodel as he approached the camp. Then, we saw that his right leg was completely red. His boot and lower leg were soaked through with blood. With a cheerful grin he said, "A couple of big ones came through while I was rappelling. I dodged most of 'em but one sucker got me." We pulled up his windpants leg and found that he had an implosion injury, exposing five inches of his tibia. We helped him down to advanced base camp, where we learned that Jim Morrissey had returned from successfully evacuating Sir Edmund

Hillary back to Beijing. Jim looked at Dan's leg and decided it would not be possible to move him back to base camp. He would remain with Dan in advanced base camp after sewing Dan's leg closed in three layers with thirty-eight stitches.

The rest of the team began carrying loads back across the glacier from advanced base camp to base camp while we sent a messenger out for yaks to evacuate camp. While waiting for the yaks, George Lowe asked me if I would like to make a first ascent on a peak called Kartse, which dominates the vista behind base camp. George and I had a perfect day, climbing a beautiful, steep ridge in perfect sunshine and calm air to the 21,390-foot summit of Kartse. I was still floating on the summits as we walked back to base camp. I felt great on top of Kartse, had learned that George was not only a great climber but a great guy to climb with, and realized that with acclimatization I could climb with him.

We returned to find base camp in an uproar. Jim Morrissey had called on the radio to say that Dan Reid, after his week of resting at advanced base camp, had popped a handful of his own medications, thus earning a new nickname, "PercoDan," and solo climbed up the fixed ropes. Jim tried to catch him but did not have the technical climbing skill, and because of having to go down with Sir Edmund Hillary, he lacked Dan's acclimatization. Dan brought an unusual assortment of gear for his solo bid, including a stove but no fuel, so he was unable to melt water, and a considerable amount of food that all needed cooking. He also brought with him a tent but no sleeping bag. I had images in my mind of Dan limping into the clouds to disappear like George Leigh Mallory. He eventually returned, having climbed for thirty-six straight hours, saying that he had gone up to retrieve the Explorers' Club flag which he had left up at the high point, and to check out snow conditions for future years. It was the consensus of everyone that Dan Reid, one of the most wonderful and warmest people we had ever met, was completely nuts.

On the trek out our liaison officer, Wang Fu Chow, who had been the first Chinese man to summit Mount Everest, expressed sympathy that we had not made the summit. Wang Fu Chow had also made the first ascent of Mount Xixibangma, the only one of the world's fourteen highest mountains that is completely in Tibet. He matter-of-factly said that it would be possible for us to attempt to climb Mount Xixibangma. George Lowe, Eric Perlman, Lou Reichardt, Jim Morrissey, and I instantly took him up on the offer. We said good-bye to the rest of the team at Kharta and headed for Xixibangma.

Xixibangma is a peak that rises abruptly from the Tibetan plateau at fourteen thousand feet to just over twenty-six thousand feet with no intervening foothills. It is probably the most dramatic relief in the world. The route we tried is technically quite easy, following a low-angle ridge line to a steep ice slope that allows one to gain the final ridge. Unfortunately, the winter jetstream winds lowered to twenty-two thousand feet. George, Eric, and Lou were poised to go for the top when our high camp tent was ravaged by one-hundred-mile-an-hour gusts. It was impossible for our team to reach the summit. However, the team experience was absolutely perfect. We were perfectly together, shared a common attitude toward the climb, and had a lot of fun. On our way back to Lhasa we all decided that with the right team and knowing the route up the initial buttress, the East Face of Mount Everest could be climbed. Jim Morrissey decided to apply for a permit to return in two years to make the first ascent of the Kangshung Face. We reached Beijing and went to the Chinese mountaineering office where Jim gave a strong presentation saying that we had figured out the feasible route, and had done all the hard work, and that the Chinese should keep the route virginal until we were able to return to try it. The man smiled broadly and through an interpreter said, "No problem, Dr. Reid already have permit."

I returned from Tibet to find that I was out of medical school. I reapplied for admission and was reaccepted with the understanding that I would not leave again. Meanwhile, Dan Reid turned over the permit for the return to the Kangshung Face to Jim Morrissey, who assumed expedition leadership under the condition that Dan remain part of the next team. Dan agreed to just be a base camp doctor and assured Jim that he would not do anything dangerous. Jim was the perfect leader for this type of trip. He had a vast amount of expedition experience, lots of common sense, strong leadership skills, and, primarily a doctor rather than a climber, he did not have a climbing ego that would clash with his team. He was thus able to listen and weigh all options and then make a decision. Tall and powerful, Jim had a commanding personality and a strong sense of self-confidence that persuaded people to follow. Jim selected a team that he felt gave the best chance for success, blending top climbers who would work well together. The common attribute was a shared belief that the Kangshung Face could be climbed.

From the 1981 team he asked Dan Reid, Andy Harvard, Lou Reichardt, Kim Momb, George Lowe, and me to return to Everest with him in 1983. Adding to this nucleus of seven, Jim invited Carlos Buhler, Carl Tobin, David Coombs, Jay Cassell, David Cheesmond, and Chris Kopczynski. The result was not necessarily the best thirteen climbers in America in 1983, but very likely the best team America could have produced. A final addition was John Boyle, a banker, engineer, and yachtsman as base camp manager. The trip again was well funded, with *National Geographic* magazine as a principal sponsor.

Climbing the last unclimbed face on Everest had become a consuming romantic quest for me. I desperately wanted to go on the trip. However, there was no chance of Harvard Medical School giving me leave to go climbing again. Then, Michael Wiedman, a professor of eye surgery, approached me and proposed that we do a research project on the physiology of high altitude. In particular, Dr. Wiedman was interested in retinal hemorrhaging at high altitude and whether an ocular exam could be used as a prognosticator of high altitude cerebral or pulmonary edema. I was thus able to schedule a research elective and did not have to apply for a leave of absence. Beyond learning to perform ophthalmoscopy, I trained for the trip by running the five miles to and from my apartment to school every day, sprinting the steps of the Harvard football stadium, and traversing a rock wall and climbing rock and ice every weekend. I easily completed the Boston Marathon in the spring and ran a complete traverse of the Presidential Mountains in New Hampshire in under four hours, normally a three-day hike. When I flew to San Francisco in August 1983 I felt prepared and confident.

An optimistic group gathered in San Francisco. We were going to climb the last unclimbed face on Mount Everest—the hardest mountaineering route that had ever been attempted, and we were going to do it with minimal supplemental oxygen and no native support on the mountain. We traveled through China as a cohesive team. Our collective mentality was similar to what I have read about the psychology of people going off to war. A macabre sense of humor prevailed with lots of "jokes" about climbers who have perished. We all knew that sixty-two lives had already been lost on the slopes of Mount Everest, that no new route had been opened on the mountain without the loss of life, that none had been climbed without native load carriers on the mountain, and that ours was the hardest and most dangerous path. Still, none of us broached the subject of whether an accident could happen to us. Interestingly, there was also a prevalent hypersexuality and much flirtation with stewardesses and other Western sojourners, perhaps our bodies' way of telling us to propagate our gene pool before embarking on the dangerous mission. I personally adopted an attitude that I had trained well enough and was with such a great team that I would be safe. I had no conscious thoughts of the risk. My mind remained completely immersed in the present, with little talk of the past or future, as we again enjoyed banquets and sightseeing.

Arriving in Lhasa I found that Tibet had changed dramatically in two years. The Chinese had eased many of their restrictions. The Potala and Jokang were now crowded with chanting pilgrims, and the streets were bustling with activity. Chinese soldiers were still present, but less obvious. We stayed in a comfortable guest house and ate well. However, there was little time for tourism. We were a team with a mission! We packed our gear on trucks and began the drive to Mount Everest after one day. The monsoon washed out the main road so we took an alternate dirt track that was so bumpy you couldn't even pick your nose. The ride was more beautiful than I remembered. We passed alongside rolling hills with layers of brown, yellow, and green bands woven into the sand. The monsoon gave a constant, unpleasant drizzle; however, the swirling clouds made the landscape all the more impressive. We arrived in Xigatse late in the evening and left for Xegar early the next morning. Despite the hectic pace we were beginning to get to know each other.

It soon became clear to me that my three-hour-per-day training regimen left me one of the weakest members of our team. Three people stood apart as being in a different physical realm. Kim Momb looked like a shorter version of the incredible hulk. He had been high on the West Ridge of Everest the previous spring and trained full time during the intervening two months. Prior to his becoming a professional climber, Kim was a top-ranked skier, motorcross racer, and a blackbelt kickboxer with an undefeated professional record. He had a ready smile and firm handshake. Carl Tobin's income was derived solely from competing as the mountaineer in a made-for-television event called "Survival of the Fittest." One look at his rippled muscular physique and it was easy to see why. He had been living in Fairbanks and consistently pushing the limits of what had been considered possible in the mountains of Alaska. Carl was quiet with a piercing sense of humor that left one slightly off balance. For instance, when the group discussed romantic movies Carl mumbled earnestly, "Yeah, I always get teary at that love scene in *Deliverance.*" When Tibetans stared at Carl, he stared back with a look of such profound, and at the same time simple, curiosity that they turned away. Carl would then follow them, continuing his study. The third powerhouse was Dave Cheesmond, a South African living in Canada. Dave had been Carl's partner on many of his hardest climbs and had distinguished himself as one of the most prolific and accomplished mountaineers in the world during the past two years. "Cheese" was gregarious and helpful and always willing to tip a beer or join in a bawdy song.

A second contingent were the older masters: George Lowe, Lou Reichardt, Andy Harvard, and Chris Kopczynski. George had already established himself as a legendary climber with a will, tenacity, and determination second to none. George had been the driving force on the route in 1981 and exuded a quiet confidence about this trip. Lou, a professor of neurophysiology, had climbed more twenty-six-thousand-foot peaks than any American. He shared George's work ethic. What Lou lacked in technical skills he more than made up for with a physiology that did not seem to be affected by altitude. Andy had been on a phenomenal number of expeditions and was a master of logistics. A lawyer by trade, he was thoughtful and articulate. Chris Kopczynski also knew about expeditions. He reached the top of Everest, via the South Col Route, in 1981 as well as making the first American ascent of the North Face of the Eiger. "Kop" was a building contractor from Spokane, Washington, who had a straightforward Western friendliness and a button with a picture of his wife and kids that he wore over his heart throughout the climb.

I thought of myself as being similar in strength to the other three climbers until we went out for a training run in Beijing. Carlos Buhler, Jay Cassell, and Dave Coombs left me in the dust. Buhler, a mountain guide from Bellingham, Washington, was a full-time climber with wider interests than just mountains. Carlos was multilingual with deep thoughts about international and interpersonal relations. He was warm, but intense, and very sensitive to "feelings" on expeditions. I found Coombs to be an upbeat man who was one of the hardest workers I have ever met. His climbing resume and background were similar to mine. He was a Harvard graduate with an MBA who trained intensively for this trip. Similar in many ways to Coombs was Jay Cassell. Jay was an MBA and ex-marine who had the least big mountain experience on the team. However, he had finished strongly in the Iron Man Triathlon and Western States 100 endurance run, and was, perhaps, our most aerobically fit member. Jay had a personality that was mentally as solid as a rock; he was a man who would break before he bent.

The final two climbers, Morrissey and Dan Reid, were both busy cardiothoracic surgeons in California. Neither was able to spend much time training. In fact, Dan had not climbed since his drug-addled solo ascent of the ropes on Everest in 1981. However, this time he came prepared. Dan had "The Little Engine that Could" embroidered on all of his climbing clothes as well as a formal kilt to wear into base camp. The final member of the team was our "Mister Organization," base camp manager John Boyle. Boyle handled the detail work before the trip and developed a winch system that we hoped would save us considerable time and effort on the mountain. To reach the top of Everest we had a three-part task: We first had to reclimb the sheer initial forty-five-hundred-foot rock and ice buttress. Next, we had to carry enough supplies up the route to support a summit climb. Then, we still had to climb a vertical mile and a half up a steep snow ridge to the top of the world. Boyle's plan was to launch a rocket attached to a cord from the top of the buttress. Next he planned to rig up a continuous nine-thousand-foot loop with high tech yachting pulleys at the top and bottom. He had a Honda engine to power our loads quickly over the difficult climbing. Most of the team was a bit dubious, but we all hoped it would work.

The trek to base camp again started from Kharta. Our gear was loaded onto yaks for the journey. It was a festive march with the colorfully robed Tibetan yak herders whistling, singing, and chanting mantras as we walked. With us on the trek were a group of seven doctor friends of Morrissey's who had donated to the cause and Jack Alustiza, the owner of a Basque restaurant whom Jim had asked to be the expedition base camp chef, our Chinese Liaison Officer who was again Wang Fu Chow, and our official interpreter, Mr. Tsao. Boyle, Alustiza, and the scientists were all a bit slower than the climbers, and we adopted a leisurely pace. The views were again stunning with bright red rhododendrons flowering in the monsoon wetness. The mornings were glorious with shimmering peaks dancing above us. By late morning clouds rolled in and covered the sky. Precipitation started before noon every day and lasted until late in the evening. As we gained altitude the rain turned to snow. Dan Reid never wore more than his kilt and stripped naked to bathe in every glacial pond.

We reached base camp at an altitude of seventeen thousand feet at the edge of the Kangshung Glacier on August 26. Everyone, including the scientists, pitched in to get camp set up. The first task was to find and mark the route across the Kangshung Glacier so that we could carry gear to the base of the buttress. I felt the effects of the altitude. My resting pulse raced at over one hundred beats per minute, double my normal rate at sea level. With exertion my pulse pounded in my temples at over two hundred beats per minute. The fourteen-mile-round-trip carry across the glacier to advanced base camp with a heavy pack made for a long, exhausting day. The entire team left early in the morning to make the carry, except for Dan Reid. We passed Dan in the afternoon. He was still a long way from the end of the glacier. We suggested that he dump his load and return with us, but he refused. An hour after dark we were organizing a search party to go out onto the heavily crevassed glacier to look for Dan when we heard him yodel. With a big grin Dr. Reid raved about how beautiful it was to be alone on a glacier at night. Jim and Dan had a talk about risk and danger and Dan agreed to stay in base camp and be good.

On September 1, the actual climb began. Lou, Carl, and I started fixing ropes up the buttress. As the climbing leader from the 1981 trip, Lou had the honor of leading the first pitch of the 1983 effort. The climbing went quickly as we knew exactly where the route should go. We were also helped by several ropes and anchors that were still in place from 1981. We regained seven hundred feet of sheer rock before noon. Dan Reid caught up to us late in the afternoon, carrying more rope. We asked him what he was doing on the route. Reid grinned. "Well, you need more rope, don't you?" Dan soon insinuated himself into the climbing rotation, carrying heavy loads in support of the leaders and helping out everywhere. Once again the crazy doc was a full climbing member of the team.

The lower part of the route climbed up steep rock that had lots of small, sharp, incut holds. We made fast progress, reaching our first campsite on the mountain on the second day. We again called it "Snow

Camp," as it sat perched on a magnificent snow ridge at the top of the first rock step. The next obstacle was a difficult ridge of enormous snow mushrooms and steep ice. Dave Cheesmond, Kop, and Coombs moved into the front. I joined Dan in the group carrying equipment up to support the leaders. The first ones up climbed the rock and ice that the mountain offered and fixed a permanent rope in place. The rest of the team used the fixed rope to safeguard themselves and climb with heavy loads. As in 1981, we used mechanical ascenders, which slide up the rope but lock when weighted, to move up, and rappelled back down using figure eight friction rings that slowed our slide down the ropes.

After five days we reached the Bowling Alley, the dangerous ice chute that gives access to the upper face. This gully was still a funnel for debris that melts out of the upper rock headwall and is again one of the scariest sections on the climb. At the top of the Bowling Alley we reestablished "Pinsetter Camp" beneath the rock headwall that was the technically most difficult section of the route. In 1981 it took three weeks to surmount the crumbly, overhanging barrier. Climbing this section required laborious and strenuous aid climbing where the leader pounds a piton into the rock and uses this aid point to advance. Looking up at the path we saw a tattered rope swaying in the breeze, a remnant from the 1981 effort. Kim volunteered to "jug" up the weather-beaten cord. He clipped his mechanical ascenders onto the old rope and methodically began climbing like a spider on a thread. We watched with horror as Kim, a couple of hundred feet above us, hastily detached first one, then the other ascender, and quickly clipped them back on to the rope a few feet higher. In four hours he regained the entire headwall. When I came up, I saw that where Kim detached his ascenders the old rope was worn 95 percent through, so that only one strand of frayed nylon, less than an eighth of an inch in diameter, remained.

I was now supposed to rotate back to advanced base camp for a couple of days of rest while Jay, Andy, Carlos, George, and Cheese moved to the front to push the route up the next section. Above the rock we had to surmount a nine-hundred-foot ice slope angled at seventy degrees that was protected by fifty-foot-high icicles at its top in order to reach the top of the buttress, a place we named the Helmut. Starting down, I met Cheese. He told me that he was not feeling well. He said that he had to turn around and descend back to base camp. Carlos and Andy were also ill. We were short of load carriers. I knew that I was very tired; however, I decided that the team needed me to stay up and work. I was still insecure about my being on this team of great climbers and believed that this was a chance for me to prove my worth. The next morning I carried a fifty-pound load of ropes and ice screws to the top of the rock. Back in the tent at Pinsetter Camp, I was too tired to help Kim with the laborious tasks of melting snow into water and preparing dinner. I crawled into my sleeping bag and began shivering uncontrollably. Kim gave me tea and helped me throughout the night. In the morning I had not slept a minute and was very lethargic. Kim and George helped me pack up and I headed down.

As I started to rappel down the rock below Snow Camp I heard a roar. Looking up I saw that a house-sized block of rock had broken off directly above me. It hit and shattered one hundred feet overhead. Car-sized chunks rained down on me. I curled up as small as possible and realized, "I am going to die." I was calm and my mind was blank as I faced my doom. Three large boulders smashed within five feet of me, but I escaped unscathed. The air was heavy with the acrid, gunpowder-like smell of the rock dust. The sound of the avalanche resonated down the valley. After a moment of calm, my heart began to race. My pulse went over two hundred beats per minute and my whole body shook uncontrollably. It was several minutes before the trembling stopped and I was able to stand and continue my descent.

Jim Morrissey heard of my shivering and lethargy. He was concerned that I had cerebral edema and insisted that I return to base camp for a rest. High altitude cerebral edema, a swelling of the brain, can quickly become fatal. Falling rock can end a climber's life in an instant. Walking dejectedly back across the glacier to base camp, I wondered if climbing any route on any mountain is worth dying for. At the same time I thought about my teammates, realizing that I had never been with a group so full of life. There was an intense prevailing appreciation for both the immense beauty surrounding us and the small joys of existence. I came to help this team climb the Kangshung Face and would return to the cause, if I could. I felt awful that I might have hurt our team's chances for reaching the top, not to mention ruined my own summit aspirations, by pushing myself too hard when I knew that I was not feeling well. I vowed to listen to my body from now on.

The rest of the team quickly succeeded in fixing ropes up to the helmet. The climbing of the buttress had been accomplished in only twelve days. Now we needed to carry our gear up the wall. We all focused on Boyle's winch system. Carlos and Jay carefully uncoiled the polypropylene trail line and aimed the rocket launcher. The first effort dribbled off into an avalanche cone and was lost in the debris. The second firing was also a dud. We only had three rockets. Jim, Lou and Boyle discussed the options. We could hazard another firing from the top station. If it failed we would have no winch support. They decided on a second option, which was to fire a rocket from Snow Camp. The route below was sheer to the glacier. They thought the rocket would surely work from there, and it did. We would get some support from the motorized winch. The second part of the plan was to install a gravity hauling system on the overhanging rock headwall above Pinsetter Camp. Dave Cheesmond and George Lowe engineered a two-thousand-foot continuous line with pulleys at the top and bottom. Haul bags were filled with rock and snow at the top station and clipped onto the rope, while the haul bags filled with our food and equipment were tied on the bottom. The upper haul bags were released and pulled up our gear. Both the gravity system and Boyle's engine-powered winch worked perfectly. We still had to man-carry the loads from Snow Camp up through the Bowling Alley to Pinsetter and from the top of the rock up the steep Helmut ice field. We needed all the manpower we could muster. So, after five days of rest at base camp, I returned to the task. I was feeling much better and hoped that I had a virus and not cerebral edema or any other high altitude illness.

With everyone putting in 110 percent every day, progress moving our gear up the mountain was steady. I again carried as heavy a load as I possibly could, plus ten pounds more every day. The monsoon continued to linger, with wet snow falling every afternoon. Still, everyone of us pushed hard, working with no rest days. We all, of course, had our own summit aspirations, and none of us wanted to burn himself out. Yet, we were in a desperate race against the winter winds and storms. Once the jet stream lowered its one-hundred-mile-per-hour wrath down on the mountain, and the winter Himalayan storms unleashed their fury, it would be impossible for anyone to reach the top. So, despite having already pushed too hard once on the trip, and feeling exhausted at the end of every day, I continued to work with every ounce of my strength. The rest of the team put in an equal effort, which inspired each of us to do more. Lou, Carl, Carlos, Andy, Dan, Jim, and I were based at Snow Camp, bringing loads up to the gravity winch at Pinsetter Camp, with Lou often making two impossibly heavy carries per day. Jay and Dave Coombs were working the bottom of the gravity winch while George, Cheese, Kim, and Kop dropped down from the Helmut to work the top of the winch and ferry loads back up to the Helmut Camp. Kim put in a herculean effort making two carries every day for a week. We slowly moved more people up as more loads accumulated at the upper winch station. Finally, on September 29 our entire team of thirteen climbers and all of the necessary gear was on top of the buttress.

After a solid month of work we were only at 21,500 feet. This is the same altitude that yaks can walk to on the north side of Everest and where advanced base camp sits in Nepal. We still had a vertical mile and a half to climb on an unknown route and little time before the weather changed for the winter. Statistically, the jetstream lowers during the first two weeks of October. Jim and Lou began to work out a tentative strategy. Everyone had to continue to push as hard and fast as he could. We would establish three higher camps: Camp One at 23,500 feet, Camp Two at 25,500 feet, and Camp Three at nearly 27,000 feet. We had a total of thirteen bottles of supplemental oxygen.

So each person would carry his own one bottle of gas up to the high camp, sleep without extra oxygen, and use the bottle of oxygen for the summit climb.

At 21,500 feet I could feel my pulse beating in my temples, even at rest. Every step upward was a new altitude record for me. On October 1, I wrote in my diary:

> I realize that I am among the weakest of the thirteen of us. I also know the risks involved, even for the strongest. Consciously, I do not think that it makes sense to jeopardize my life to climb a mountain. But, I am beginning to understand what Mallory must have meant when he said he was climbing Everest "because it is there." It is not just that the mountain is "there" externally, but it is because it is "there" internally, within me. It has become a personal quest. Yes, the beauty of the high mountains, the camaraderie, the teamwork, and the joy of movement are all reasons to be climbing here. But, in these really high mountains there is a definite element of self-realization and of learning exactly where my limits are, driving me upward. I do not want to die. But, this is my shot at the top of the world, and I'm going for it, savoring every moment of life!

The weather turned perfect and the massive team effort continued unabated. By October 5, everyone had been to twenty-five thousand feet without supplemental oxygen. Jim decided that the first summit team would be Kop, George, and Cheese. Along with Lou and Kim they headed up to establish High Camp. The group had to break trail through knee-deep snow angled upward at thirty degrees. With their loads they moved at a pace of four breaths per step with many rests. Digging out a tent platform from the steepening ice at over twenty-seven thousand feet was exhausting. They took turns working until they were gasping, then passed the shovel on to the next climber. It required three hours to chop out space for a single two-man tent. All were too exhausted to stay at the High Camp. Cheese, who had been the strongest and the hardest worker on the team, developed a wet cough at the end of the day. He worried that he might be developing high altitude pulmonary edema and elected to drop back all the way down to Helmut Camp. Kop had a bad headache and decided to descend to Camp One. George felt exhausted and realized that he also could not continue without a rest.

Jim hastily reorganized summit plans. He moved Lou, Kim, and Carlos into the first try. George, Jay, Dan, Kop, and Andy were the new second team. Dave Coombs, Carl, Jim, and I would be the third summit team. It sounded great to me. I could use the extra day of rest that being on the third team would afford. Moreover, with two parties ahead of us we wouldn't have to break trail through deep snow, making it much easier for us. Finally, it was exactly the team I wanted. I liked the concept of a Tabin-Tobin summit team. Carl's razor-sharp wit, laid-back personality, and incredible strength made him a joy to climb with. Dave Coombs was as mentally tough as anyone I've ever met and the most safety-conscious member of our team, which is a great asset for an Everest summit partner. Jim was a person I admired greatly with whom I would be honored to share the big day.

The plan was to rotate the three teams to the top in three days. We had two tents at twenty-five thousand feet and a two-man tent at High Camp. You can descend quickly from the High Camp to Camp Two by sliding on your butt in the snow, breaking with an ice axe. The first team would go to High Camp, sleep without supplemental oxygen, and use their bottles to go for the top. They would then descend to the second camp where the third team would have hot drinks waiting for them. Meanwhile, the second team would have moved to High Camp. The next day, team two would summit and descend to Camp Two where the first team would take care of them. Meanwhile, the final team would move into position for a summit bid. On the third day my group would climb to the top of Mount Everest and descend as far as possible. An air of excitement engulfed us. In three days we would have either made it or failed.

• • •

On October 8, Carlos, Kim, and Lou set out for the summit of Mount Everest at two o'clock in the morning. George, Dan, Andy, Kop, and Jay headed for High Camp. Jim, Carl, Dave Coombs, and I set off for Camp Two. The first big news was that Andy had a sharp pain in his chest and a deep cough. Jim's diagnosis was an inflammation of the lining of the lungs. Andy headed down to base camp. Jim decided that as a doctor he had to stay with Andy and turned around. Next, Carl found that his toes were freezing and he could not warm them. He had developed frostbite in Alaska the previous winter and decided that the summit of Everest was not worth the risk for him, as he would surely lose his toes and the frozen foot would add to the danger of a fall. Next, Coombs developed a terrible headache and was unable to hold down food. Worried that he was developing cerebral edema, he turned back.

My entire summit team had disintegrated on me. We all returned to Camp One. I was very upset and confused as to what to do. I felt good enough to go for the summit, but was afraid to try it alone. Then, Cheese called on the radio to say that he was feeling healthy again and was keen to make a bid. Dave Cheesmond and I thus became the new third team. We planned to move to Camp Two, at twenty-five thousand feet, the next day. Meanwhile, the weather remained perfect with a cloudless calm sky. Jay, Dan, and George reached High Camp feeling strong. We all eagerly awaited word from the first summit team. The second team reported that the snow was deep above camp. Trail breaking must have been exhausting for Kim, Carlos, and Lou.

At noon we got an excited radio call from our Chinese interpreter, Mr. Tsao, who was watching the progress from base camp via a high-powered telescope. "I see climbers on ridge! Climbers are on ridge!" he reported. This was at 28,000 feet where our route merged with the Southeast Ridge. The East Face had been climbed! Now we only needed to follow the ridge to the top. In the background on the radio we heard Tibetans chanting mantras for our success. The next message we heard was bizarre. "Seven climbers, seven climbers going to get them!" We had no idea what Tsao was talking about. We later learned that a Japanese team climbing the South Col route from Nepal met up with our team just below the South Summit at 28,500 feet. The Japanese were climbing without supplemental oxygen and soon fell behind our climbers.

The final climb to the South Summit was steeper and scarier than expected. The angle was over forty-five degrees with a hard crust over sugar snow. It would have been impossible to self-arrest a fall. To save time and weight they were climbing unroped. Any slip would be fatal. Above the South Summit a heavily corniced knife-edged ridge led to the short vertical obstacle known as the "Hillary Step." This thirty-foot wall was passed by strenuously bridging one foot on rock while kicking the other foot's crampon points into the ice. Finally, at two-thirty in the afternoon, twelve hours after starting out from High Camp, Kim's voice crackled on the radio, "We're on top of this fucker!"

Back at Camp One we whooped with joy and hugged all around. Kim, Carlos, and Lou walked the final steps to the top together. Kim was openly weeping on the top of the world. The three spent forty-five minutes in perfect sunshine and air calm enough to light a candle, enjoying the view and taking photographs. All three were out of supplemental oxygen when they cautiously headed down. They encountered the Japanese, still stumbling upward, at the South Summit. None of them had a pack. This meant that they did not have any extra clothing, sleeping bags, water, or stoves for a bivouac. It was past four o'clock in the afternoon. Our team suggested that it was too late and that the Japanese should turn around. They shook their noticeably blue faces and continued upward. A Sherpa climbing with the Japanese then fell and started sliding ten feet above them. Lou looked directly into the terrified man's eyes as he tumbled past, missing Lou by only a few inches, before accelerating into a seven-thousand-foot drop into the Western Cwm. A few minutes later one of Lou's footholds gave way and he flipped upside down, suspended by only one foot punched through the hard crust in the snow. He hung, unable to right himself, with just a couple of toes keeping him from falling off the mountain. If his foot had let go he would have torpedoed seven thousand feet, head first, following the path of the Sherpa to certain death. Carlos climbed fifteen feet back up to help him. Badly shaken by the near fall and having watched the Sherpa perish, Lou and Carlos faced into the slope and backed slowly down the steep ice.

Kim continued descending alone, unaware of Lou's slip and reached High Camp at six o'clock. He came down all the way to Camp One, joining me in my tent at 23,500 feet at eight o'clock. I had never seen a human being who looked as exhausted as Kim. His eyes were sunk back into his face and he was barely able to whisper. Meanwhile, Carlos and Lou still had not returned to high camp. Our team became progressively more anxious. Kim postulated that they may have opted to descend the easier route down to the South Col in Nepal and stay with the Japanese. We worried that they had fallen. Finally, at nine o'clock, George reported that they had staggered into High Camp. Six people were crammed into the tiny two-person tent, so that any movement by one person affected everyone else. Lou had terrible nightmares and coughed incessantly. Carlos had full-body muscle cramps and convulsions. No one got any sleep. Dan later said that, physically, the hardest part of his summit day was holding Carlos' arms and legs during the night.

At two o'clock in the morning, on October 9, George started brewing up, melting snow into water. At three-thirty he was set to go. Kopczynski had had a bad headache all night and felt it was getting worse. He was also concerned about Lou and Carlos going down alone. Kop volunteered to help them. Dan and Jay wavered a bit, then decided to go for the summit. Since the track had partially blown in, they decided that George should start out breaking trail and they would catch up. The wind picked up toward morning. After an hour George stopped and looked back. He saw no one behind him. He later wrote in his diary:

> Wind whips snow across my face. Can't even tell if I'm standing up straight. Complete vertigo! So alone! Have never felt such an alien environment, clearly a place where man was not meant to be. Why haven't Jay and Dan

started? Storm is increasing—will just continue 'til it seems unreasonable.

Dan and Jay discussed what to do for a long time. When they finally decided to go for it, Dan found that the oxygen fogged his glasses, and they were delayed further as Dan struggled to clear his vision. Meanwhile, down at Camp One, I brewed up for Kim and enjoyed a celebratory breakfast of tinned cake and pudding. Jim Morrissey came over to our tent. He was elated at the team's success and said he now just wanted to see everyone safely off of the mountain. Cheese joined us in great spirits, totally optimistic about our summit bid. "The track will be in so we'll just walk up the steps. We'll have a perfect summit day, Geoff," he said. I was feeling great and was very happy to have Dave as my summit partner. We headed up to the next camp carrying our oxygen bottles and personal gear. At Camp Two we had a great reunion with Lou and Carlos coming down. Both were wasted, but healthy. Kop was also feeling better. His headache was gone and he opted to join me and Cheese and go back up. This increased my confidence. Not only was Kop strong and safe, but he'd been to the top before. I only wished that Jim, who had also been powerful and fit, had decided to join us.

The wind increased in intensity as the morning wore on. Clouds began to build down in the valley and move up the mountain. Up high, George was continuing to climb solo and he was finding very hard snow and a steeper slope than he expected. He climbed cautiously as he knew that he could not self-arrest a fall. Then, he saw a figure above. In his diary he wrote, "He moves incredibly slowly, taking a few steps, then collapsing on his ice axe to rest. I am going up and he is coming down. Yet, we are covering ground at about the same rate. I ask the Japanese climber if he is okay. He replies, 'bivy,' and points up. He is very blue and his motions uncoordinated. I have no rope to help him, so just pat him on the shoulder and continue."

Dan and Jay were now struggling up the lower slopes finding that George's steps had already disappeared with the wind. Cheese, Kop, and I watched the weather carefully. Dave reassured me that the clouds were just down in the valley and conditions should hold a few more days. I still worried about my own summit chances as I watched the mist slowly creep up the mountain.

The climbing steepened for George. Just below the South Summit he turned up the rate of his oxygen flow. At the South Summit he found a movie camera left by a Japanese climber the day before and he wondered how many had to bivouac. George moved onto the dramatic upper ridge and over the Hillary Step. He continued in his diary:

> Above the Hillary section is a steep bulge of snow. It feels awkward moving over it, especially since I can't see well with the mask and goggles. Immediately above is an ice axe sticking in the snow. Looking down I see scrape marks in the snow until they end at steep rock a few meters below. The realization hits that one of the Japanese died here yesterday. I push on, now just wanting to be finished.

George reached the summit just before ten o'clock in the morning. He spent a half hour surveying the view, turned up his oxygen, and started the descent. He picked up the Japanese ice axe for added security on the steep sections. At noon he met Jay and Dan just below the dangerous part. George told them about the Japanese and urged them to set a turnaround time. He recalled, "Dan says they will turn around by one-thirty. Knowing Dan does not give me any confidence in that prediction."

George stopped briefly at our top tent and left his extra oxygen. He also turned on his headlamp and left it suspended from the top of the tent in case Dan and Jay returned after dark. He then zipped down, stopping for a quick congratulatory hug and a brew at our camp, and reached Helmut Camp by four o'clock in the afternoon. I was very psyched by George's fast ascent. Our team had already achieved great success, and I began to believe that I would reach the top of Everest. During the next two hours the clouds continued to surge up the mountain and the wind began to whip the tent. I began to worry about my summit chances. George's footprints were already invisible outside our tent. Then the realization hit: Dan and Jay were still out there! The storm intensified into a white out blizzard as the sun set. "Death-pact PercoDan" had not been on a mountain in two years. This was Jay's first trip to the Himalayas. Worry gave way to panic, made all the worse because there was nothing we could do. It would be impossible for anyone to survive a night out at this altitude, in this storm. Then, at nine o'clock, Dan and Jay came on the radio to say they had just returned to the High Camp tent.

They, of course, had ignored the turnaround time. Jay and Dan reached the summit at three-fifteen, out of supplemental oxygen. They stayed on top until four o'clock and started to descend, just as the storm hit them. For psychological support they took a small length of rope that Dan had carried and tied themselves together so that if one fell they both would die. Both were totally exhausted and disoriented in the blizzard. It was completely dark. Both were freezing. At eight o'clock they argued about where to go. Dan felt that they must have passed the tent and advocated going back up. Jay was too tired to ascend and insisted they must have lost the ridge and that they should move laterally. Then, the storm abated for an instant and they saw a glimmer of a light beneath them. An hour of desperate struggle later they found the High Camp tent and crawled inside. George's headlamp battery had gone dead, but it lasted just long enough to help Jay and Dan survive.

Dawn on October 10 revealed the full fury of the mountain. The blizzard still raged. High winds and two feet of new, windblown snow made it difficult to move, and the avalanche danger was extreme. There was no question. We had to go down. Kop, Cheese, and I waited for Dan and Jay, then begin breaking trail down to Helmut Camp. Jay's right hand had fingers black with frostbite, but he never complained. Dan was having visual problems from his glasses becoming covered with snow, but he kept on smiling, even after he wandered off the trail and tumbled twenty feet, stopping only a few inches from a fatal drop.

I descended down the avalanche chute, tied Dan to a rope, and helped him out. We crawled, wet and miserable, into Helmut Camp after seven hours of hard work. The next day we rappelled down into the swirling tempest, having to dig out icy ropes which had frozen into the buttress. Forty scary times we slid down the slick ropes with freezing hands barely able to work the braking device. We were trying to bring all of our gear and garbage off of the mountain with us and it was difficult to balance the enormous loads. At the top of the Bowling Alley I slipped and my pack flipped me upside down. Spindrift avalanches swept over me. I couldn't breathe and couldn't untangle myself. Just as I started to drown, Dr. Dan returned my favor of the previous day and came back up a rope to save my life.

Eight hours later our entire team was reunited at advanced base camp. Everyone was safe. With the exception of Jay, who would lose a couple of fingertips to frostbite, all of us were healthy. Six Americans reached the top of Mount Everest via the first ascent of the largest, steepest, and most difficult face on the mountain. We did it with a minimum of supplemental oxygen and no native support or porters on the climb. More importantly, we did it as a team of brothers who were all leaving the mountain as friends, bonded for life.

from # Beyond Everest
by Patrick Morrow

The icefall near the bottom of the original route up Everest

is a morass of ice towers and crevasses that by 1982 had

claimed 11 climbers' lives. Canadian Pat Morrow (born

1952) describes his 1982 expedition's experiences there.

T he expedition reached Base Camp on August 15, several days after
Peter Spear, the Base Camp manager, and climber David McNab
had arrived to start erecting a comfortable camp in a most uncomfortable location. The site, a rubble-strewn stretch of glacier at the
foot of the Khumbu Icefall, has been used by expeditions for 30 years.
Garbage from past climbs littered the ground, and it seemed that the
camp was no more than a historic fecal deposit. The situation was little
improved by the fact that, along with several others, I was suffering from
a spiteful strain of dysentery. This, combined with the effects of altitude,
laid me up for a whole week until I wondered if my body would ever be
able to recover from the malaise at this altitude. Out of curiosity, when I
had regained my health, I took my resting pulse rate at Base Camp. It was
119. I didn't even bother to measure it above that point.

We shared the site with a team of Catalans attempting Everest's highly technical West Ridge route. Together with the Sherpas from both teams, we observed a Buddhist ceremony and then proceeded to help the Catalans drain some of their magnificent stock of Base Camp cheer, which amounted to 500 cans of *cerveza*.

On August 17, while several members of the team conducted a training session with the Sherpas to standardize climbing techniques and rescue procedures, Bill March, Lloyd Gallagher and Alan Burgess scrambled up a short distance to reconnoitre a route through the icefall. The climbing, at last, had begun.

The overall strategy was to lay siege to the mountain in the classic fashion of past expeditions. The team would establish a series of camps up the mountain, stocking each with the supplies needed to push up to the next camp. This style of climbing is considered necessary whenever a mountain presents an obstacle, such as the Khumbu Icefall, that might require many days to surmount. Unlike almost any other popular mountain in the Himalayas, Everest sits right on the Tibet-Nepal border and so the only easy access from Nepal is through the Khumbu region. Because Tibet's borders were closed to foreigners at the time we were planning our expedition, we chose to approach the mountain through the treacherous icefall, a route that makes no mountaineering sense at all and would normally be avoided at all costs. Since the Khumbu Icefall was considered almost a separate climb in itself, we needed a large climbing and support team. In spite of our manpower, we soon found out how vulnerable we still were to the dangers of the ever-shifting mass of ice.

Moving on Air

The climb assumed a pyramidal structure—a wide base of supplies and climbers at the bottom that gradually tapered to a carefully selected cache of provisions and one or two climbers at the highest camp. The high camp might require a scant 10 loads to stock, while the one below needed 40 or 50, and so on down the mountain. Consequently, our Base Camp consisted of 700 loads of supplies, 15 Canadian climbers, 5 support personnel and 29 high-altitude Sherpas.

To facilitate movement on the mountain, polypropylene ropes were fixed between camps and anchored by ice screws or, in the case of deep snow, snow flukes and pickets. Also known as "dead men," snow flukes resemble snow-shovel blades and are pushed into deep snow, as are the T-shaped aluminum pickets, to offer resistance to any tug on the rope. Together, the ropes constitute a mountain lifeline to which climbers attach themselves as they shuttle supplies from camp to camp. If a climber slips or falls, the rope will secure him, thus eliminating the need for two or more climbers to rope themselves together and move as a unit. During the course of the expedition, we fixed more than five miles of rope on the mountain.

Everest's first challenge, the icefall, was to be one of its most severe. From the bottom, it appeared impassable, a tumbled confusion of massive seracs (pillars of ice formed as a glacier moves down a steep incline of bedrock and splits apart) and gaping crevasses made all the more menacing by the continual reshuffling of glacial elements. Taken one step at a time, however, possibilities appeared and lines of approach opened up, and it became feasible, if nerve-racking, to move gently through the frozen, creaking maze.

The first 1,000 feet (304 m) went smoothly enough, but then we encountered a severely broken section that was dubbed The Traverse, and progress literally slowed to a crawl. There was nothing there but 30-foot-high (9 m) seracs above and 150-foot-deep (45 m) crevasses below, which forced us away from the centre of the icefall and into a position of vulnerability under the west shoulder of Everest. Our route lay across chunks of ice that had fallen from the seracs and become wedged in the crevasses, meaning we were moving more or less across air, rather than substance. As our Sherpa porters struggled upward under heavy loads, their breathing came in gasps for not only did they have to suck in enough air to breathe, but they also had to force a continuous stream of mantras through their clenched teeth as they exhaled. Their prayers ceased higher on the mountain, and it was hard to determine whether that was a sign the hazards had lessened or whether there was not enough oxygen to fuel them.

Fixing ropes through the traverse involved inching delicately down a rib of ice, leaping across a crevasse, tentatively working up the far side, crawling across a yard of serac crumbs to another gaping chasm and then starting all over again. To make subsequent progress easier, eight-foot aluminum-ladder sections were used to bridge the worst spots; several of the crevasses needed three sections.

Despite the severity of the task, our team, working in pairs, penetrated the icefall in three days and secured the route with ropes and ladders in five, a record time that surprised and delighted us. One climber would usually lead the route, another would fix ropes and ladders, and one or two would improve the passage somewhere below. On August 22, Jim Elzinga, still limping from a fall suffered in Kathmandu, and Laurie Skreslet moved beyond the icefall to establish Camp One at 19,600 feet (5,974 m). The next several days were devoted to improving the route and carrying loads to Camp One. Almost without exception, we were all well acclimatized, strong and working hard. The team leaders had to threaten to tie David McNab down with a rope before he would take a day off. By the end of the month, the team had ferried more than 130 loads of food and supplies to Camp One and had selected a site for Camp Two at 21,000 feet (6,400m). "The way we were going," said Lloyd, "I thought we were going to be up the mountain by the end of September. That would have been a little embarrassing, since we were supposed to be gone until the end of October."

Bubble of Immortality

The passing days brought an easing of the initial apprehension about the ice-fall. The dangers were still obvious—so much so, in fact, that we began our day's work by headlamp at 3 o'clock in the dark, cold early morning when the glacier was least active and the chance of avalanche minimal—but as Rusty noted, "The team was building up a nice little bubble of immortality."

The bubble was not to last. On the morning of August 31, I set out from Base Camp with Rusty and two lightly loaded Sherpas to break a trail through snow that had fallen the previous evening. A larger complement of Sherpas, accompanied by Peter Spear, freelance cameraman Blair Griffiths and Bruce Patterson, our Southam reporter, was to follow. A short distance into the icefall, we found one of the crevasse-bridging ladders beginning to twist, but we were used to such phenomena by then and measured the icefall's motion by the torque on the ladders and the tension on the ropes. Rusty and one Sherpa decided to straighten it while I moved ahead with the other Sherpa. By the time we reached the traverse, the snow was boot-deep. More troublesome, however, was the strength of the wind: whatever snow had accumulated would be wind-deposited and thus prone to avalanching.

Moving out of the traverse, I thought of turning back and decided to do so if I came to a slope where my feet disturbed the surface of the snow enough to release its bond with the glacier and trigger a slide. I rested in the darkness, eating a chocolate bar and drinking water, trying to get a feel for the situation. It was still early, still cold. We had worked in fresh snow for the past two weeks, but nothing we had passed through so far had been avalanche-prone, and the disconcerting roar of big avalanches high up on Everest and its satellite peaks seemed to go on regardless of the time of day or the weather.

I decided to press on but radioed up to Camp One, where Bill, Alan, Tim, David McNab and three Sherpas—the first team to spend a night above Base Camp—were just awakening. As I talked on the radio to Bill about the possibility of his group's breaking trail down to meet us, Blair and six Sherpas caught up to me. After exchanging a few words, they moved upslope, but I only got 30 paces before being enveloped in a tremendous hissing of wind and snow. The snow was being driven so hard that it felt like grains of sand, and the rush of wind tore the breath out of me. It was very confusing, and I became totally disoriented. I couldn't see, I couldn't hear, and I couldn't breathe. I tried to shield my head with my arms and dived for the shelter of a serac I knew was in front of me, but I kept being dragged out from behind it. I was clipped into the fixed rope, and every time I got behind the serac, the rope, which was being torn off the mountain, would drag me back out. "Well," I thought, "this is it. It's finally caught up with me."

As suddenly as it hit, the avalanche passed, and I could see and breathe again. I first spotted Blair a bit below me on the edge of the avalanche path and slid down the rope to see if he was all right. Assured that he was, I worked back up to the Sherpas. They, too, were intact, although one had a badly bruised leg. Then, just minutes after signing off from the first call, I radioed back to Camp One to say that we had been hit by an avalanche but that everyone seemed all right. Next, I radioed down to Base Camp and, after a quick conference with Lloyd, decided that it would be best to evacuate the mountain immediately. A major avalanche is sometimes followed by another, and we wanted to leave the zone as quickly as possible.

Mountain Grave

As we picked our way back across the 200-yard-wide (182 m) swath of debris, we found ourselves crawling over cakes of ice the size of refrigerators. The avalanche had been massive: it had picked up entire seracs and beaten them into smaller pieces as it roared down the mountain. We later estimated that it had begun almost 3,000 feet (914 m) above and, at its widest point, measured well over a mile. The snow that had swept over our team was one small tongue of a much larger slide.

On the far side of the avalanche path, the radio crackled again with the message from Base Camp that Rusty, Peter and three Sherpas had narrowly escaped serious injury on the downslope side of the avalanche. Rusty had been knocked down the mountain and buried up to his chest, and Peter, spinning on the fixed rope, had been completely buried except for one foot. Rusty and one of the Sherpas were able to dig him out. Three other Sherpas were missing. The snow had stopped just 150 feet (45 m) below us, and we couldn't believe that there were three men somewhere in there. Disregarding the threat of another avalanche, Blair and I began a frantic search, but the wet snow had settled like cement. It was impossible to probe the debris, and shovels bounced off the surface. Although we were soon joined by others from Camp One and later from Base Camp, it was well over an hour before we found the only body the slide was to yield—Pasang Sona. Stephen Bezruchka, our team physician, had come up from Base Camp and arrived in time to help recover the body. Pasang and the two others had been together and were buried just a couple of yards into the edge of the avalanche path. If they had been able to walk back down the fixed rope just a few more paces, they would have been missed by the slide as closely as Blair and I had been.

Stephen recalls the moment: "The grim reality became clear when a hand was uncovered near the bottom end of the fixed rope. It took an eternity to clear the snow away from the body, and while Pasang was being uncovered, James Blench asked me if I had any idea what to do. I suggested I try CPR [cardiopulmonary resuscitation]. It seemed so hopeless, and there was so much frustration that I was at the point of tears; but I knew that if it were me, I'd want someone at least to try. We put him in a sleeping bag, and Rusty and I climbed in with the body to try to warm it. We worked on him for about 30 minutes, but Pasang never came back."

Premonition of Disaster

The loss of the three men was an immense blow. The single recovered body, bound in a sleeping bag, was lowered to Base Camp and placed in a rock enclosure with a burning light to guide its spirit into the next life. With no place to go, we wandered around camp disconsolately, trying to sort out what had happened. "It was shattering," says Rusty. "It's one thing to sit in a bar in Calgary and say, 'Geez, you know 11 men have died in that icefall; we'll have to be careful in there,' and quite another to be carrying the body of a friend down through it. I don't think we truly understood the full implication of what we were up against until that moment."

In the afternoon, we gathered in the cook tent to analyze our situation. Although we were unable to isolate any particular reason for the accident (other than being on the mountain during the post-monsoon season when the Himalayas are heavily snow-laden), we did decide to travel in smaller groups; to spread out more; to use the radios to make scheduled early-morning weather reports; and not to make any subsequent climbs during snowfalls, no matter how mild it was. A year after the climb, I came across an eerie reminder of the occasion in a calendar photograph taken by Jonathan Blair, who himself was later killed in an avalanche on a Chinese peak. Jonathan had been at the site of our Camp One when he had photographed a massive, billowing release of snow along the identical path ours had taken. But the photograph had been taken at midday, under a clear blue sky, indicating to me that this was a haphazard occurrence that could take place in any weather. It was simply bad luck that we had blundered into, and nothing short of a premonition could have averted the disaster.

More than just adding to the nuts-and-bolts aspect of climbing the mountain, the avalanche added a tremendous emotional burden to the climb. "It was about the worst possible accident," recalls Tim. "Not only had we lost three expedition members, but those members were Sherpas who were on the mountain solely because they could help us, the crazy Westerners, get to the top. It's true that most of them really do like to climb and that they are paid very well for it and that those who are successful become heroes among their own people, but that doesn't diminish the responsibility you feel for them on the mountain. And all this is in addition to the fact that they are such a warm, gentle people, so loyal in a way Westerners can barely comprehend that you just don't want them to be hurt." Those killed were Ang Tsultim, 20, who had worked with trekking groups before but was on his first climb; Dawa Dorje, 40, who had extensive climbing experience and had joined our training climb on Annapurna IV; and Pasang Sona, 40, also an experienced Himalayan climber.

Their deaths raised an old question that every climber must consider sooner or later: is any mountain worth the loss of a single human life? The team had decided back in Canada that the expedition would continue despite a serious accident, but it now seemed that the matter deserved reconsideration. Stephen, remembering the Japanese ski expedition of 1970 in which six Sherpas died, recalls: "I always resented that expedition for continuing. Now I was suddenly asking myself if three were so many fewer than six that we could continue ourselves." Rusty, a fine climber with a long history of dangerous, difficult ascents, surprised us at the meeting when he announced that he was considering quitting. Donald Serl, who could not reconcile recreation with death, said it was definitely over for him.

The following morning, a party of eight Sherpas carrying the body of Pasang Sona headed down the trail to Lobuche, a high-summer yak pasture that has recently become inhabited year-round to serve trekkers. Bill, Stephen and John Amatt went with them—Bill and Stephen to look after details concerning the Sherpas' deaths, John to move farther down the valley to Namche Bazaar to radio out news of the accident. The powerful Base Camp radio had a faulty antenna, and it was thanks to Teleglobe Canada technician Dick Cushing, who arrived a couple of weeks later, that we were finally able to establish a radio link with Kathmandu. The men had been in Lobuche only a short time before the bereaved relatives began to assemble, Pasang Sona's widow and youngest daughter arriving first, their wailing audible for a great distance. Next came Ang Tsultim's father, a middle-aged man with a limp, leaning on a stick for support and silently weeping. Dawa Dorje's widow was slow to appear—she had one infant and was pregnant with another, and no one had wanted to break the news to her.

Serene Setting

The next few hours were the hardest of the entire climb for Bill: "My official responsibilities were to meet with the families, express the expedition's condolences, explain the insurance policies we had on the Sherpas' lives and give them some money and what we had of the men's personal effects. Unofficially, I wanted to do all I could to comfort them, which meant sitting with them while they mourned—and they mourn long and hard, day and night. They are a very emotional people; they don't hold much back. Three of us—Gyalgen, the Sirdar, or head Sherpa, Kshatri Pati Shrestha, the liaison officer, and I—took turns in two-hour shifts. The mourning went on for two or three days, but it seemed like months. The sorrow was overwhelming."

On the morning of September 2, Pasang Sona's body was carried down from Lobuche for cremation on a ridge below the settlement. It was a serene setting: the world opened up below to the south, and the majestic peak of one of the most beautiful of the Himalayas, Ama Dablam (meaning Mother's Jewel Box) rose against the sky. A lama who had arrived the day before to help guide Pasang Sona's soul into the afterlife chanted while the body was washed, ritually fed, then braced as rhododendron wood was piled around it. Once the fire was lit, the group of mourners moved to a spot where food had been prepared. Distraught, Stephen talked to the lama about the calamity. But the lama's words caught him off guard: "This is just one of those things. It just happens."

At 2:30 that afternoon, as Bill and Stephen were preparing to move back up to Base Camp, two Sherpa runners arrived with more of the deceased Sherpas' equipment and a note for Bill. The message from Peter was short and to the point: at 9:15 a.m., there had been a collapse in the icefall. Blair Griffiths had been killed by a falling serac at the upper end of the traverse. The climbers had decided to recover the body and carry it down to Lobuche for cremation.

Antidote to Sorrow

Two days earlier, after Bill had left for Lobuche with the Sherpas, the team had regrouped, resolving to move back onto the mountain. Action, it was agreed, was the best antidote to sorrow, and besides, the weather had become perfect for climbing.

Despite the momentary optimism born of the continuation of the climb, Tim described his feeling of apprehension in his diary: "In the hours preceding the full moon of September 2, 1982, I was awakened from an uneasy sleep by ominous rumblings in the Khumbu Icefall. It was shortly after midnight, the night clear and still, cold but brilliant with reflected moonlight—and filled with the sound of thousands of tons of ice slowly stirring, groaning in its steep glacial bed, restlessly moving at up to a yard per day toward the valley below. The noise was distressing, for the icefall was our choice approach to the mountain's summit, 12,140 feet [3,700 m] above, and our team had been nervously threading its way through the maze of precariously balanced blocks and spires almost daily for two weeks."

On the morning of September 2, a party of five Canadians, of which I was one, and 10 Sherpas had moved up to occupy Camp One, carrying loads, while Rusty (who had decided to stay on after all), Dave Read, Blair and two Sherpas went into the traverse to repair a two-section ladder that was badly twisted. Dave and Nima Tsering were working at the base of the ladder, Blair and Pasang Tenzing at the top, and Rusty was sorting out ropes just behind Blair. At 9:15, just over an hour after 15 of us had passed through this same spot, "the whole glacier started to shudder and shimmy." Caught in the midst of the movement, Dave remembers the next few minutes clearly: "I thought at first that it was an earthquake, but then I realized the entire glacier was moving around me. The piece I was standing on started to slide into the crevasse, and suddenly, there were these big blocks of ice all around my head, and I was passing them, and they were going over the top of me, and I thought, 'This is it, mate. Too bad.' " Above him, Rusty and Tenzing were scrambling from toppling block to toppling block.

Rusty later recalled that when the collapse began, his major concern was that he die with dignity. His one thought was, "I want to go calmly." Then, when the first wave of falling ice missed him, he began to work at avoiding the next onslaught.

Seconds later, as the ice stabilized, Dave found himself still alive, wedged in a domino assortment of snow and ice within the crevasse. Two large blocks of ice had fallen against each other above him, leaving a space for his upper torso and head. While trying to orient himself, he saw a wool tuque lying in the rubble, and reaching out with his one free hand to retrieve it, he was startled to find it attached to a head. Gently, he scooped snow away from the face and cradled it with his left hand, pulling the head back. Sputtering out a mouthful of snow, Tsering came back to life with a shout. Panicking, the Sherpa freed his arms and shoulders and began struggling against the snow, using Dave as a combination ladder and pull-up bar. Dave, with little means of resistance, was pushed deeper into the unconsolidated debris beneath him, until only his head, shoulders and left arm were clear of snow. The two men's struggles were interrupted when a face appeared in a small hole 20 feet above, where Rusty, hearing the noise, had discovered the site of their entombment.

"My God! You're alive!" said Rusty.

"Right, mate. But I won't be for long if this Sherpa has his way."

Rusty lowered a rope and managed to pull Tsering out. With the aid of a snow stake, knife and ice axe, it took Dave another 15 minutes to cut the ropes binding his left leg and to clear the ice from both. Finally liberated, he asked Rusty how Blair was.

"Sorry, Dave," came the reply. "He's dead."

Emerging from the crevasse, Dave had found Blair a scant 15 feet away, pinned between two large cakes of ice and remembers, "He had a very calm look, as though he were going to talk, to say, 'Hey, you know I'm only joking.' " Dave walked over to the body, shook Blair's hand and said, "I'm sorry about that, Blair." With that, the three climbers turned away and began to struggle through what was left of the traverse. The remnants of the fixed rope they had been following now dangled 25 feet above them.

I was sitting at the entranceway to my tent at Camp One when the news reached us on our hand-held radio. Dwayne slumped over and began to weep. "It just isn't fair," he said. Jim reached over to console him, and I turned to Laurie who was staring in disbelief down on the top of the icefall that had so recently taken three other lives. I had never felt my own mortality more than at this moment, looking around at my friends and knowing that any one of us could have shared Blair's fate.

As the news reached Base Camp, the remaining climbers stumbled into the cook tent for yet another meeting. With the spectre of the Sherpa deaths still haunting it, the team was faced with another numbing loss, and the accumulated pressures were reaching a flash point. The decision was made that four men would move into the icefall the following morning and meet us descending from Camp One, and then the entire team would carry Blair's body down to Lobuche. This plan, however, met with stiff resistance from Bill, and in an afternoon radio conversation, Bill advised the climbers to leave the body on the mountain. From a practical point of view, he felt that it was a completely empty gesture: the icefall had twice proved itself deadly, and to traverse it for any reason other than absolute necessity was to jeopardize more lives needlessly. Also, as Bill had learned from his recent descent to Lobuche, transporting a body down the steep, rocky trail from Base Camp was physically exhausting and dangerous in itself. Another consideration was that Blair was a Catholic, and Bill was uncertain whether cremation was compatible with that religion. The body, Bill insisted, could be given a fitting burial on the glacier, in a long-accepted tradition among mountaineers.

Several of the climbers, however, insisted on following their plan, and to keep the peace, Bill asked for time to think it over. After scheduling another call and signing off, he and Stephen retired to a sod-walled hotel named "The Promised Land." Stephen pleaded the climbers' case for catharsis, and following much discussion, Bill relented. In his second call to Base Camp, he agreed to the plan, provided risks to the climbers were minimized. The Catalans assured him that cremation was in fact suitable for a Catholic, and inquiries in Lobuche confirmed that there was an adequate supply of wood.

The following afternoon, the team arrived in Lobuche. As Bill had predicted, the journey had been exhausting and dangerous. Laurie, having injured several ribs in a fall, was in considerable pain. The trip down was—not surprisingly—an emotional forum, for the doubts that had arisen in the aftermath of the avalanche now gathered like storm clouds. It was a time for each man to wrestle with personal demons, to contemplate his commitment, to try to separate the emotional from the practical.

Blair was cremated the next morning on the site that had been used for Pasang Sona. It was a cold morning, full of mist and blowing clouds, a day suitably sombre for the task at hand. The team had a small service before the lighting of the pyre, and each member stepped forward to pay tribute to the man, the mountain and the nexus between. Blair had been very well liked, respected for his enthusiasm and hard work, admired for his quiet self-assurance. On the trek to Everest, at the Tengboche Monastery, he had spent an afternoon gazing toward the mountains of Ama Dablam and Nuptse and the valley below and had written in his journal: "I don't want to die, but if the pale horse should decide to come along, there isn't a better cathedral to stay in." Knowing Blair's love of poetry, Tim wrote a verse for the ceremony:

> *This is the way of all eternity;*
> *As we see him now, so shall we be.*
> *When the time comes to follow him*
> *To where the mountain wind blows,*
> *Go as he does, with a good heart.*

from Fragile Edge
by Maria Coffey

Maria Coffey's (born 1952) three-year relationship with climber Joe Tasker ended in May, 1982 when he and Peter Boardman disappeared on Everest's Northeast Ridge. A few months later, Coffey traveled to Everest with Hilary Boardman, Peter's widow.

Leaning precariously out of the truck, I craned my neck to look up at the steep, fluted, colorful walls and down to the tumbling river rushing through waterfalls and rapids. The gorge opened out onto a wide plain, so flat it must once have been a lake. Villages rolled by, cornfields splattered color across the aridity, and cows tethered to stakes grazed hopefully among the windswept, stunted grasses. Denny became agitated in the back of the truck, his photographic desires frustrated by the relentless movement of the bumpy vehicle. Despite his periodic banging on the cab roof, Tele, encouraged no doubt by Dong who was anxious that we reach Rongbuk before dark, drove purposefully on. I sympathized with Denny, who needed photographs for a travel brochure, but for myself I didn't mind. The images forming and transforming before us, day after day, were being imprinted on my memory. And it felt right to be pressing onwards, skirting the mountain in a long loop to reach the northern side before the light faded.

We stopped briefly at a dusty village where Zhiang tried to bargain for a sheep. I was dumbstruck to realize that he planned to put the live animal in the back of the truck and slaughter it at Base Camp. My relief was great when the deal fell through, but Zhiang had been delighted by my dismay and from then on would bleat at me regularly.

Pieces of a bridge recently washed away lay scattered along the banks of a wide, meandering river. Zhiang leaned forward for a rapid discussion with Dong and Tele in the cab, and the truck plunged in. I watched water rise almost to the top of the tires and recede again as we began to climb the far bank, before the unmistakable sound of wheels spinning in mud signaled a sudden halt. We clambered over the cab roof, across the bonnet and stone-hopped to land. Tele, his feet bare and trousers rolled up, lowered his skinny legs into the icy water. He threw ropes to us and we heaved on them as he revved the engine until the truck came free and mounted the bank, dripping from its undersides. Tele climbed down again, still shoeless, folded his arms and smilingly surveyed the river, obviously delighted by the maneuver and its success.

"Like a rock climber looking at a route he's just done," laughed Hilary.

Late in the afternoon, as light was fading, we reached the Rongbuk Valley. It is windswept, stark and cold, and totally dominated by the vast bulk of the mountain at its head. Chomolungma, silent and majestic, seems to emanate an ancient power. I imagined what Joe must have felt on this approach, seeing the scale of the challenge he had taken on. I remembered how the yak drivers and porters in the Kharma Valley stopped to pray and leave offerings to the mountain.

"Can you see?" said Hilary, as we balanced against the cab in the back of the truck and scanned the Northeast Ridge through binoculars. "They were almost at the part where it levels out. They'd done the hardest stuff. It would have been a long snow plod to the summit."

There were no clouds on that side of the mountain: It stood hard and clear against the sky. Seeds of understanding were slowly, slowly germinating in me. I had been tortured by unanswered questions— why were they so drawn to this mountain, why did they push the limits instead of turning back and coming home? But, little by little, the puzzle was beginning to fit. Le Grand Combin had begun it and now, the closer I drew to Chomolungma, the more I began to feel that perhaps their deaths were not as senseless as they had seemed.

> "He is a portion of that loveliness
> That once he made more lovely."

Familiar words slightly adapted and carved on a granite bench atop the windy hill behind Chris Bonington's house in Cumbria. They are there in memorial to a local boy, Mick Lewis, who died at sixteen in 1944. The first time I walked up High Pike with Hilary, Chris, Wendy, and the dogs, and we rested on the bench and read the words, I had been moved; now, in the Rongbuk Valley, the sentiment seemed right for Joe and Pete. As the sun was dipping out of sight and an orange glow spread over the mountain, we arrived at Base Camp.

Joe had described the site to me in letters and once enclosed a photograph: He posed against a backdrop of gray, moraine hillocks with Changtse and Everest beyond, and held onto his hat to prevent the wind whipping it away "This is a desperate place," he wrote. We pulled up outside a large tent where a small group of Dutch climbers and Chinese officials stood waiting to greet us. There was a pile of trunks and cardboard boxes full of canned food. A generator hummed and two trucks, identical to ours, stood next to it. One man tents were dotted about the flat, dusty site. It was an orderly scene, set in a wilderness. Mr. Wang, the Chinese liaison officer, made the introductions and insisted that we eat with them in their food tent. Hilary and I quickly withdrew to erect our tent before the light was gone, choosing a spot next to the wide and shallow glacier river that formed a boundary on one side of the Base Camp. Close by was a hillock, another boundary.

"Ladies on left, gentlemen on right!" Mr. Wang had said, referring to the large boulders, on either side of the rocky outcrop, which afforded a little privacy. And on the top of the hillock stood memorial cairns for climbers who had lost their lives on the mountain. I smiled at the intimacy of the connection.

There was barely any soil to catch the tent pegs, and we paused from hammering to watch the last rays of the sun on the ridge. I hugged Hilary; it seemed a long time since the morning she had suggested the journey to Everest Base Camp, and our friendship had grown deep and enduring along the way, through all the highs and lows.

Our names were being called, a meal was ready. Inside the spacious tent a circle of picnic chairs was illuminated by a single light bulb, and several propane stoves formed the kitchen area. Porters lounged in the darker recesses, resting and eating. We were ushered in, seated, and served with delicious food. Mr. Wang talked kindly to us of Pete and Joe, whom he had met earlier in the year. But it was not an easy evening for us to socialize, and we soon thanked him and left. Night had fallen and the outline of Chomolungma was just visible against the brightly starred sky.

"It's strange to think of them here, Hilary."

"Pete described it so well. It's exactly as I imagined."

"How do you feel?"

"Close to Peter."

"I wish . . . I wish Joe had got my last letters. And my birthday cards." I had sent him two, one funny, the other romantic. They, and the three letters, had been returned unopened.

"You must stop worrying about that, Maria. It doesn't matter now."

"It's horrible to regret so much. You're lucky in that way."

"No, I'm not. I regret that Peter's baby isn't growing inside me."

We were nearly at the tent. I knew she had begun to cry.

"In one letter he joked about sending frozen sperm. I was sure I was pregnant before he left. I had to write and tell him I wasn't. I wish I were pregnant, I wish I had been left with a part of Peter."

"Hilary, Hilary." I soothed her. "It's cold. Let's get inside."

We crawled into the small nylon shell that had become a familiar home. Two insulation mats were laid out to give some protection against the cold, stony ground, and at night we made an extra layer with our clothes. On top were the voluminous feather-filled sleeping bags. At the end of the tent stood two rucksacks and along the sides, in the limited space next to the sleeping bags, were diaries, water bottles, tissues, wash bags, towels. Hilary's belongings were organized, but I still tended towards a frenzied scramble of unpacking whenever I needed something. With the onset of darkness the temperature, at 17,500 feet, was dropping rapidly and we wriggled into the sleeping bags still wearing thermals and socks and drew the hoods tightly around our faces.

"Let's go up to the cairn in the morning."

"Yes. At first light."

My sleep was disturbed by dreams and I tossed and turned until the alarm finally startled me fully awake. We dressed quickly and gathered together the things we had brought to leave at the cairn. Hilary had a piece of gritstone, the Derbyshire rock Pete had loved to climb on, and some poppy seeds to scatter in the hope that they might germinate and bloom. Joe's family had given me a religious medal and a prayer card to leave there, and I had brought pressed flowers and the translation of a Chinese poem. Suddenly I was reluctant to leave the tent and my stomach knotted with tension. As two mourners we were about to take offerings to a grave, to perform one of the rituals of death, and this had an air of finality that I still resisted. Angry, frustrated tears fell on what I held, the papers, the flowers, and a round of metal. This was all that was left, memories and flimsy representations.

"Come on, Maria," urged Hilary. "We must go before everyone gets up."

The morning air was sharp and frosty and rocks crackled under our boots as we climbed the hillock. They had not been the only ones to perish on the mountain—there were several mounds of stones holding memorial plaques. We found the granite slab on which Charlie Clarke had chiseled their names:

"In Memory of Peter Boardman and Joe Tasker May 1982."

I traced the letters and numbers with my finger, wiping away ice crystals, and thought back to May 17th, four months before. I had been taking my course then; I walked to the college and called in for a friend on the way. We sat outside in the morning sun of that unusually warm spring, waiting for classes to begin. My thoughts must have drifted during a lecture because in my diary page for that day there is a complicated doodle of snowcapped mountains with the sun setting behind them.

Three days later, while spending a weekend in the Lake District with Sarah, I had had a vivid nightmare. I was running down the windswept streets of Ambleside, rain was washing over my upturned face, and I was screaming. She remembers me sitting up in bed, rubbing my eyes and saying, "I dreamt that Joe is dead."

There had been no way that I could allow myself to dwell on the possible implications of that dream. It had to be a manifestation of the fears and worry I had been tamping down into my subconscious for weeks. Or so I had assured myself, and Sarah. And maybe it was. Or perhaps I did pick something up, some disturbance through the realms of time and space that are not yet understood. Because, as far as we know, the dream had been accurate. By then he was already dead.

Hunkered before the cairn, looking beyond it to Chomolungma, I felt no more anger and frustration but simply a great sadness. On May 17th I had been so excited about Joe coming home. The house was almost finished, he would be delighted by the transformation, he could retreat there while his building work went on. We had a whole summer ahead of us . . . But it was over, everything was over. I missed him so much. Hilary was planting poppy seeds; it was time for my private ceremony. I stood up and quietly read the prayer, and then the poem:

> ". . . Oh that I had a bird's wings
> And high flying could follow you . . ."

Papers, flowers, metal; I slipped them into a plastic envelope and dropped it inside the cairn. A breeze blew up, lifting my hair and raising a little dust. No other movement, no sound, no bird cries.

"Are you finished?"

The question pulled my gaze away from the memorial cairn. Hilary was standing very close, and speaking in a low voice. Our ritual was over.

"I can see Denny coming."

We sat against a nearby boulder. Denny reached the top of the hillock, nodded to us and took off his cap before standing in front of each of the cairns. One was for a girl, Marty Hoey, a climber with the American expedition that had been trying a different route on the mountain at the same time as the British team. Within days of Joe and Pete's disappearance she slipped from a harness and fell 6,000 feet to her death. There were other plaques for Japanese climbers. And somewhere on the Northeast Ridge were the bodies of Mallory and Irvine, names I was familiar with as a child, never dreaming that some day I would be a tiny part of the weft and warp of the history of Everest. Denny put his cap on, saluted us and left. The camp was stirring below us, it was time to go down.

"Sometimes," I said, "when you do things that you were really dreading, they turn out to be much easier than expected."

Hilary smiled.

"Joe's making sure you learn that lesson, isn't he?"

Over breakfast we discussed plans. Hilary and I wanted to get to Camp Three on Joe and Pete's route; we should really have stayed at Base Camp for a few days to acclimatize, but time was short and our driving force strong. I had no idea of how I would fare, trekking at that height, but I was ready to push myself. To the perturbation of Dong and Zhiang, who were not allowed to accompany us beyond Base Camp, we decided to set off that afternoon.

We were blessed with fine weather and Chomolungma looked benevolently down on us as we laid out sleeping bags, clothes, and the tent to air, in preparation for the trek. Concealed behind a boulder on the riverbank we stripped off and bathed in icy waters that ran straight off the glacier. My head ached from the cold as I washed and rinsed my hair, but within minutes the pain was replaced by an invigorating glow. As we packed our rucksacks a Dutch climber hesitantly approached. We had decided to avoid contact with the team as much as possible, fearing that our presence and the reasons for our journey might unsettle them.

"I just want to wish you well," he said, "on behalf of all of us."

Lin, the Chinese cook, was already spoiling us, and for lunch he had prepared his specialty of *momos*, spiced meat wrapped in pastry. It was 2 p.m. before we set off across the plain towards the jumble of moraine at the end of the glacier. Clambering over and around the big boulders was exhausting, but before long the path began to cut through the loose rocks of the valley sides and become easy. Below us the rock- and mud-strewn glacier was zig-zagged by wide, shallow crevasses, and above us stood sandstone pillars, high and wind-eroded. Shadows fell across the slope—our guide and interpreter were coming up behind me.

"But, I thought . . ." I began.

"We will take your packs. Follow us to Camp One," said Dong. They were bending the rules to give us moral and physical support. Before we could begin to thank them they had hurried on ahead.

Camp One was next to a tiny blue lake; the tents were already erected and Dong and Zhiang had a brew of tea ready for us, but as soon as we arrived they left quickly, making their goodbyes for the second time that day. The Dutch climbers were using the same site and some of them were spending the night there before going back up to their Camp Five on the North Col of the mountain the following morning. On most expeditions a camp system is set up, as the altitude, the terrain, and the weather make it impossible for the mountain to be scaled in one straight push. Tents, with supplies, are erected at various stages up the mountain and are sometimes replaced, very high, by caves dug into the snow. This allows the climbers to work a relay as they gradually establish their route, going increasingly higher up the mountain and often leaving fixed ropes. A team goes a certain distance,

sets the ropes and perhaps a camp, and then retreats to a lower altitude, sometimes as far down as Base Camp, to recuperate.

One of the Dutch men came over to our tent as we finished a
meager dinner of canned ham and bread. Johan's head was swathed
in folds of white cloth, and his gingery beard framed a face prematurely lined by wind and sun exposure. He knew who we were and
talked sensitively of his plans to climb Changabang, following the
route Joe and Pete had taken and described in Pete's book, *The Shining
Mountain.*

"They were remarkable men," said Johan. "It must be strange for
you to be here."

We accepted his invitation of tea and biscuits and joined a cheerful
group of climbers all squashed inside a four-man tent. The nylon was
picking up the rays of the setting sun and made us all appear to be suffering from advanced sunburn. They told us that the site of the British
expedition's Camp Three was easily identifiable.

"Just look for the empty whisky crate!"

Their camaraderie and the ease with which they accepted us on the
mountain was reassuring. They offered us the use of their large food
tent at Camp Two, a thousand feet below the point we hoped to reach.
This meant we could reduce the weight of our packs by leaving the tent
and cooking equipment behind, and we accepted gratefully.

Outside the tent the spectacle of the night was spine-tingling. The
sun had slipped behind the western, snow-peaked horizon and an
ethereal light of deepest orange spread over the surrounding mountains. Stars were beginning to twinkle in the darkening blue sky and
the air was sharp, impossibly clear and totally still. I caught my breath
at the beauty of it and had a strong sense that something was about to
happen. Just before he left for Tibet, Joe and I had watched *Close
Encounters of the Third Kind*, and the appearance of strange ships in the
sky on that night would not have surprised me: We were in the perfect
setting. Hilary laughed when I shared my thoughts.

"This *is* close encounters!" she said.

I lay with my head poking out of the tent door for a while, watching as the night stole across the sky, and the purity of the atmosphere allowed the heavens to display their full celestial beauty. We were finally on the mountain that Joe and Pete were part of, and I wondered if they were somehow aware of us. It was hard to believe that all their vitality, talent, and joy in life had been blotted out. Surely it had been absorbed into the energy of Chomolungma, an energy I imagined I could feel as I lay on my back, star-gazing. My eyelids grew heavy and my face numbed with cold. I slid into the tent, zipped it shut, and snuggled down into the sleeping bag, happier than I had been for a long time.

The reflection of snow peaks rippled and broke when Hilary dipped a can into the still lake. I watched her light a stove and boil water, but the tea she handed over did little to rouse me from the tired and sluggish state in which I had woken up. She waited impatiently as I floundered about, misplacing things and packing up slowly. It was a clear and warming morning and we wore britches and sweaters, and put scarves on our heads for protection from the strong sunlight. The track to Camp Two was along the glacier. It was easy ground and the crevasses were obvious, but Charlie had warned us to watch out for stonefall from the rock towers and steep scree slopes high above. He and Adrian had nearly come to grief on this first section when high-speed missiles narrowly missed them. I walked along with sharp eyes and ears, and the eerie sensation that the slope above me had a mind and an evil intention of its own. Despite our steady pace across this dangerous section we were overtaken by Johan and then a succession of Dutch climbers who, far fitter and more acclimatized to the altitude than we were, trotted by with chirpy greetings. Beyond the menacing section of the track was a forest of ice pinnacles, remnants of the slowly dying glacier. These teeth-like formations of white and blue ice towered to thirty feet, bright against the grayness of the surrounding rock and sparkling with prisms of light.

The sun was high and strong; we peeled off sweaters, pushed down socks, and rubbed sunblock onto the exposed parts of our limbs. Hiking at 19,000 feet was a strain to the lungs, but we pushed on up the slope, following the small cairns that marked the route. The valley narrowed, below us a stream ran along one side of the glacier, coursing through tunnels and bridges of ice.

"Is it the altitude getting to me, Hilary, or is that a telephone wire?" I couldn't believe what my eyes were seeing: something that snaked along the ground among rocks and gravel.

"I thought I'd told you about those," she said. "Pete wrote about them in his diary. They were put down for one of the big expeditions, Chinese or Japanese. At least we're going the right way!"

But by mid-afternoon we were no longer sure of that. Hilary went ahead to check our position, leaving me to rest. She moved behind a hillock and out of sight.

It was a welcome stop. Several hours of walking in hot sun at such an altitude had left me weary and I had begun to watch my feet, fearful of stumbling and spraining an ankle. I sat down on the loose, gray scree. Boulders lay scattered all around. Nothing was growing, not even lichen. A total wasteland. With Hilary gone and my own body unmoving at last, the air became utterly still. Such absolute silence was unnerving. I glanced anxiously to either side, drew my knees up and hugged them against my chest. I was afraid. It was like my childhood fear of the dark, which I had never really overcome. There were nights when I still lay awake in bed, wanting to go to the bathroom but paralyzed by an abstract terror that only the flicking on of a light could dispel. I reassured myself—there's nothing to be afraid of, stand up, stretch, do something to blot out the anxiety. Some crevasses nearby hovered on the edge of my vision; I moved over to them and peered down at the solid blueness below their lips. They yawned into black space and I felt that strange urge one gets on the top of cliffs, wondering what it would be like to jump. A sudden rustling swung me round in alarm—who's there? No one, of course not, pull yourself together, Maria. It was ice slithering from a slowly melting pinnacle.

Creak! The glacier shifted imperceptibly far below me, but the noise traveled up through hundreds of feet to where I crouched. Blood began to throb loudly in the veins of my ears. The demons of loneliness and isolation crept nearer. Hilary was not far away, logically I knew that, yet it could have been a million miles as far as my oxygen-starved brain was concerned.

"Maria! This way! Round the back of the crevasses!"

I moved cautiously towards the voice. Her scarfed head appeared; she turned her face up and grinned widely.

"Nearly there!"

We had miscalculated after all: We were too high. But three tents were in sight, and a Dutch flag fluttered from one. We bent our stiffening knees and set off down the steep slope.

The camp made a desolate picture. It sat on one side of the narrow valley, and was diminutive amidst a stark and massive landscape. A wind blew down the glacier, flapping the partly unzipped door of the bungalow tent as we approached. I was suddenly overwhelmed with tiredness.

"Hello?" called Hilary.

"There's no one there," I snapped. "Johan said they were all going up the hill this afternoon."

As if responding to his name, he appeared in the doorway and welcomed us in.

"The others have already gone up to Camp Five. I will leave at first light in the morning. I'll get there in time for breakfast."

He had stayed behind to ensure that Hilary and I arrived safely, although he obviously did not wish it to be alluded to. I felt reassured by his presence.

"Relax," he said. "I will make tea and some soup."

Relaxing at 20,000 feet did not prove to be easy. My head was heavy and aching, I felt listless and irritable and could not find a comfortable position in which to sit or lie.

"I feel like an old woman," I grumbled.

Johan laughed. "Yes, you look like one, too!"

He paused from stirring the soup, delved into a bag and passed me a mirror.

"See?"

The face reflecting back at me had deep lines that ran from nose to mouth and were etched between and around the eyes, and the skin underneath the sunburn was a pallid gray. I knew this to be only a temporary change caused by altitude, but it did nothing to improve my feeling of ill health. At 8 p.m., Johan made a radio call to Base Camp. Something was wrong. Although he could hear the incoming calls they were not receiving him.

"Is your group expecting you to call?" he asked.

"Not unless there's a problem," I heard Hilary answer.

My headache was worsening and we realized that we had left the aspirin at Camp One. It was impossible for me to join the conversation. I lay in a stupor and listened to them discussing Joe's and Pete's books, and to Johan describing the avalanche which had injured Eelco Dyke. Restless, uncomfortable, and helped only a little by a sedative, I dropped into a fitful sleep. With the silence of the night came the sounds of the glacier—loud cracks, bangs, and creakings from beneath us would start me awake and I would feel freezing air on the exposed part of my face; I would move my tongue around my mouth to try to relieve the dryness, and wriggle about on the insulation mat to seek a comfortable position. Once it was a pressure on my bladder that drew me out of sleep. I lay for a while trying to will it away. Frosted plumes of breath rose from the mounds of the other two sleeping bags. Hilary was closest to me, she sounded hoarse. It was no good, I had to get up. I wriggled out of the bag, pulled on inner boots and a jacket, unzipped the tent, and squatted right outside it, my teeth chattering. Relief. Another sound began as I settled down again and tried to sleep. *Rustle.* Silence. *Rattle.* Silence. *Crunch, crunch.* Of course. It was the mouse. Johan had talked about it earlier. No one knew where it had come from, but it was presumed to have followed the team up to the camp and moved into the bungalow tent, lured by the feast of dried foods left there. By morning it had munched and nibbled its way through several sesame-seed bars and a packet of dried soup. The idea of the soft little animal busily feeding close by was comforting, it took my mind off the cold and the effects of altitude, and I drifted off into a dream. I was in Derbyshire, dozing in bed at Joe's house. He was pottering about downstairs. I could hear him opening and shutting doors. He had often got up very early, leaving me to sleep while he worked on his slides or his writing, bringing tea and joining me some hours later. He let one door bang shut so loudly that I jolted awake. Where was I? Another door creaked open; where *was* I? I groaned aloud, recognizing the sounds of the glacier below me, and distressed to leave the comfort and familiarity of the dream.

At 5 a.m., in the dark, Johan got up and made tea. We slurped down the hot liquid and mumbled our thanks and goodbyes as he left, then snuggled back into the sleeping bags for three more hours. The sun was creeping up in the sky by the time we roused ourselves, but my contact lenses were still frozen into their solution. I was grateful for the inners of my plastic boots, warm from being inside the sleeping bag with me all night, as I watched Hilary trying to defrost her solid, leather ones. Breakfast was just a cup of hot chocolate, as neither of us could stomach solid food. As I sipped it I thought about the thousand more feet to the site of Camp Three. I wanted badly to get there but my body was not functioning well, every movement was an effort and my head still hurt.

It was an easy walk up the glacier, a gentle gradient across loose stones. But each step was painful. I inched along like an old, old lady and my head pounded dangerously. Hilary was getting smaller and smaller. She came back to where I had sat down, clutching my forehead.

"I don't want a case of cerebral edema on my hands, Maria. You have to decide if you can go on."

The words were firm, but kindly spoken.

"I'll be all right. I will. I'll just take my time."

"OK, I'll wait for you. But if your headache gets worse, you must tell me."

Very slowly, with many rests, I continued up that slope. The whole of the Northeast Ridge came into view and then, over a final knoll, we reached the site of Camp Three.

Circular areas cleared of sharp stones showed where the individual tents had been. The team spent a lot of time here, it had been their Advance Base and they had tried to make it as comfortable as possible. Pete had been proud of his temporary home, and in one letter to Hilary he described his search for flat stones to use as the foundation for his tent. She picked these out immediately and sat down on them, looking up to the Ridge. I didn't know where Joe's tent had been, although perhaps it was where I found the label from a movie-film canister. Scattered about the site were the singed remains of the bon-fire Adrian must have made hurriedly when packing up camp. A tin opener, a few paperbacks, a film box, the whisky crate, odds and ends that proved they had been there not long before, eating, laughing, working, and sleeping before setting off together towards the Ridge. Hilary was crouched immobile in Pete's tent area. I felt disorientated, physically uncomfortable, and I didn't know if I should sit or stand or walk. I leaned against a boulder and surveyed the site and the Ridge above. It seemed so close now. We could go no further along the route, from that point on we would be on snow, we would need equipment, I lacked experience and neither of us was acclimatized to the altitude. I remembered the slide projected onto a wall in Chris's house, the pic-ture he had taken of Joe and Pete setting off for the summit attempt. Their backs were to the camera and they carried big rucksacks. I could see where their path must have been. That was May 15th.

"There is a big job for Pete and me to do," Joe wrote in his last letter, "but hopefully it could go well . . . and if fortune, weather, and spirit favor us we could be up the mountain in a few days from when we start."

Before they left there was a celebration for Joe's birthday at Advance Base. They had a party and champagne. He was thirty-four. I thought ruefully again of my cards sent from England that did not arrive in time.

"You and I will age," Hilary had said to me when we looked at the slide of them laughing and catching the fizzing wine in a jug, "but they won't. They will always stay as young as this."

And the last photograph, the very last one, taken with a powerful telephoto lens. Two tiny dots in the col between the First and Second Pinnacles, mere pinpricks on a vast and forbidding landscape of snow and upward-thrusting rock. 27,000 feet high, with no oxygen, climbing difficult ground for hours, since dawn. The Pinnacles—we had talked about those so much since June. "They were last seen moving behind the Second Pinnacle." Time and time again I had said that without understanding the full import of the words. Over the past days I had looked at those rocky towers standing up from the Ridge, looked and looked, from the truck, from Base Camp, from our trek up here and now, finally, from this place. And still it was impossible really to understand what it had been like for Joe and Pete up there, so totally and ultimately alone, to glean anything of what might have befallen them or to grasp the fact that it could be a long, long time before anyone else gets that far along the route, and that even then they may find no trace.

I slid my back down the boulder and sat on the stony ground. My feet looked big in the plastic boots. Hilary had still not moved, and yet I was so restless. I thought of the others, Charlie, Chris, Dick, Adrian. How it must have been for them when Joe and Pete set out. Dick was on his way back to England by then, with Charlie accompanying him as far as Chengdu. Chris and Adrian went up towards the North Col to leave supplies for Pete and Joe on their way down. They had the last radio contact with them on the evening of May 16th. The following day, back at Advance Base, Chris and Adrian watched their progress along the Ridge, through a telescope. At three o'clock they opened up the radio but Joe and Pete did not come through. They were still visible at 9 p.m., two tiny dots moving very slowly at the foot of the Second Pinnacle. But when the night closed in there was no sign of any light from a tent up there, and Chris presumed they had moved behind the Pinnacle to camp on the eastern side of the Ridge. The morning of May 17th dawned clear. A perfect day for climbing. Good conditions for Joe and Pete. But there was no sign of them. Chris and Adrian went back up towards where they had left supplies. And all day they watched the Ridge. No sign. On May 19th they reached the North Col. The hope they had been clinging to, that Pete and Joe were delayed on the east side of the Ridge and would reappear at any moment, began to fade. Charlie had returned from Chengdu and was at Advance Base. They talked to him by radio, told him what had happened. He wrote in his diary, "I think we must prepare for a disaster. But there is still hope. If the situation is the same tomorrow I shall have almost given up."

It was the same the next day, and the next. Weeks later, Adrian wrote to me, "My thoughts have been with you since that awful moment on the mountain, when we finally realized that our hopes and prayers were in vain."

I remembered Chris's tears in my house, when he first came to see me after the accident. He cried because he had not followed them up the Ridge. Because he had not gone to help, to rescue or at least to discover what had happened. But he was already stretched beyond his resources by the mountain, and Charlie and Adrian were not experienced enough to go with him. He could not have followed Joe and Pete alone, even if he had been stronger. Poor Chris. He had never really forgiven himself, and yet it would have been suicide. Sometimes he gave me the impression that he felt guilty to be alive. But I was glad he had survived. For Wendy and their boys. And for me and Hilary. We needed him, just as we needed Charlie and Adrian and Dick, for they were our links to the final part of Joe and Pete's lives.

Adrian had stayed in wait at Advance Base while Chris and Charlie hurried round to the east side of the mountain, to scan the Ridge and the Kangshung Face through binoculars and telescopes. They must have known Joe and Pete were dead; I think they did it for all of us left at home. Closing my eyes I could see the photograph of the Face they took, blown up to show detail and projected against the wall in Chris's cottage. Even though the clouds did not lift for us on the other side of the mountain, I still knew of its scale and of its great slabs of fluted snow. If the snow had given way beneath Pete and Joe, as Chris thought it had done, they would have fallen a great distance, down to the steep glacier below. He and Charlie scanned the Ridge and the Kangshung Face for a day. No sign. While they were gone Adrian packed up the camps. A ghastly task, I thought, to collect up Joe and Pete's belongings and to know that bringing home the news of the tragedy was their responsibility alone. Not far from where I sat lay the singed remains of a book I had given Joe, the story of a train journey through Patagonia. I fingered its blackened pages. It was comforting to think of him reading it in his tent. I imagined Adrian making a bonfire to burn debris and surplus gear that could not be carried down the mountain, watching the flames and looking beyond them to the Pinnacles . . .

Back in Britain we had endured three weeks of silence from Everest. As day after day passed, I screwed down my fears and worked feverishly on the finishing touches to the house. And then opaque messages began to arrive on Jardine Matheson's telex machine.

"Expedition about to leave Base Camp."

"Arriving in Hong Kong, June 9th."

I talked to Ruth, Charlie's wife, in London.

"Maria, they are all dead," she said.

Ruth was always dramatic, she was overreacting, it was impossible that anything had gone wrong. Wendy Bonington expressed disquiet. I listened to her quiet voice on the telephone and told myself not to worry. And Dick, back in Cardiff with Jan and their little boy, was hesitant in reply to my questions, but then he usually sounded like that.

Sarah and I had then gone to London to see a production of *The Oresteia* at the National Theater. For over four hours masked actors had conveyed to us the timeless realities of death and grief.

> "Suffering comes first then after awareness
> The future's the future you'll know when its here
> Foreseeing the future's to weep in advance . . ."

Coincidence or not, it was a portent. Within a week I had received news of Joe's disappearance, and a few months later, Sarah heard that Alex had died on his descent from Annapurna.

Now, high on Chomolungma, gazing at the Ridge, my head began to swim with the memories of the day in June when Dick had appeared on my doorstep. My fears for Joe had been so tightly coiled up by then that I had asked Dick what he was doing in Manchester, almost 200 miles from his home. His first words, "I've got some tragic news," ran through my mind again and again, as if he were sitting next to me on the rock, speaking into my ear. The suddenly-frozen faces were all around me again as I backed away, into the yard, to be alone.

Hilary stood up and began to walk slowly around the site. We hadn't spoken since arriving. She seemed very calm and concentrated. But I was besieged by memories and thoughts, my head hurt, I wanted to cry yet did not have the energy. I felt as if all emotion had been sucked out of me. It's time to leave, my body was saying, it's time to go lower. I called to her that I was moving. She turned and nodded. At the hillock I attached a piece of Joe's scarf to a pen I had found at the site, and stuck it into a little marker cairn. My tiny prayer flag fluttered towards the summit of Chomolungma. I took a long, hard look at the Ridge and the Pinnacles, before turning away.

A tingling sensation spread from the left side of my face and down my arm as I moved weakly along the glacier. This warning sign of altitudinal damage to the body registered only faintly in my brain amid the overwhelming desires to stop, lie down, and drink. The tents appeared and grew larger as I stumbled along. I unzipped the door of the bungalow, reached for the water bottle and fell onto my sleeping bag. The thudding in my head and my heart gradually quieted. I must have dozed off because Hilary was suddenly sitting next to me, cross-legged.

"Here," she said, handing the an unopened packet of Panadol. "This was left up there for you."

I stared from her to the packet, astonished.

"See?" she laughed. "They knew we were coming!"

We were expected back at Base Camp that day, but it was too late and we were too tired for more exertion. Repeated efforts to call Dong and Zhiang failed; we could hear voices over the transmitter but they were obviously not receiving us. It was Hilary's turn to be flattened by altitude and I, from some inexplicable source, found a short burst of energy, which I used to collect water from the stream and make soup. By seven o'clock we were deep in our sleeping bags; I was more relaxed than the previous night and the drug had eased my headache. We chatted and began to drift into sleep. Suddenly, from above us on the glacier, came footsteps. A tension stretched between us as we strained our ears to listen to the feet crunching across freezing stones. There were two people moving towards the tent. My mind snapped into a fantasy I could hardly bear to recognize, and I held my breath as the tent door was unzipped. A dazzling flashlight beamed around.

"You are the English girls? Has our mail arrived?"

An accented voice.

The fantasy, mercifully short-lived, crumbled around me as two Dutch climbers, arriving from Camp Five, came into the tent. They got tea going and made another, unsuccessful attempt at a radio call.

"They are asking what has happened to you," one translated for us. "They want to know if you are here."

Curled in a ball inside my sleeping bag, my face almost covered by the down hood, I slipped again into fantasy about Joe and Pete emerging from the darkness. Since their disappearance I had imagined them returning, after some miraculous survival. I would open my door in England and find Joe there, or they would be alive in Hong Kong, in Lhasa, at Kharta, or Base Camp. As time progressed, the dream would adapt to the circumstances I was in. Allowing myself to indulge in these fantasies gave comfort and a respite from the ache of grief. And each time I returned to the reality of my situation, each time I pulled myself out of the daydream and faced the fact that I would not find Joe at an airport, in a hospital, or hotel room, or remote village, I gained a fraction more of acceptance and was a little further down the road towards emotional healing.

My sleep was calmer that night, but was still disturbed by the sounds of the glacier and the rustling of the mouse, and by a dry racking cough which was echoed by the others in the tent. All that Joe had told me about the harshness of life at altitude became a reality over those two nights: the unrelenting environment, the effort of the simplest of tasks, the awareness of physical deterioration. And for him this had been a resting place, a relief from the higher camps.

It was a long, long trek back to Base Camp the following morning, trying to hurry, aware of the concern that would be growing for us. We lingered by the ice pinnacles to rest before moving as quickly as possible across the unstable moraines. Hilary made me run across a steep gully— I scrambled up the far side, lungs heaving, and through the sound of my panting heard the tumbling, crackling, and bouncing of a rock fall behind me. Before long she turned to me.

"I can see Camp One. There's someone there, we can stop for a brew." It was Denny and Jacques, waiting with coffee and biscuits. There had been anxiety the night before when we failed to turn up, they told us, and we should get back to Base Camp as soon as possible. The awareness that shelter, food, and rest were close by seemed to allow my mind to accept the exhaustion of my body and I staggered along the track, high above the jumble of crevasses, stopping repeatedly to drink orange juice and trying to stomach a sesame-seed bar. I thought about Joe descending from Dunagiri, going for days without food or water. He had persevered in far more weakened states than this. I wondered what he would think, if he could see me, straggling along behind Hilary beneath the peaks of Pumo Ri and Nuptse. Zhiang was waiting at the strenuous, boulder-strewn section.

"Hello! Hello!" he said, and he took both our rucksacks.

Back on the dusty plain, walking slowly towards the tents, a despondent feeling grew in my chest and made my throat ache. This should have been Joe and Pete returning from the summit instead of Hilary and me from the remains of their Advance Base Camp. Dong and Mr. Wang came to greet us. There were no admonishments for the concern we had caused them but, instead, congratulations that we had coped with the altitude and reached our goal.

The shade of the big food tent was a great relief. Hilary answered questions while I drank green tea and tried out a few of Lin's *momos* on my shrunken stomach. In a corner two large bowls were piled high with lumps of marinating meat and Lin was busy skewering them for a barbecue. Zhiang caught my eye.

"Baaaa! Baaaa!" He was gleeful.

In our absence he had returned to the village and had finally been successful in his quest for a sheep.

"Well, I'm glad I didn't have to get to know it," I said.

We were dusty, sweaty, and in need of a wash, but we couldn't face the icy river. Taking some water from a cauldron that was always on the boil in the food tent, we retired to a large empty wigwam to strip off and bathe. A wind suddenly blew up, threatening to lift the loosely-secured tent.

"I bet Peter and Joe are doing that," said Hilary

While she went back to our tent to read Pete's diary, I walked up to the memorial cairn. Someone, probably Zhiang, had left two cans of lychees there. The gesture moved me, more deeply than I could explain. I returned to the tent and wrote a long letter to leave behind in the cairn, disconnected thoughts of love and grief and hope to Joe, or in his memory, I didn't really know which. The act of expression settled me, and when Zhiang called us for dinner I was ready to face everyone. The meal was delicious: tasty, tender lamb kebabs and potatoes boiled in their skins. My appetite was restored, I was suddenly ravenous and the Chinese cook laughed heartily.

"He says—one shish kebab eating many shish kebabs!" translated Dong, setting off much good-natured bantering about my skinny frame. A group of Dutch climbers sat to one side of the tent, sharing the meal but involved in their own discussion. Near them, out of the light, was a group of high-altitude porters, wild-looking men, dark and striking, whose eyes flashed across the tent at us. As the sun was setting we stood outside in our down jackets drinking coffee with Dong and Zhiang and watching the changing colors of Chomolungma. Our guides were relaxed and began to talk a little about their personal lives. Dong's wife was studying in Australia for a year and Zhiang was married with a small baby. Chinese etiquette demands great social reserve, and these disclosures displayed a sense of trust by which we were very flattered.

We had one more day and night at Base Camp. Our Swiss companions left early in the morning for a trek, and we arranged to pick them up on our way out of the valley. It was good to relax around the tent and to soak in the atmosphere of the place. The wind had dropped, and we sat outside in warm sunshine listening to the river, which had swollen in our three-day absence. The truck that had taken the Swiss men down the valley reappeared, raising clouds of dust all around it, and rolled into camp. Zhiang jumped down from the cab, strode purposefully over to where we sat, handed us each a posy of tiny yellow flowers tied with a red shoelace, and left, smiling shyly at our thanks. We taped the posies on either side of the memorial stone, and between the cans of lychees placed a foil-wrapped cake that Lin had baked and asked us to leave there. I slipped a piece of the silk scarf underneath one of the cans so that a corner fluttered out in the wind. Hilary began to dig up plants with her hands and a stone.

"Help me to make a garden."

After an hour's work we sat back to look at the result. Ringed by rocks were two types of mosses, a miniature edelweiss, a strong-smelling green herb and a delicate plant with tiny purple flowers. These were age-old and instinctive rituals, beautifying a grave and leaving offerings to the spirits of the dead. I sometimes wonder what has happened to the cairn, its garden, and the things we left. Friends have gone on expedition to Chomolungma since then and used that Base Camp, but I have never asked them about it. The cairn and the stone will eventually fall and be weathered down, the articles will rot or rust or blow away, the plants have surely died, but above them all the mountain stands as steadfast as ever, and it is the true grave.

In one of the emotional swings that I had come to accept as a natural part of grieving, over lunch we laughed and sang and played music with our Chinese hosts. Dong and Zhiang had been curious about the tapes we listened to on our Walkmans, so we brought them to the food tent and watched their bemused expressions as rock music blared from the portable stereo. Mr. Wang put on some Chinese popular music. "Sing along! Sing along!" he urged us, and our efforts reduced them all to helpless laughter.

At the start of their expedition, Joe and Pete's team had picnicked at the site of Mallory and Irvine's 1921 Base Camp. We tried to cross the river by foot to reach the picnic spot, but the water level had risen too much. I trekked up the cairn from the far side of the hillock, suddenly hit by the realization that in the morning we would be gone.

"How will you ever leave the mountain?" several people in Britain had asked, and I had replied that when the time came it would be a simple, inevitable, and timely step. Sitting by the cairn, I realized that I would indeed have to turn calmly away the next morning. Joe was gone, he was no longer moving about the earth, he was frozen somewhere on that beautiful mountain looming above me, never to be called back. I had come to be close, to make my peace with Everest and with him, and now I had to leave accepting all. My questions about our relationship remained unresolved, but I had reached one simple conclusion. We had not had the time together that we needed to work things out, and regretting that was of no use. The important thing now was to continue to face the fact of Joe's death. It was not possible to "get over" it, instead I had to accept all that had happened without anger or bitterness or remorse, and reconstruct my life around this acceptance.

Hilary was reading Pete's diary in the tent when I crawled in. She looked up and smiled.

"Shall we build a house here?" she said, and we laughed to think of the horror it would cause if we were to sell our properties in England and set up home in the Rongbuk Valley. She had become so dear to me. Her strength, wisdom, and complete generosity were only part of what made her a special person. It was easy to see why Pete had loved her so. She began to read to me from his diary, the symbol of the closeness and resolution of their union, and as I listened it struck me that for the first time I was not experiencing pangs of envy and sadness over this. Those were early days; I did not know as I sat in the tent, arms around my knees and watching my friend read, just how long it would be before I felt happy and whole and able to see the past as a part of life's pattern, but I could tell I was on my way.

"Come in! Tea? Tea?"

Mr. Wang ushered us into his "house" tent. It was warm and friendly in there; foam mattresses on the floor were covered with heavy, fur-lined coats, a tape machine played Chinese music, and a card game was in progress. We had come with thanks for his kindness and generosity but he waved these aside and pressed us to sit down and talk for a while. He told us stories of other expeditions he had worked on. In 1975 four hundred people were camped at Rongbuk during the Chinese attempt on the mountain, there were seventy "house" tents, a makeshift volleyball court was set up, and a Tibetan dance troupe performed. As we left he gave us each a dried lotus flower head.

"Come back to Tibet, you come back soon?"

We smiled but did not say that no, we would probably never return.

We lingered outside for a while in the cold air. Electricity from the generator illuminated the large food tent, and laughter and people spilled in and out of its flapped door. Smaller tents glowed with torch or candlelight as climbers settled down for the night. Beyond these spots of brightness the night was dark, still, and silent. The sky was full of stars and one fell and burned out.

"Make a wish, Hilary."

"I've made it. It won't come true, though."

Within hours we would leave, but all this would still go on. Expeditions would arrive and set up, some lives would be lost and others, like ours, would be enriched by being on the mountain. I was glad we had made the journey. I slept deeply and peacefully and imagined Joe there with me—we were curled up like two spoons throughout the night.

During breakfast in the food tent, heads popped around the door in farewell. We packed up and threw our rucksacks onto the truck. Then quickly to the cairn for a final goodbye to the pile of rock that had become somehow significant and symbolic to us. I reached in for the plastic envelope, slipped my letter inside and pushed it back deep among the frosty stones. One fell and hit my finger, and the blood-blister it caused was a reminder of that morning for days to come. I looked at the little garden, the cans of lychees, the silk peeping out, the names carved onto granite, and the mountain beyond. Words from the poem among the stones ran through my head, "In my dreams I see the light of your face."

Swallowing hard and blinking back tears, I walked steadily down and climbed onto the truck.

A little group formed to wave us off. Mr. Wang and Lin reached up to grasp our hands and I was glad we had said our goodbyes the previous night, because neither of us could manage any words at the moment of departure. The truck pulled away, then stopped abruptly as Wilhelm, a handsome Dutch climber, ran out of his tent calling to us and stuffing a letter into a hastily-addressed envelope. "Please, could you post this for me in Hong Kong or London?" Probably to his girlfriend, I thought sadly. And we were off, bumping and jerking out of Base Camp, the two of us alone in the back. Dong and Zhiang, sensitively, had climbed into the cab with Tele, allowing us private space to watch the mountain recede. I stared hard at Chomolungma. I was leaving calmly, as I had wished. The image of the mountain at the head of the valley filled my eyes and my heart, and I knew I would carry it with me for a long time to come.

Absent Friends
by Chris Bonington

Chris Bonington (born 1934) led a series of ground-breaking Himalayan expeditions during the 1970s and '80s. Several of his expeditions ended with the death of one or more climbers. Three of those climbers died on Everest: Mick Burke in 1975, and Peter Boardman and Joe Tasker in 1982. Bonington was 51 years old when he returned to the mountain in 1985 for his own attempt on the summit.

The South Col was far more extensive than I had imagined, a flattish expanse the size of a football pitch and littered with the debris of previous expeditions: discarded oxygen bottles, skeletons of tents, clusters of old food boxes—unsightly memorials to the ambitions of our predecessors. On the far side rose the final slopes of Everest, and although they are called the South-east Ridge they were less of a ridge than a face of snow and broken rocks that looked steep and inhospitable.

I was pleased to be sharing a tent with Pertemba, who had already climbed Everest twice before. I could feel his friendship and at the same time was spoilt, for he insisted on doing the cooking. It was essential to drink as much as possible through the afternoon, to guard against the dangers of dehydration, and we also ate tsampa, the traditional Sherpa dish of roast barley flour, boiled into a thick porridge and spiced with chilli sauce. It was a great improvement on the dried high-altitude rations we had been consuming.

I didn't sleep very much—I doubt whether any of us did—although I was excited rather than apprehensive. There was none of the stabbing fear that had preceded climbs like the North Wall of the Eiger or the Central Tower of Paine in Patagonia so many years before. I drifted into sleep, to wake to the purr of the gas stove. Pertemba had started to heat the water he had melted the previous evening and stored in a thermos.

Two hours later we were ready to start; boots, kept warm in our sleeping-bags, forced on to our feet; outer windproofs and down jackets turning us into Michelin men as we wriggled out into the bitter cold of the night. It was minus 30°C and the wind gusted around the tents. A struggle with oxygen equipment, last-minute fitting of the Sherpas' face masks, and we were ready.

There were six of us: the two Norwegians, Odd Eliassen and Bjorn Myrer-Lund; the three Sherpas, Pertemba, Ang Lhakpa and Dawa Nuru; and myself. The South Col is at just under 8,000 metres, so we had some 850 metres left to climb. It was 1.30 a.m. when we set out across the flatness of the col, crampons slipping and catching on the stones underfoot, then on to a bulge of hard smooth ice that slowly increased in angle as we approached the ridge. Each of us followed the pool of light cast by our headtorch. Pertemba was out in front—he had been here before. I was bringing up the rear and it wasn't long before the gap between me and the person in front increased. We were now on a snow-slope, a tongue reaching up into the broken rocks that guarded the base of the ridge. At the top of the snow was rock, crumbling steps, easy scrambling but unnerving in the dark with all the impedimenta of high-altitude gear.

I was tired already; not out of breath but listless, finding it progressively harder to force one foot in front of the other. Three hundred metres, an hour and a half went by. God, I was tired. I had dropped behind, the lights of the others becoming ever distant glimmers, weakening all the time. They stopped for a rest but, as I caught up, started once again. I slumped in the snow and muttered, almost cried, 'I'll never make it'.

Odd heard me. 'You'll do it, Chris. Just get on your feet. I'll stay behind you.'

And on it went—broken rock, hard snow, then deep soft snow which Pertemba ploughed through, allowing me to keep up as I followed the well-formed steps made so laboriously by the people in front. The stars were beginning to vanish in the grey of the dawn and the mountains, most of them below us now, assumed dark silhouettes. The crest of the ridge, still above us, lightened and then the soaring peak of the South Summit was touched with gold from the east as the sun crept over the horizon.

By the time we reached the crest, the site of Hillary and Tenzing's top camp in 1953, all the peaks around us were lit by the sun's low-flung rays. The Kangshung Glacier, still in shadow, stretched far beneath us. The Kangshung Face itself was a great sweep of snow, set at what seemed an easy angle. Just below us some fixed rope protruded, a relic of the American expedition that climbed the face in the autumn of 1983. Across the face was the serrated crest of the North-east Ridge. I could pick out the shoulder where we had excavated our third snow cave in 1982 and, above it, the snow-plastered teeth of the Pinnacles where we had last seen Pete Boardman and Joe Tasker.

It was 5 in the morning. We were at 8,300 metres and it was time to change our cylinders. We set out again, plodding up the crest of the ridge, our shadows cast far into Nepal. Ever steepening, sometimes rock, mostly snow, it was much harder than I had imagined. It seemed to go on for ever. Glancing behind me, the black rocky summit of Lhotse, fourth highest mountain in the world, still appeared higher than us. A last swell of snow, with the wind gusting hard and threatening to blow us from our perch, and we were on the South Summit. We gathered on the corniced col just beneath it, the very place where Doug Scott and Dougal Haston had bivouacked on their way back in 1975.

There was a pause. Pertemba had broken trail all the way so far but the ridge between the South Summit and the final steepening of the

Hillary Step looked formidable, a knife-edge of snow clinging to the rocky crest, with an intimidating drop on either side. Odd was worried about our oxygen supply. It had been three hours since we had changed bottles and he questioned whether we had enough to get back. The others had been climbing with a flow rate of three litres per minute, but I had found that this had not been enough. I had been turning mine on to four and so would have even less. But at this stage I was prepared to risk anything to get to the top.

Pertemba said decisively: 'We go on'.

Bjorn took the initiative and pushed to the front. Ang Lhakpa got out the rope, 20 metres between the six of us, and Bjorn tied one end round his waist so that it trailed behind him, more of a token than anything else, as we followed. The going to the foot of the Hillary Step was more spectacular than difficult, but the step itself was dauntingly steep.

Odd took a belay and Bjorn started up, wallowing in the unconsolidated snow, getting an occasional foothold on the rock wall to the left. Pertemba followed, digging out an old fixed rope abandoned by a previous expedition. The step was about 20 metres high and Bjorn anchored the rope around a rock bollard near its top. The others followed, using the rope as a handrail.

I was last, but Dawa Nuru waved me past. I gathered he had run out of oxygen—he and Ang Lhakpa had been climbing on just one bottle while carrying our spare bottles to the crest of the ridge. As I struggled up the step, panting, breathless, apprehensive, I felt what was almost the physical presence of Doug Scott beside me. It was as if I could see his long straggly hair and wire-rimmed glasses and could sense his reassurance and encouragement, pushing me on. Then Les, my father-in-law, appeared too. A man of quiet wisdom and great passion, he had thrown the I Ching just before I left home and predicted my success. This was something that had given me renewed confidence whenever I doubted my ability to make it.

Doug and Les got me to the top of the Hillary Step and disappeared. I seemed to have the mountain to myself, for the others had vanished round the corner ahead. I felt as if I had to squeeze out my last bit of will power to join them. Push one foot in front of the other, pant hard to capture what little air and oxygen was flowing into my mask, and then take another careful step along the corniced ridge that led to the summit.

A break in the cornice and there, framed below me to the right, was the North-east Ridge, with its crazy ice towers and snow flutings, seeming to go on and on. I thought again of Pete and Joe—perhaps their bodies were still down there. Another step, and the ridge was hidden by a curl of snow. Now I was at the spot where Pete Boardman had last seen Mick Burke in 1975. Pete and Pertemba had been on their way back down; Mick—that cocky, aggressive, very funny figure I remembered so well— was going for the summit on his own. He never came back. Thoughts of other lost friends from Everest came flooding in: Nick Estcourt who forced the route through the Rock Band in 1975 and died on K2; and Dougal Haston, who died skiing in Switzerland the year after going to the summit with Doug Scott.

Suddenly I was nearly there. Odd, Bjorn and Pertemba were beckoning to me, shouting, their voices muffled by their masks. I crouched in a foetal position and cried and cried in great gasping sobs—tears of exhaustion, tears of sorrow for so many friends, and yet tears of fulfilment for something I had so much needed to do and had done with people who had come to mean a great deal to me. Everything was dropping away from me on all sides—I had at last reached the summit of Everest. I hugged Pertemba, who crouched beside me. Odd and Bjorn, who were raising and photographing the Norwegian flag, came over and embraced me.

It was time to look around. The summit is the size of a pool table, but we could move about on it without fear of being pushed over the edge. To the west lay the Tibetan plateau, a rolling ocean of brown hills with the occasional white cap. In the east rose Kangchenjunga, a huge snowy mass, and in the west the great chain of the Himalaya, with Shisha Pangma, China's 8,000 metre peak, dominating the horizon. Immediately below us, across the Western Cwm, was Nuptse, looking stunted now. To the south was a white carpet of cloud covering the foothills and plains of India. We were indeed on top of the world.

Another figure appeared, moving slowly and painfully. It was Dawa Nuru, coming to the summit without oxygen. I still felt numbed, took pictures automatically, without really being aware of what I was taking. There was no sign of the Chinese maypole Doug and Dougal had found in 1975. There were, however, some paper prayer flags embedded in the snow which must have been left there the previous autumn.

Pertemba had brought with him the T-shirt that Pete Boardman had worn to the summit in 1975. It was a hand-painted one that Pete's local club, the Mynedd, had presented to him. Hilary, Pete's widow, had given it to Pertemba when he had visited her in Switzerland, and now he had brought it to the top of Everest once more in honour of his friend.

We lingered for another 20 minutes before starting the descent. I was first away, pausing to collect a few pebbles of shattered rock. The limestone had been formed many millions of years ago at the bottom of the ocean from living organisms and had been thrust up here, to the highest point of earth, by the drift together of the two tectonic plates of India and Asia. The thrust continues. The Himalaya, the youngest of the earth's great mountain ranges, is still being pushed up. Each year Everest is a few centimetres higher.

from Everest: Alone at the Summit
by Stephen Venables

English climber Stephen Venables (born 1954) and three Americans in 1988 set out to climb Everest's formidable Kangshung Face. They climbed the Face—a tremendous achievement—but only Venables made it all the way to the summit. Here he describes the team's epic descent from the mountain.

I had work to do. First I had to photograph myself. I took off the camera belt, removed the big camera, cocked the self-timer, and, gasping with the effort, knelt down to prop it on its case about three metres from the summit. I was too tired to lie right down and frame the picture in the viewfinder, so I just put the zoom on wide-angle and pointed it in the general direction of the summit. Then, as the self-timer whirred, I stepped back up and sat by the ornamental oxygen bottles. I thought that I heard the shutter click. I knew that I should take more frames, bracketing the exposures for safety, but I did not have the mental or physical energy to reset the camera.

Robert had the summit flags and trinkets from Norbu, but there was one small ritual for me to carry out. I reached into one of my inside pockets and pulled out a tiny polythene bag. Inside were the two miniature envelopes given to me in Bombay by Nawang and Sonam. I carefully took out the flower petals and scattered them in the snow, then placed the two envelopes beside the oxygen bottles. Then, panting with the effort of concentration, I took two pictures on the compact camera.

The film in the SLR with the self-portrait was either not wound on properly or was lost on the journey home, for I was never to see the photo of myself on the summit. However, I do have a picture showing the little envelopes. Each envelope is decorated with the face of one of the teachers at Geeta's ashram in Pondicherri, staring up from amongst the radio boxes, yellow cylinders and wisps of prayer flag on the summit of Everest.

I rested again, slumped in the snow. The air temperature in this second week of May had been getting steadily warmer and even at 8848 metres there was still very little wind. I felt comfortable and I was almost tempted to linger, for I was aware that this was a terribly important event in my life and I wanted to savour that precious moment, storing away what memories I could in my feeble oxygen-starved brain. It would be nice to say that it was the happiest moment of my life and that I was overwhelmed by euphoria; but that would be a gross exaggeration, for at the time there was only a rather dazed feeling of—'Isn't this strange? You really have done it, after all those weeks of watching and waiting and worrying. It would have been better if everyone had made it but at least someone has actually reached the summit—and a rather special summit . . . So this is what it's like.'

It was a turning point. Even in my befuddled state I knew that this would inevitably alter my life. But I also knew that it was far more urgently critical as a turning point in the climb, the point where I no longer had to struggle upwards but had to start down immediately, fleeing from this bewitching dreamlike place and hurrying back down to Earth before it was too late. It was now 3.50 p.m., Nepalese time. I was just ahead of schedule, but the clouds were closing in fast and in three hours it would be dark. I stood up, took the ice axe in my mittened hand, had one last look down Mallory's ridge, then hurried away back south.

After descending a short way I stopped for my final summit task. Just below the top there was an exposed outcrop of shattered rock, where I knelt down to collect some pieces of limestone and stuff them in a pocket.

The wind was mounting now, starting to blow spindrift in my face. I hurried on, using gravity to speed myself back towards the Hillary Step. As I came over the last hump the clouds enveloped me completely. Suddenly I realised that I was heading too far to the right, down towards the South-West Face. I headed back up to the left, peering through my iced-up sunglasses at the swirling greyness. I was utterly alone in the cloud and there was no sign of the South Summit. I felt disorientated and frightened, remembering the tragedy of 1975 when Mick Burke, the last person to complete the South-West Face, went alone to the summit and never came back. Somewhere up here, in conditions like this, blinded behind iced glasses, even more myopic than me, he had made an unlucky mistake, probably falling through one of those fragile cornices overhanging the Kangshung Face. I suddenly noticed the dim outline of one of those bulbous overhangs just in front of me and veered back right. For God's sake don't do a Mick Burke. Just concentrate. You've gone too far left now. Head for that rock—must be solid ground there. Now I could pick out some tracks— my tracks almost filled with spindrift already, but tracks nonetheless. This is right. But it's so difficult. Must have a rest. I sank down and sat in the snow. Then I continued wearily, too slowly, legs sagging, head bowed. I stopped after only a few paces but forced myself not to sit down, leaning instead on my ice axe. Then I took a few steps again, willing my legs not to sag and crumple.

It was snowing now, stinging my face and encrusting my glasses. I had to wipe them with a clumsy mitten, clearing a hole to peer through, searching for landmarks. I recognised clumps of rock and followed them to the pinnacle above the Hillary Step. Then came the hard part, taking off mittens, pulling up some slack in the fixed rope and clipping it into my waist belt karabiner with an Italian hitch. I pulled mittens back on and started to abseil down the cliff. Even though I was moving downhill it was exhausting. Possibly the waist belt was pulling up and constricting my diaphragm, for I had to slump and rest during the twenty-metre abseil, gasping for breath. I continued in a frantic blind struggle to the bottom of the Step where I fell over and collapsed on the side of the ridge, hyperventilating furiously.

It had never happened before and I was terrified. This was quite new —this ultra-rapid panting, like a fish out of water incapable of getting oxygen into its gills. I panted harder and harder, clutching at the air, frantic to refill my lungs. But nothing seemed to get beyond my throat and for a ghastly moment I thought that I was going to suffocate. Then the air started to get through, and I gasped great sobs of relief as my breathing slowed to normal again.

I had to move. Get off that rope and continue. Take mittens off and unclip from the rope. Now, quickly get those mittens back on again. The first one is always easy but the second one won't go. I can't grip it—can't make those useless numb fingers work. It's all too difficult. I'll never get it on and my fingers will freeze solid. No more piano playing. But I must get that mitten on or I'll never get down. Concentrate. That's it, ease it up the wrist.

I slumped over again, gasping with exhaustion. The wind was flinging snow at me and I was starting to shiver. I was completely blind and tore at my sunglasses, letting them hang down round my neck by their safety leash. At least I could see a little now, only blurred shapes, but better than nothing. There's a bit of a clearing. That's the South Summit up there on the far side of the bridge. No sign of Robert or Ed. They must have gone down by now. Crazy to continue to the top in these conditions and no reason to wait for me. There's no-one to help me. Either I get myself down or I die. It would be so easy to die—just lie down here and rest and soon the wind would kill me. It would be the easiest thing in the world but I'd look so bloody silly. No use to anyone climbing Everest then lying down to die. No, pull yourself together and move. It's not possible to get out the other pair of glasses without taking off mittens again, so we'll just have to move very carefully on half vision.

My invisible companion, the old man, had reappeared and together we moved forward, determined not to die. We stumbled half-blind along the ridge, crouched over the ice axe, peering anxiously through the driving snow, almost on all fours, laboriously dragging ourselves across the rocks, clinging carefully to avoid the death slide down the South-West Face. Fear and instinct kept me moving over the rocks. Then I recognised the dry hollow by the overhanging rock where Boardman and Pertemba had waited in vain for Mick Burke to return. I wondered briefly whether I should bivouac there, but decided to continue, determined to get right back across the bridge to the South Summit. That was the critical point beyond which I was confident that I could survive.

The visibility was still atrocious and I strayed too close to the crest on the left. Suddenly my left leg shot down into a hole and I collapsed in another fit of hyperventilation. I may have trodden on the cornice fracture line, but I think it was just a deep snowdrift. Whatever it was, the jolt almost suffocated me; but I regained my breath and forced myself on up the fifteen-metre climb to the South Summit. I collapsed again and this time, as I regained my breath in great anguished gasps, I was filled with pity for the poor old man who was finding it all a bit too much.

We floundered eventually up to the crest of the South Summit where my mind must have gone almost blank, for I can only recall blurred images of snow and cloud and the gloom of dusk. I can remember nothing of the descent of the knife-edge ridge, I only have the vaguest recollection of slithering back over the bergschrund and then I was back on the big snowslope, sitting down to slide, because it is easier to sit than to stand.

We were racing the darkness, using gravity to hurry down towards the safety of the South Col. But even sliding is hard work, because you have to brace your legs and brake with your ice axe. It was somewhere down here that Peter Habeler, during his phenomenal one-hour descent from the summit to the South Col, spurred on by his fear of permanent brain damage, almost flew out of control down the Kangshung Face. I was anxious about the big slope below me and kept stopping to walk further right towards the ridge. Then on one slide the old man became very frightened. We were gathering speed in a blinding flurry of powder snow. The surface underneath felt hollow and unstable and seemed to be breaking off in avalanches. We were sliding faster and faster down to the east and the old man was hating it. He had suddenly become a musician. Musicians hate this. The composer is sliding on his cello, riding the avalanche to his death. Please stop! Now!

I dug my heels in and leant over hard on my ice axe, dragging the ferrule deep into the snow, and came to a halt. We were about to collapse and had to rest as soon as possible, but we could not sit down here. Too steep and insecure. Quick, cut a ledge. Ice axe and burrowing hand—that's it. Quick. Just enough of a hollow to sit down. Must rest. Must have a pee. The old man says do it in your pants —it'll keep you warm.

I could wait no longer and with one last frantic effort I plunged the ice axe deep into the snow and used it to heave myself up onto the ledge. Then my strength gave out and I collapsed, wetting myself and suffocating in another fit of hyperventilation.

Poor old man . . . that's better now, he's breathing again. He just needs to rest. What was all that business about music—cello music? What has that got to do with avalanches? Who is this composer? Dvorak wrote a cello concerto. Kate plays the cello—but she's a woman. It's all too confusing. Better to concentrate on reality—on me sitting here on this precarious ledge in the snow. And why did I believe that nonsense about peeing in my pants? All wet now. It must have been the shock.

I was getting chronically exhausted and it was now virtually dark, so I decided to stay where I was. I sat there for about an hour, shivering as the cold pressed through from the snow. Then I decided that my precarious perch was too dangerous and that I should try to continue down to the South Col where Ed and Robert would be waiting in the tents. I lowered myself to my feet, faced into the slope and started kicking steps carefully across the snow, back towards the crest of the ridge. There I tried to orientate myself, climbing backwards and forwards over the rocks, trying to recognise individual outcrops from the morning. But it was dark, there was no moon and, although the afternoon storm had blown over, there were still drifting clouds to confuse my vision. Even after putting on glasses and switching on my headtorch, I found it very difficult to judge shapes and distances. I started to worry that perhaps my glissade had taken me lower than I thought and that I was now below the point where I had to turn right into the couloir.*

After about half an hour of wandering about, the old man suggested that we should stop here for the night and wait for daylight to re-orientate ourselves. I decided that he would be warmest sitting on a rock and soon I found a ledge on the ridge where we could sit down. But it was precarious and sloping and we both longed to lean back properly, so we traversed back out onto the snow and dug a horizontal ledge where we could lie down properly. At about 9 p.m. we settled down for the night.

The emergency bivouac had many precedents. During the American traverse of Everest in 1963 Willi Unsoeld and Tom Hornbein completed the first ascent of the West Ridge, reaching the summit just before dark at 6.15. Two companions had reached the summit by the normal route the same afternoon and were waiting near the South Summit when Unsoeld and Hornbein started to descend the South-East Ridge. When they met, Hornbein tried to persuade the other three to continue down to the top camp but they soon became lost in the dark and had to resign themselves to a night out in the open at about 8500 metres. They survived the intense cold and descended safely the next day, but afterwards Unsoeld had to have nine frostbitten toes

---

* On the way up, at dawn, about 16 hours earlier, the team had found an abandoned tent at about 27,300 feet—the top camp of the Asian Friendship Expedition—next to a prominent feature sometimes called the Black Tower. Not realizing that from here most parties traverse rightward to reach the Southeast Ridge at a point known as The Balcony, Venables had continued straight up a steeper, more direct gully, to break out onto the ridge well above The Balcony. Now, in the dark, it was finding the top of this gully which was causing him so much anxiety.

amputated and one of the South-East Ridge duo, Barry Bishop, lost all his toes.

In 1976 two British soldiers, Bronco Lane and Brummie Stokes, were also forced to bivouac on the same slope just below the South Summit, descending in bad weather. Twelve years later in Kathmandu, Stokes was to show me his mutilated toeless feet. Lane had to have fingers as well as toes amputated, but at least both of them were alive, unlike the German climber, Hannelore Schmatz, who in 1979 insisted on stopping to bivouac before dark, even though her Sherpas were urging her to carry on down to the safety of their top camp. She died sitting in the snow and for several years her frozen body was a grisly landmark on the South-East ridge, until it was recently buried or swept away by an avalanche. I also knew about the Bulgarian climber who had died whilst descending the difficult West Ridge in 1984. Meena Agrawal, who had been doctor to another Everest expedition that year, had later told me how she had talked to the Bulgarian on the radio, trying to comfort him and persuade him to live through the night; but eventually the man had been unable to hold up the receiver any longer and had presumably died soon afterwards.

I had no intention of dying that night. I was alone just above 8500 metres (about 28,000 feet) but the wind which had frightened me so much by the Hillary Step had now died away and the air temperature was probably not much lower than minus 20 degrees centigrade. I was lucky with the conditions and I knew that I could survive in the excellent clothes I wore, but I had to resign myself to the probable loss of toes. Six months earlier, caught out high on Shisha Pangma, Luke and I had dug a snowhole and crawled inside to take off boots and warm each other's toes. But now I was nearly a thousand metres higher, I was alone and I barely had the strength to cut a ledge, let alone a proper cave where I could safely take off boots. I had climbed with the specific intention of not bivouacking, so I had no stove to melt snow. Only a trickle of half-frozen juice remained in my water bottle and in the last twenty-four hours I had drunk less than a litre. Dehydration was thickening my blood, already viscous with the concentration of red blood cells necessary to survive at altitude, and circulation was sluggish to the remote outposts of the vascular system, particularly my toes.

If the weather had been worse, I would probably have found new reserves of strength, either to dig a snowhole or to search harder for the correct descent route. But as the air was calm I lay inert, huddled up in the snow with my spare mittens providing meagre insulation under my hips and my ice axe plunged into the slope in front of me, like a retaining fence post.

I was not really alone. The old man was still with me and now there were other people as well, crowding my tiny ledge. Sometimes they offered to look after parts of my body. At one stage during the long night the old man became rather patronising towards a girl who was keeping one of my hands warm. Perhaps it was then that Eric Shipton, the distinguished explorer so closely involved with the history of Everest, took over warming my hands. At the end of the ledge my feet kept nearly falling off where I had failed to dig a thorough hollow in the snow. I was aware of several people crowding out the feet, but also trying to look after them. They were being organised by Mike Scott.

I had never met Mike Scott but I knew his father, Doug, who had bivouacked even higher than this, right up on the South Summit in 1975. He and Dougal Haston had been half-prepared for an emergency bivouac, carrying a tent sack and a stove. When they emerged from the South-West Face late in the day, they had started digging a cave and had made a hot brew before climbing the final ridge to the summit. After photographing the magical sunset from the summit they returned to the snowcave where their oxygen ran out and they settled down for the highest bivouac ever. Scott had no down gear— only the tent sack and a rucksack to sit on, yet on that bitterly cold autumn night he had the strength not only to survive but to concentrate on 'the quality of survival', warming and talking to his feet throughout the night. When he and Haston descended to the haven of Camp 6 the next day, neither of them had any frostbite.

I drifted in and out of reality, occasionally reminding myself that I was actually alone, before returning to my confused hallucinations.

Towards dawn, as I started to long for warmth, my companions teased me by announcing that there were some yak herders camping just round the corner with tents and food and hot fires. They left me alone with the old man and went to investigate. It was good to be left in peace for a while and I reminded myself that yak herders could not possibly be living up here at 8500 metres; but later the people returned to tell me that while the insidious cold of the snow had been creeping through my body they had been enjoying hot baths and food. Now I longed even more desperately to be warm.

At some stage during the night I stood up to enlarge my ledge. After that I felt slightly more comfortable and less precarious. Eventually I think that I must have slept, for I remember an actual awakening and sudden realisation that the long night was finally over.

I sat up shivering. There was pastel light in the sky and only a soft blanket of grey cloud remained in the valley far below. All the people, even the old man, had gone but I had survived my night out. My body was stiff and my feet were dead, but my fingers were still alive inside their down mittens. The hairs on my eyebrows, moustache and beard were stuck together with great lumps of ice and a frozen film encased my wooden nose. My iced sunglasses still hung useless round my neck, but my other glasses were clear, so that I could see the route down.

I could not believe that it had all seemed so strange in the dark, now that I could see the shoulder just below me, with the little dip where one had to turn right into the couloir. If only I had seen better in the dark I could perhaps have descended to Camp 3 and saved myself all that shivering!

The sun was rising over Kangchenjunga as I stood up shakily, picked up my ice axe and set off wobbling and sliding down the slope. Soon I was back in the couloir, daring myself to sit down and slide wherever possible. Once I went too fast and gave myself another alarming attack of hyper-ventilating, but after that I stayed in control. The world was sparkling in morning sunlight and life was wonderful. I was alive and warm again, I had climbed Everest and soon I would be back in the valley.

Suddenly I saw two people in the couloir, down by the Dunlop tent.

It took a while for my dulled mind to realise that they must be Ed and Robert, who had also failed to reach the South Col in the dark and had taken shelter in the Asians' abandoned tent. They turned round and saw me sliding towards them and a few minutes later we were reunited. I cannot remember what we said. Only a few words were spoken and they were probably banal; but I remember vividly Ed and Robert's relief at seeing me alive and a deep warmth of friendship as the three of us roped together for the final descent to the South Col.

Robert led the way down to the col. I followed, sitting down to slide whenever possible, and Ed came last. On the bottom easy section of the couloir we unroped to slither and stagger independently. Then we just had to walk across the plateau.

Ed photographed Robert towering over me with a welcoming arm over my shoulder, then me on my own, with my torch still on my head and camera equipment and sunglasses tangled round my neck. I just managed to rise to the occasion, forcing a smile out of my iced-up face and holding up the ice axe in my left hand. Before Ed put his mittens back on he showed me his fingers: 'I think they're frostbitten. I didn't really notice yesterday, but I think it must have happened at sunrise. I took about twenty frames. Wasn't that light amazing? Kangchenjunga, Makalu . . . They're going to be some brilliant pictures.'

We continued towards our two tents. Robert and Ed were moving quite strongly but on this last stretch I sank every few metres to my knees or just sat down, waiting for the willpower to move my legs again. We knew that we should really continue straight down the East Face to the safer altitude of the Flying Wing, but we were desperate for liquid and sleep and by the time I reached Camp 3 on the South Col Robert was already crawling into his tent. Soon Ed and I were nestled amongst down sleeping bags in the warmth of our tent, with the first batch of snow melting on the stove while we started to remove our mittens and boots to inspect the damage.

My fingers were fine, apart from a touch of frostbite on the right thumb; and the right foot looked all right apart from slight discoloration on the big toe and heel. The left foot was worse but I was relieved to see that the damage was limited to the heel and toes, which were starting to turn a purplish colour. The demarcation line between live and frozen tissue curved from the base of the big toe to the tip of the little toe. By some inexplicable coincidence Ed's right foot was also virtually undamaged and the injuries were much worse on his left foot, almost identical to mine. However, it was the fingers that were now worrying him. He explained again how he had exposed them at sunrise the previous morning.

'I had on liner gloves but even so my fingers must have been frozen by the metal camera. I thought that they had just gone numb and would warm up again. What do you think?'

'They'll be all right,' I assured him. 'They're certainly frostbitten but they don't look much worse than Luke's did on Shishers and he didn't lose anything. What does my nose look like? It feels completely dead.'

'It's a sort of purplish grey colour.' As soon as the melted snow was ready, Ed started to bathe his fingers in warm water. With considerable difficulty I did the same with my toes, twisting my foot to get it in the mug. Later I was to be reminded that one should avoid thawing frozen tissue until one is safely down; but at the time we lacked the sense to realise that our digits were about to be refrozen descending the East Face. After our thirty-two-hour ordeal on the summit ridge we just wanted warmth and comfort and it did not occur to us to keep our damaged digits firmly frozen, which would have meant keeping our left feet and both Ed's hands out of our sleeping bags.

The tent was a haven of bright warmth seducing us into staying on the South Col. We knew that this was our third day above 8000 metres and that we should leave the 'death zone' as soon as possible, but we decided that we would wait till the next morning, by which time we would have rested and rehydrated a little. It felt wonderful just to lie back, warm and content, drinking the remains of our tea, sugar and hot chocolate.

Ed told me a little about what had happened to him and Robert up on the South Summit, but we were too tired to talk properly and it is only now, three months after our summit climb, that he has searched his memory for the details and written from Colorado to tell me what happened.

Like me, he kept falling asleep on the long slope up to the South Summit, but always forced himself to wake up and continue, drawing closer to me. When I pushed on again he followed at a distance. Ever professional, he tried to photograph me on the final slope, but by the time he had the exposure adjusted I was disappearing over the crest. That was the last he or Robert saw of me until the next morning.

Ed eventually reached the false top just below the South Summit. The clouds were now closing in and, like me, he remembered Mick Burke. He stared along the final precarious snow arête leading to the South Summit and decided that he did not like it. If the three of us had been together, giving each other moral support, he might have considered it; but he was alone, Robert was about an hour behind him and it was too late. He had a strong gut feeling that if he continued he would either lose control and fall off, or at the very least have to face an open bivouac near the summit. However, if he turned round now, at about 3.30 p.m., he could descend safely to our Camp 3 on the South Col.

Ed started back down and soon met Robert, who announced that he wanted to go a little higher. Ed replied that he would wait on the shoulder at the top of the couloir leading down to the South Col. Robert, with his usual determination, forced himself slowly up to the South Summit. He arrived at about 4.30 p.m., while I was battling to find my way back down from the summit to the Hillary Step. Everest was enveloped in swirling cloud and Robert became disorientated. As he explained later, 'After I'd walked round in a circle once, I realised that if I tried to continue I wouldn't come back.' In 1985 he had retreated from the West Ridge 250 metres below the top, after weeks of hard work. Since then he had spent three years dreaming of his return to Everest and now he had to take the same painful decision less than a hundred metres below the summit.

Ed had a long wait at the shoulder, staring up at the murky slope leading down from the South Summit. Frequently he hallucinated, seeing Robert and me descending out of the mists. Sometimes the two figures were too far to the right or had already descended past him and Ed would yell to them, trying to warn them of danger. But there was never an answer and the figures always disappeared. Ed grew steadily more cold, tired and frustrated until, at dusk, Robert finally appeared in bodily form. Ed was angry with him, because they now had only about fifteen minutes of daylight left.

They thought that they would be unable to reach the South Col in the dark, so they were resigned to a night out without sleeping bags. However they remembered the Asians' tent and rushed off down the couloir, peering through the fading light to find the way and race the darkness. Ed just managed to find the tent before it became totally dark. A few minutes later Robert arrived and they both crawled inside. There was no insulation other than the tent groundsheet, but Ed managed to sleep intermittently. Robert had a worse night and kept waking Ed, asking to go down to the col; but Ed told him each time that it was too dark and cold outside and that they should wait for the sun. Finally the sun appeared and Ed gave permission to leave. They crawled out of the tent and a few minutes later saw me 'staggering down the gully like a drunk'.

The extraordinary thing about Ed's decision to turn back by the South Summit the previous afternoon was that he felt no regret. Having analysed the dangers so rationally, he set off down with the patently absurd notion that he would simply rest a day at the South Col, then come back up for another attempt. Now, a day later, we were back on the col. We felt warm and secure, but Ed certainly realised now that there was not the slightest chance of another summit attempt and we were both becoming dimly aware that even the descent was going to be a hard struggle.

We talked idly and dozed and soon it was dark. By the evening our last gas cylinder was now empty and I had to quench my thirst by sucking lumps of ice. It was a strange confused night and, although there was nothing to compare with the hallucinations of the previous night, I slept badly, wandering in and out of troubled dreams. In the morning I lay half-conscious, waiting for Robert to bring us water. Time was moving with unchecked speed and several hours passed as we waited for our drink. Occasionally we would shout: 'Robert, what's happened to that water?' and he would answer from the other tent in a dreary slurred voice, 'Just wait. It's coming soon. The stove's not working properly.'

It must have been nearly midday when he eventually brought over the water to relieve our thirst; but still we delayed our departure. It was pitiful to witness our own deterioration as we sprawled on our backs, mumbling feebly about the imperative need to descend but failing to do anything about it. Eventually Ed forced me to start the first exhausting task—sitting up, getting out of my sleeping bag and, with many pauses for rest, packing it into my rucksack. Then I lay down for half an hour, delaying the awful effort of putting on boots.

I knew that this was all wrong. It was now the afternoon of May 14th and we had spent almost four days above 8000 metres. We had broken the rules and we were asking for trouble. We should have left early that morning to descend all the way to Camp 1, but now we would be pushed even to reach Camp 2 before dark.

It was nearly 4 p.m. when we eventually left. A combination of laziness and the intention of glissading most of the way down meant that we did not bother to rope up. We did not have the strength to take the tents we had carried up from Camp 2 and left them standing on the bleak plateau; we would have to manage without them when we got down to the Flying Wing. I left my Therma-Rest, my spare mittens, my down sleeping boots and the windsuit which had saved my life two days earlier. I could manage without it now and I had to keep weight to a minimum. Before he left, Ed asked, 'What shall we do with this?'

'Ah—the mail packet. Perhaps the Australians will wander over here and pick it up, if they're still on the mountain.'

'I'll leave it here in the tent. You never know, even if no-one picks it up now, the tent might still be standing in the autumn, when the next lot comes up here. Right, I'm going. Make sure you and Robert come soon.' He left quickly, determined to escape to a safer altitude.

Robert was still nurturing his last few ounces of gas, making one final brew of tepid water. I concentrated on my crampons. When they were safely on my feet I sat drinking half a pan of water, watching Robert staggering over to the edge of the plateau to start down the East Face. About ten minutes later I managed to stand up, put on my rucksack, pick up my ice axe, fit its safety loop over my wrist, put one foot forward and start walking.

I did not get very far before sinking to my knees to rest. That was better than sitting down, because it required less effort to stand up again from a kneeling position.

The afternoon had closed in, it was snowing and the South Col seemed even more forlorn than usual. I knew that if I failed to follow the other two I would die, but still I dallied, stopping to rest every few steps. When I reached the brink of the plateau and looked down the East Face Robert was resting far below. I saw the furrow where he had slid down and yelled, 'Is it all right?' I took his garbled shout to mean 'Yes' and jumped over the edge, landing in a sitting position and glissading off down the slope.

It was steeper than I remembered and I accelerated rapidly. I leaned hard over to one side, braking with the ice axe, but it made little difference. I was sliding faster and faster, then suddenly I hit submerged rocks. The ice axe skidded on the rocks; then it was plucked up in the air. I felt a sharp crack on my hip bone, I bounced faster and faster and then I was flung up in a rag doll somersault, spinning over and landing on my back to accelerate again. I was shooting down the slope, but now I was on snow again and could dig in my heels, braking desperately and finally coming to a gasping halt, coughing and spluttering in a shower of powder snow.

I lay there, battered, bruised and helpless, almost succumbing to terror before finding the courage to stand up. Luckily I had broken no bones but my one ice axe had been wrenched off my wrist, almost taking the Rolex with it, and now I had no tool to safeguard my descent. I was blinded by snow and frantically took off mittens to wipe clear my glasses, irretrievably dropping one mitten in the process. Now I had to split the remaining double mitten, wearing the flimsy down mitt on one hand and the outer on the other.

Robert was still a long way below watching impassively and Ed was far ahead, out of sight. Again I felt weak and helpless and in a fit of terror I yelled down, 'Robert, wait. Please wait! Don't go without me.' Then I started to kick shaky steps down towards him, holding my useless penguin arms out to the side.

Robert waited patiently and when I reached him he explained that he had also slid out of control. 'I never saw those rocks at all. Then the snow below avalanched, carrying me all the way down here.'

'Can I borrow your spare tool?' I asked. 'You had two tools with you, didn't you?'

'Sorry, I've lost both of them. The ice axe was ripped off my wrist and the spare ice hammer fell out of my holster. Now I just have this ski stick. I could break it in half . . .'

'No, it's all right.'

We carried on down, Robert leaning on his ski stick, I holding out my mittened hands for balance. Dusk was falling as I followed the others' tracks across the big slope above the Flying Wing. That traverse seemed an interminable purgatory. Robert and Ed were now out of sight and I was sitting down every few steps, finding it harder and harder each time to stand up again. Snow was still falling and everything was cold and grey.

I suddenly remembered a winter evening in 1976, in Italy, returning exhausted to the roadhead after an abortive climb above the Val Ferret. I longed to be back there, taking off snowshoes and walking into the little bar where I had sat on a high stool and made myself gloriously dizzy with a tumblerful of dark sweet Vermouth and a cigarette. Then I thought about skiing in bad weather, succumbing to temptation and ordering an overpriced Swiss glühwein. Which took me back to the soft green twilight of an evening in January 1986, camping amongst the primeval tree heathers of Bigo Bog in the Ruwenzori Mountains of

East Africa. It had been a long wet day and after changing into dry clothes we had lit a fire to make mulled wine. Soon the air had been infused with the hot steam of wine, lemons, Cointreau and spices, sweetened with heaped spoons of sugar.

Darkness fell and there was no restorative hot drink. I wanted help to remove my sunglasses and I shouted out to Ed and Robert; but they were too far ahead, so I had to manage on my own, fumbling with wooden fingers to take off sunglasses, open the zipped lid of my rucksack and take out clear glasses and headtorch. Now I could see where I was going but I still felt lonely and frightened that I would not make it to Camp 2. I kept shouting 'Robert! Ed!' as I trudged laboriously over the little crevasse, past the marker wand, down into the dip, then back right, following the shelf under the Flying Wing, longing for warmth and rest and the reassuring company of my friends.

At last I saw their lights at the site of our Camp 2. They had already fitted one of the cached gas cylinders to the burner Robert had carried down and the first brew was on the way. The instant coffee and milk which they had found in the Asians' tent two nights earlier tasted disgusting but we drank it anyway, hoping that it would give us some strength. For an hour I just lay in the snow, too feeble to get into my sleeping bag. When I eventually made the effort I kept boots and over-boots on my feet, deciding now that it would be best to disturb the frozen toes as little as possible. I had left my inflated Therma-Rest on the South Col but my down sleeping bag kept me warm enough in the snow. Robert produced one or two more brews before we all fell into a deep sleep.

Thirst and a croaking cough woke me at dawn on May 15th. For ages I lay inert, coughing up foul lumps of phlegm from my throat. Then I tried to rouse Robert and Ed, begging them to light the stove. I tried several times but there was no response. In the end I had to do it myself. It was a big effort, leaning up on one elbow, scooping snow into the pan, setting the stove upright and struggling with my slightly frostbitten right thumb to work the flint of the lighter. Fifteen minutes later I had to replenish the snow, then I dozed again. Eventually we had a full pan of dirty tepid water but the stove fell over and we lost it. I started the laborious process again, forcing myself to repeat the whole exhausting routine, but after about forty-five minutes the stove fell over again.

The day was now well advanced. The weather was fine again and the open cave under the Flying Wing was a blazing suntrap. The heat was appalling, pressing down on us and intensifying our thirst. I managed to haul myself out of my sleeping bag and unzip the legs of my down bibs but I could not find the energy actually to take them off.

The third attempt to make a drink was successful. Then Robert's slurred zombie voice suggested that we should eat some food. The bag we had left here five days earlier contained chocolate, freeze-dried shrimp and clam chowder and potato powder. 'No—I couldn't,' croaked Ed. 'Not the chowder.'

'Can you make some potato then, Stephen?' Robert asked.

He managed to eat a reasonable helping, and I forced down a few spoonfuls but Ed could not face it. He was more concerned about getting off the mountain and kept urging, 'We must go down! Soon we won't be able to move.' We knew that he was right, but each of us was lost in his own private world of dreams, sprawled helpless in the stultifying heat, powerless to face reality.

'We should signal to the others.'

'Yes, we should stand up so that they can see us.'

'Maybe they saw our lights last night. Anyway, they'll see us when we start moving.'

'We should go soon.'

'But I want to sleep.'

'We'll go soon.'

'We need another drink. It's so hot!'

The heat grew worse as the East Face was covered by a layer of cloud, thin enough to let the sun through, but also just dense enough to reflect the white heat back onto the snow. We were imprisoned in a merciless shimmering glasshouse and it was only in the afternoon, when the cloud thickened and snow started to fall, that we felt cool enough to move.

Ed urged us on as usual. His frostbitten fingers had now ballooned into large painful blisters, but he still managed to be ready first. Again we had wasted nearly a whole day and it was after 3 p.m. when Ed set off, wading through the deep heavy snow below the Flying Wing. I followed last, nearly an hour later. It was snowing and visibility was bad. After I had descended about 150 metres I heard Ed's voice further below, shouting up through the cloud to Robert.

'This is scary—I can't see a thing and I've just slipped over a cliff. We're not going to make it to Camp 1 tonight. If we try and continue we're just going to get lost. We'll have to go back up to Camp 2, where we've got shelter and gas. We'll just have to spend another night there and make sure we leave early in the morning.'

I knew that Ed was right but groaned with despair at the horror of having to force my body uphill. It was a slow painful battle to climb back up that slope and Ed quickly overtook me. He had our one remaining ice axe and moved alongside me as I balanced my way up a 50-degree bulge of ice which we had slipped over on the way down, sweeping off the snow. Ed would drive his pick into the ice as high as possible, then I would use it as a handhold to step up higher, before letting go and balancing on my tiptoe crampon points, with the mittened palms of my hands just pressed to the ice, while Ed moved up alongside and placed the axe higher. Robert was approaching the bulge from below and shouted gloomily, 'What am I supposed to do?'

'I'll leave it here—halfway up!' Ed shouted encouragingly.

'Thanks a lot. How am I meant to reach it?'

'Jump—I suppose.'

It was dark by the time Robert eventually joined us under the Flying Wing. Ed and I were sprawled once again in our sleeping bags and I was starting to melt snow. We had no tea, coffee, Rehydrate or sugar—nothing to flavour our water except the remains of the potato powder. After the first cup of water I promised to produce another solid meal of potato, knowing how desperately our bodies needed fuel, but the meal never materialised for I fell too soon into an exhausted sleep.

When we woke at dawn on May 16th, we knew that this was our last chance. If we stayed another night at this altitude with virtually no food we would probably become too weak to move. It was now five days since Paul had left us on the South Col. We knew that he and the others would be worried, but once again we were too apathetic to take advantage of the cloudless morning and stand up to wave; instead we lay hidden under the Flying Wing, reasoning that the others would see our tracks of the previous evening and realise that we were on the way down.

Ed's blistered fingers were now agonising and Robert's finger tips, though less badly damaged, were also painful, so I prepared the morning water. Everything smelled and tasted disgusting and the other two refused to eat the chocolate-coated granola bars that I had found. However I managed to sit up and eat two bars, concentrating stubbornly on the unpleasant task and swilling them down with sips of dirty melted snow. All this took time and we failed to leave before the sun hit us. This time I found it even harder to struggle out of the stifling oven of my sleeping bag and the down bibs. Beside me, Ed looked like an old man. His face was lean and haggard, his hair hung lankly and the light had gone out of his eyes as he stared in horror at his swollen blistered fingers. His voice too was the dry croak of an old, old man, repeating over and over again, 'We've got to go down. We *must* go down. If we don't go down today we're going to die.'

Robert, like me, was almost silent, fighting his own private battle against lassitude, building himself up for the great effort of departure. Ed, the most sensitive member of the team, seemed more deeply affected by the trauma of our descent and actually said that it was going to take him a long time to get over the psychological shock of this experience. However, because he was so sensitive to the danger threatening us and because he so urgently needed to reach Mimi's medical help, he had become our leader.

The only help Ed could give us was his insistent croaks of encouragement. We were powerless to help each other physically and I thought with detachment how our situation was starting to resemble the 1986 tragedy on K2, when the storm finally cleared, allowing the Austrian climbers, Willi Bauer and Kurt Diemberger, to bully their companions into fleeing the hell of Camp 4, after eight days at nearly 8000 metres had reduced them all to emaciated wrecks. Julie Tullis had already died in the storm. Alan Rouse was only semi-conscious, incapable of moving, pleading deliriously for water. Diemberger and Bauer could do nothing and had to leave him lying in his tent. The other two Austrians, Immitzer and Wieser, collapsed in the snow soon after leaving the camp. The Polish woman, 'Mrufka' Wolf, managed to keep going but died later that day on the fixed ropes. Only Bauer and Diemberger, both large heavy men with enormous bodily reserves, crawled down alive.

Our experience had not approached the horror of K2: we had only spent four days, not eight, above 8000 metres; we had been hindered slightly by poor weather, but we had experienced nothing to compare with the horrendous storm on K2; we had failed to make adequate brews but we had at least been drinking something, our gas at Camp 2 was still not finished and there were further stocks at Camp 1; nevertheless we were now in danger of re-enacting the K2 tragedy and as I lay flat on my back, delaying feebly the moment of departure, I realised how easy and painless it would be just to lie there until I died.

'Come on you guys, we've got to move! It's clouding over already.' Ed was right: it was only 9 a.m. and the clouds had arrived earlier today with their crippling greenhouse effect. I reached out for the things I wanted to take—cameras, torch, down bibs and jacket. The sleeping bag would have to stay here, like Ed's and Robert's. It seemed monstrous to litter the mountain with $1500-worth of sleeping bags, but they weighed two and a half kilos each and the less weight we carried the greater chance we would have of reaching safety.

At 10 a.m. Ed was ready. Again he urged me to move. 'Don't wait long, Stephen. You've got to get up and move: if you don't get down alive you won't be able to enjoy being famous.' Then he left.

Robert made his final preparations and I fitted my crampons. Everything was now ready but I wanted another rest so, while Robert set off, I sat on my rucksack. I sat there for nearly an hour, bent over with my elbows on my knees and my head cupped in my hands. My eyes were shut and I swayed slightly, almost falling asleep as I dreamed of life after Everest. Ed was right: life would be fun when I returned to earth. People would be surprised and pleased by our success. I would be so happy and everything would be so easy. I would be able to eat delicious food and I would have that sweet red Vermouth, with great crystals of ice and the essential sharpness of lemon. And I would drink orange juice, cool tumblers full of it, sitting in the green shade of a tree. That life was so close, so easily attainable; all I had to do was reach Advance Base—just one more day of effort and then the others would take over.

I tried to stand up and failed. It was a feeble attempt and I told myself that next time I would succeed. After all, I *wanted* to descend, didn't I? I was just being a little lazy. I would have to concentrate a little harder on the task: lean forward, go down on my knees, shoulder the rucksack, stand up and away! Easy. Let's try now.

Nothing happened.

I began to worry. It was nearly an hour since Robert and Ed had left and I knew that they would not have the strength to climb back up for me. It was 11 a.m. and I had to leave now and catch up with them. I just had to take that simple action to save my life but I was finding it so hard. I was also frightened now that when I stood up my legs might be too weak to remain standing.

There was only one way to find out and with a final concentrated effort I started to move. This time it worked. I went down on my knees, reached round behind me and pulled the rucksack onto my shoulders. Now came the hardest part. I pressed a mittened hand to one knee, pushed up with the other knee, held out both hands for balance and stood up. I managed to stay upright and took a few wobbly penguin steps to the edge of the shelf under the Wing. It was so tempting to sink back down onto the shelf and fall asleep, but I forced my mind to concentrate on directing all energy to those two withered legs. The effort succeeded and I managed six faltering steps down the slope, sat back for a rest, then took six steps more, then again six steps. It was going to be a long tedious struggle, but I knew now that I was going to make it.

Ed led us down the mountain. Paul's tracks had long since disappeared, obliterated by successive afternoon snowfalls. The warm air currents which heralded the Monsoon's approach from the Bay of Bengal had made the snow damp and heavy and there was no possibility of sitting down to slide, as we had done in the dry powder two weeks earlier: this time we had to descend on our feet, wobbling down the deep furrow which Ed ploughed for us.

Ed also had to navigate, guessing his way through a confusing blur of half-remembered shapes shrouded in mist and falling snow. He was terrified of losing the way and plunging irrevocably down towards the ice cliffs of Lhotse, because each time he reached an orange marker wand he had to continue blind for quite a distance before the next one came into view. Then he veered too far to the right and I heard his voice calling out of the mist, 'We've got to go back up left, to the snowbridge.'

I started to break a trail back left, wading through the clogging knee-deep snow. This was hell—having to climb up round this crevasse, step by laborious step, resting sometimes for three or four minutes between steps. It was my fifth day with virtually no food and I craved for rich flavours. I dreamed that someone organised a lunch stop. We came across the crevasse and there was a striped pavilion, cool and clean inside, with a large pink-faced Frenchman welcoming us. There was a huge tray of cheeses—Camembert, St Nectaire, Gruyère, Roquefort and, out of deference to my Englishness, a slab of Stilton. Our host had already opened bottles of rich dark claret but he knew that we would be thirsty, so he had also laid on a great jug of fresh orange juice.

Fantasies like this were to continue all day. Sometimes I would be coming in after a day's climbing to sandwiches and unlimited cups of tea; at other times it would be pints of beer on a summer's evening in Wasdale. Meanwhile, on Everest, we ploughed our way down. Ed caught up and led across the snowbridge. For a long time I sat in the snow, wondering whether one of these times I really would sit down and find, like those Austrians on K2, that I could not stand up again. I also worried about Robert, who was out of sight behind, but I decided to continue and give Ed a break from trail-breaking.

Once we crossed the snowbridge the route-finding was easier and the visibility improved, so we became almost certain that we could reach the safety of the fixed ropes. Nevertheless on several occasions we reached a marker wand and asked, 'Where the hell do we go now?' Then Ed or I would wade off down some steep bluff, horribly laden with unstable snow. At the top of one bluff I dithered on the brink before waddling down over the edge, with my useless penguin arms held out either side, waiting for the snow slab to give way. Suddenly the surface cracked with a horrible breathy 'hhrmmmphh' and I was away, riding a wave of snow, all arms and legs as the wave flung me over a steeper ice bulge and poured me down into the hollow below, where I came to a standstill, buried up to my thighs.

Fear was a thing of the past. I calmly dug myself out, looked up at the little silhouetted figure of Ed, fifty metres above, and shouted, 'Yes, this is the right way,' before ploughing manically onwards towards the ropes.

The snowfall had stopped, the clouds were clearing and the daylight was fading when Ed joined me at the wand marking the first anchor.

'Let's dig out our stuff,' I suggested.

'We didn't leave anything here, did we?'

'Of course we did. We need our harnesses and descendeurs!'

'But we're not at the ropes yet.'

'Yes, we are. Look—down there. Can't you see that little bit of rope sticking out of the snow? That's the bit past the Jumble.'

Then Ed realised that we had made it to safety. Nothing now would stop him descending the ropes that night and he started to dig feverishly with his frozen claws, while I watched feebly, too lazy or too stupid to stop him damaging the delicate blisters on his fingers. Robert had lent me his spare mitts at Camp 2, but my hands were cold, and I found it very hard to buckle on my harness and organise my descendeur. God knows how Ed managed.

Soon Ed was away down the first rope. I was anxious about Robert, but he appeared a moment later, wading down our trench a few hundred metres above. I asked, 'Are you all right, Robert?'

'Yes,' he shouted. 'See you at Camp 1.'

'No, we're going all the way,' yelled Ed, digging his way across the Jumble. 'All the way to Advance Base!'

I followed across the Jumble and the Hump. Then I looked down the twilit slope to the Jaws of Doom and saw with immense relief that the lower jaw was intact, for I had been terrified that it might have gone, ripping out our safety line as it crashed down the Buttress and cut off our retreat. However, Ed was now sliding safely across the dark gap and a thousand metres below him the clouds had drifted away from the Kangshung Glacier. It was almost dark, but surely the others would be up and looking, seeing our figures against the snow? Surely they would see us and know that everything was all right? In a few more hours, by 10 p.m. probably, we would be down with them, drinking buckets of fruit juice and tea.

For the last time I made the exciting whoosh across the Jaws of Doom, transferred to the rope below, slid, fell and rolled my way across to the next anchor, transferred ropes again and abseiled down the Fourth Cauliflower Tower. It was almost dark now but I could see that more of the tower had disintegrated, littering the terrace below with great ice boulders.

Ed was busily searching for the rope over Webster's Wall. It was buried deep in the snow, so we advanced unprotected right to the brink of the wall, hoping to unearth the rope there. For a few minutes I suffered the torment of believing that it must have gone, leaving us stranded above the overhanging wall, but eventually Ed hacked it out with his ice axe and clipped in his descendeur.

He rushed on past Camp 1, but I stopped to collect some things. While rummaging in the sack of cached gear I noticed a huge furrow, gouged by a falling ice boulder right through the spot where our tents had been pitched, but I hardly took in its significance. I grew bored with searching for my equipment and the thriller which I had been reading a week earlier, but I did make a point of collecting my helmet. It would make the final descent safer and in any case I was damned if I was going to leave it behind: it was a good helmet and it had cost a fortune, even with the Alpine Sports discount.

Before leaving on the final climb, Paul, Ed and I had always argued that we should make every effort to clear all our equipment from the mountain. Now, faced with the reality of our nightmarish descent, all those good intentions had to be abandoned. We were only just managing to get ourselves off the mountain alive, and there was no question now of removing the detritus of our climb. Not only that—I was not even waiting for Robert. Like the Polish girl, Mrufka, on K2, he was being left to find his own way down the ropes. If he chose to stop at Camp 1 that was his problem; Ed and I were rushing on headlong to Advance Base and nothing was going to stop us now.

I buckled on my helmet, waded across to the next rope and clipped in for the first abseil into Big Al Gully. Ed was waiting at the anchor fifty metres below, unable to clip his descendeur into the next section of rope. It was ridiculous for him to go first and I insisted, 'I'll have to go first and clear the ropes; otherwise you're going to shred your fingers.' It was hard work, straining on the rope, pulling and pulling, until it came unstuck from the ice below and gave me enough slack to clip in my descendeur.

I abseiled down that rope, clipped my safety loop into the next anchor and shouted up, 'Okay, Ed, you can come!' Then I was off again, excavating the rope below, down to Paul's letterbox, where I perched for ages, pulling desperately on the next rope. I could not get enough slack to feed into the descendeur, so I had to go down with the rope just wound round my wrist, until I could free more slack from the imprisoning ice. Then I could abseil normally, down, down the big icefield to the next anchor where everything was buried and confused. I searched and searched for the next rope but could not find it and, as the snow was compacted by wind, I had to wait to dig until Ed arrived with the ice axe. His torch had gone out, so he asked me for my spare bulb, but in the numb-fingered confusion we lost both bulbs. Now we had to descend in total darkness.

We never considered stopping. We were too close now. We would just fight on down the ropes, groping our way by memory along the 1600-metre lifeline. It was weird, repeating all those familiar changeovers, section by section, relying just on feel and the faintest glimmer of starlight. Nearly every metre of the ropes had to be pulled out from the snow and ice, as I fought my way back across the shattered wall to the Terrace and down to the big traverse, and on, slithering sideways on my knees, past all Paul's anchors to the cave above the Scottish Gully. It had been slower than I expected but I hoped at least to be back by midnight, and I shouted as loudly as I could, 'Mimi. Joe. Paul. TEA!'

The gully was hideous. The ropes were buried in knee-deep soggy snow and every few metres I had to stop and pull out the next section before I could continue. We had now been on the move for twelve hours without water and we had hardly eaten for five days. I was struggling again, stopping repeatedly to close my eyes. But I had to get down, had to fight just a little longer and soon we would be lying in our tents, drinking all the fruit juice and tea in the world.

'Joe. Paul. Mimi. TEA!'

Columns of ice ensnared the rope over the headwall. There was no hope of feeding it into my descendeur, so again I had to rely on the friction of the ice hawser wrapped round my wrist. Midnight passed and I was still on the lower part of the Buttress. Once I stopped for half an hour with my head lolling on the snow and almost fell asleep before continuing the painful excavation, metre by metre, fighting the heavy snow until at last I reached the bottom of the last rope, and there was the spare ice axe for the glacier, which I had left clipped into the end of the rope nine days earlier.

When I reached the glacier I lay down and waited for Ed. He arrived at about 1.30 a.m. and we tied on to the short length of rope we always left here for the crossing.

The fight with the fixed ropes was over now and all we had to do was plod. We thought happily that we would be back at Advance Base in an hour; but the mountain would not let us escape that easily. Soon we lost our way, strayed from the usual easy route and started to wander through a maze of hummocks and crevasses. The darkness was confusing and we stumbled back and forth, pulling each other in and out of crevasses, crying and cursing with misery as we staggered about like impotent drunkards.

At last we fought our way out of the maze and reached the final smooth section of glacier. Surely now it would be easy? But no, it was a warm night and the snow had not frozen properly. Time after time the crust gave way and suddenly I would plunge waist-deep into a pit of slush. I screamed with rage as I flung myself back onto the surface, yanking furiously at my trapped feet until I could crawl out on my hands and knees, displacing my weight to try and avoid another col-lapse. Then I would stand up gingerly and walk again, waiting for the next unannounced plunge.

Ed followed slowly, dragging on the rope, and taking an intolerable age to crawl out of each pit. Now I seemed to be even more desperate than him to reach camp and eventually I grew tired of waiting, so I just untied from the rope and left him to follow at his own pace. I was sure that the glacier here was safe, but it was still a callous thing to do and I tried to assuage my guilt by telling myself that I had to hurry on and find the others.

Where were they? Why hadn't they come out to meet us? I tried shouting again.

'Joe, Paul, Mimi. TEA!'

Surely they could hear us? Surely they would have water heating by now? We must be nearly there. I can't go on for ever. I just want to be comforted and cosseted.

'Mimi! MIMI! Why don't you answer?'

Where are they? Do I still have to walk? At Camp 2 I thought that I might not be able to stand up and yet now, sixteen hours later, I'm still coping; but surely there comes a point when the body stops? At least the snow's better now, no more hephalump traps. And the air down here is so rich and thick. Just as well, otherwise I would have given up long ago. There's that buttress on Peak 38. Almost level with it now. And this strip of frozen lake on the left. It's all collapsed at the edges so I must keep my distance. It would be so stupid to get down this close to safety then die of drowning or hypothermia in a puddle.

Now this is it, surely? The moraine on the left curving slightly. 'MIMI! JOE! PAUL!' Please be there—if they've left Advance Base we'll never cope. It must be up on those rocks to the left. Just got to drag the legs a little further. First a little rest: bend over and lean on knees, but don't sit down—fatal. Now up the hill, dragging one leg after the other, stumbling on the rocks, left . . . right . . . left . . . right . . . almost there . . . Now, we're on the crest of the moraine. It's somewhere round here. But why is there no sound? It all looks different. What's happened to the lake? Are those lumps over there tents? Please—they must be! I can't go any further. 'WHERE ARE THE BLOODY TENTS?!'

I heard a scuffle, then, at last, the sound of startled voices. A dark shape materialised, a torch was lit and Paul came rushing across the rocks towards me. I remembered all those pre-dawn departures from this camp, the shivering breakfasts and dark journeys across the glacier, in that other life when we climbed the Buttress; I remembered my impatience on all those load-carries, and now that it was all finally over I shouted out a feeble joke, 'Four o'clock in the morning, Paul. Time to go up the ropes!'

Paul reached me and put an arm on my shoulder. He shone his torch in my face, stared in disbelief at my sunken eyes, swollen lips and lumpy black nose and he gasped, 'Venables! Where the hell have you been?'

from **Sheer Will**

by Michael Groom

Michael Groom (born 1959) in 1987 lost all of his toes

and portions of both feet to frostbite on Kangchenjunga,

the world's third-highest mountain. He returned to the high

mountains and in 1996 served as a guide on Rob Hall's

Everest expedition.

found myself joining a commercial expedition to Mount Everest in the spring of 1996 when Rob Hall needed another guide. Guiding clients up mountains has been an occupation for the last century, most notably when Edward Whymper employed two Swiss guides to make the first ascent of the Matterhorn in 1865. Unfortunately this ascent ended when four of their party fell to their deaths. In recent times some degree of criticism has been aimed at commercial expeditions for poor service and unsafe practices, or at guides who drag inexperienced climbers willing to pay large sums of money to the summit of their whimsical dreams. The situation also raises the question: Where does a guide's responsibility for a client stop in a life-or-death situation? I gave it considerable thought as I mulled over Rob's offer, but could not find a confident answer.

The days of sponsored expeditions are well and truly over and the large sums of money needed to mount an expedition to any of the world's highest mountains have to come from somewhere. Any climber with the experience and motivation to attempt Mount Everest must also have a network of like-minded climbing friends, all with disposable incomes and plenty of time, not only for the climb but for the planning stages as well. Anyone lacking any of these requirements is forced to look at other options. One is to look for a private expedition willing to sell off positions on their permit. This sometimes means a number of smaller teams operating under the one expedition permit, often with little overall planning, a mishmash of experience levels and to the detriment of such things as safety, food and equipment. Such expeditions can become a risk to other teams on the mountain, as well as to themselves. Of course, it can work well, as I have experienced, but it is far better for someone who does not have the network of resources and a high level of experience to join a professionally run (commercial) expedition.

In the world of commercial expeditions Rob Hall had an aura of respectability that was hard to match. I had become friends with him on the K2 climb and had enjoyed his generous hospitality at various base camps in the world's greater mountain ranges. Rob had shown me the impressive list of climbing résumés, but the final incentive came when a friend of mine, John Taske, was accepted on the climb as a paying member. In fact a few of the climbers had more experience than some of the members of the noncommercial expeditions I had been on in the past. I would be the third guide along with Rob and Andy Harris, a professional guide, whom I had not met but who, by all accounts, was an excellent guide and a likeable fellow. I would need no introduction to the quality of an expedition Rob organised and, as I had witnessed on many occasions, there would be no shortage of good food, worldwide satellite phone and fax communications, and the best equipment money could buy. It would be sheer luxury compared with my previous expeditions. As a guide I would be using oxygen, a foreign experience for me, so much so that I was embarrassed to admit I could not screw a regulator onto an oxygen bottle. Rob had to show me in the privacy of our mess tent. To compare an ascent of Everest using oxygen to one without was an interesting experiment.

I had been in Nepal for most of March co-guiding a trek to a couple of smaller peaks that unfortunately became a non-event due to a heavy snowfall. I left the trek a couple of days early, in the capable hands of my co-leader Mike Wood, to be in time to meet the Everest team in Kathmandu. The bus trip back from the foothills of the Himalayas was a dusty and exhausting ride, and to test my patience further I had difficulty finding a hotel room when I arrived. Looking worn and grubby means you are a less likely victim of streetside salesmanship, so it was with considerable ease that I made my way through the backstreet alleys to the barber. My barber friend knows me well from many visits and I have always felt comfortable in his rickety chair, even though we can only exchange a few words of greeting. I had only just submitted to his razor, when John Taske bounced in to have his pre-expedition haircut. He had climbed with me a couple of times in Nepal and Tibet and had a million and one questions about the pending climb and regaled me with gossip from home. I could only afford the occasional response, as the barber did battle with my two-week growth.

On my way back from the barber I called in to Rob's hotel to announce my arrival. It was then that I met the first of our eight members, Stuart Hutchison. I took an immediate liking to the tall, handsome Canadian who was working in the USA as a cardiologist. His considerable mountaineering experience had seen him on Broad Peak, Denali, K2 and the North Face of Everest.

Food fantasies are a common torture on climbing expeditions and why climbers persist in tormenting themselves by talking about food they cannot have until they return to civilisation, I do not know. On this expedition there would be no such problems. Helen Wilton, our BC manager, took great pride in overseeing the preparation of every lavish meal and she had a shopping list of fresh vegetables, meat, bread and the occasional beer brought in on a weekly basis. As this was my first luxury expedition, I was determined to make the most of the food, but I met tough competition from Lou Kasischke, a US attorney with numerous ascents of the world's smaller but better known mountains to his credit. He liked his food as much as his climbing, and as he had a big engine to run it was usually Lou who won the silent battle over the last piece of tomato or dollop of chocolate mousse.

With the spring climbing season in full swing a record number of teams had gathered at the southern side of the mountain. It represented an enormous social scene which I normally enjoy but on a much smaller scale. Catching up with old friends and making new ones is part of the social activities at BC. But with any community of between 100 to 150 people there are inflated reputations, egos, one upmanship and the inevitable false rumours. These elements I deplore in such a fine setting and I purposely avoided them by keeping to myself.

BC had more home comforts than I was used to. A hot shower on call was just one of the many luxuries. It only made it difficult to leave and start up the hill. These comforts were thanks to Rob's meticulous planning and Helen, who took care of everything each time we came off the mountain. Caroline MacKenzie was our qualified doctor and at any given time of the day she could be seen treating someone, often from other teams. Her speciality, to use another doctor's expression, was coughs, colds and sore holes.

I had now been away from home for two months and I took full advantage of the phone and fax on a daily basis. This alone made being apart for so long a little more bearable. Little did we know what a key role our small phone would play towards the end of the climb.

Beck Weathers, a pathologist from Texas, and I had something in common—we liked to start the day with an early breakfast. Often it would be only Beck and I enjoying an early bite together in the BC mess tent. Without doubt Beck had the gift of the gab and my only opportunity to change the subject would come when someone else entered the mess tent. His unmistakable southern accent could often be heard on the mountain while he climbed—a considerable talent at altitude.

I first met Doug Hansen the year before when Veikka and I shared the same BC area while attempting to climb Lhotse. It was his second opportunity to attempt Everest with Rob. He had previously reached the South Summit but was forced to turn around due to bad weather. This time he was determined to climb the last 80 metres.

Jon Krakauer was a journalist on assignment for an American outdoor magazine. With considerable climbing experience at lower altitudes, his brief was to cover the increase in popularity of commercial expeditions to the world's highest mountains. Jon certainly had a way with words as his sign on our BC toilet shows. YO! Dude! If you are not a member of The New Zealand Everest Expedition Please don't use this toilet. We are a way serious bunch of shitters, and will have no trouble filling this thing up without your contribution. Thanks, The Big Cheese.

Despite popular public belief that Everest has become a giant rubbish dump modern day climbers have taken it upon themselves to clean up the rubbish left behind by expeditions who believed no-one would be following in their footsteps. Everest is cleaner now than it has been for a long time. Every expedition is obliged to take out what it takes onto the mountains otherwise heavy fines are enforced. In the case of our expedition we included the removal of human waste from BC.

Rounding out our team of eight clients were Frank Fischbeck and Yasuka Namba. Frank was a middle-aged Hong Kong publisher who seemed to be very much at ease with climbing Everest. He had attempted it 3 times before. I liked his reserved manner and after sharing a tent with him at C1 I discovered he was a real gentleman.

Yasuko Namba was a Japanese woman of feather weight build and gritty determination. She was the hardest to get to know. Although everyone tried to draw her into a conversation she responded with limited English. At times I felt for her, hoping she wasn't a raving extrovert bursting to have a conversation with someone.

The heavy work for our team settled on the shoulders of the strongest Sherpas around. The team of Lhakpa Chiri, Kami, Arita,

Norbu, and Chuldrum were led by Ang Dorje. Over the next four weeks our group of individuals grew to become a harmonious team.

Scott Fischer's American expedition and ours had decided to team up for a combined effort in the belief that we would make a powerful force in trail-breaking to the summit. We met to finalise a date both teams could work towards for a summit attempt. As we discussed the next five or six days, it seemed increasingly likely that 10 May was the big day. As it happened, Rob and I considered the 10th to be our lucky date. Rob had summited Everest twice on that day, and I had summited a collection of the world's highest mountains on that day too.

Frank Fischbeck and I were the last to arrive at C4 late in the afternoon of 9 May, having spent most of the day climbing up from C3. It was windy on the South Col with light snow falling; this did not surprise me, nor was it cause for concern for our summit attempt beginning at 11.30 p.m. Although the day had started off under exhausting conditions weighed down with a heavy pack of personal gear plus rope and oxygen bottles, once I started to breathe bottled oxygen from midday onwards, the climb became a cruise. I experienced little of the stress I was used to when climbing without it, and I could see how climbers who become dependent on bottled oxygen can run off the rails when the supply abruptly runs out.

Arita, the designated cook at C4, shared a tent with Chuldum to prepare the basic noodle soup and cups of tea. It was far easier for them to do this and pass the mugs of hot drinks from door to door than each tent try to do their own. Ang Dorje, Lhakpa, Chiri, Kami, Norbu and Chuldum would accompany us to the summit.

The calm that I was hoping for arrived a couple of hours before our departure. Rob asked me to lead. We aimed to keep our eight climbers, three guides and five Sherpas within a distance of 100 metres from front to back. Ang Dorje, our head Sherpa, explored the climbing route ahead of us. Scott Fischer's group of a similar size would leave fifteen to twenty minutes after us. Frank had been considering an early failure for the last 24 hours but I had urged him to at least make a start for the summit in the hope that he might find some new lease of energy and motivation as I had done on previous attempts. Frank's gut feeling told him that today was not the day. He turned back early in the night, too tired to continue, but the rest plodded on in the light of a half moon and the occasional flurries of snow.

Certain landmarks prompted memories of my 1993 ascent and the debilitating cold which at the time froze any thought of reaching the summit. Now with oxygen I was comfortably warm and progress was relatively easy. At some stage, surrounded by many of the summits I had climbed, I marvelled at the luck which the 10th had brought me. On the eastern horizon was Kangchenjunga, climbed on 10 October 1987; then Everest, climbed on 10 May 1993; around the corner, Cho Oyu, climbed on 10 May 1990; and now, with the coming of dawn, 10 May 1996 was shaping up to be another great day. I quickly reprimanded myself for using luck to climb on. So brilliantly clear was the dawn that I stopped frequently to take in the view, something I was rarely able to do in 1993 when I could barely find the energy to take the next step.

This climbing was fun, and when we broke out into sunshine on the crest of the South East Ridge, I must confess feeling so confident that I put the summit 'in the bag'. We changed our oxygen cylinders and the sun was so warm I could change mine with bare hands.

Rob's arrival on the ridge meant we were together again as a team. Everyone had coped well with the pre-dawn hours, which psychologically can be the toughest, and after a long rest we set off for the steepest part of the climb to the South Summit. It was such a great day that it was almost deceitful in its promise of continuing good weather.

Summit fever. I have seen it in others on many occasions and have experienced it personally on my earlier climbs. Sometimes it can be the boost needed for that final push to the summit but often it can be a dangerous state with fatal consequences. Yasuko had told me she was well known in Japan and hoped to emulate her country-woman, Junko Tabei, the first woman and the only Japanese woman to have climbed Mount Everest. I could see signs of summit fever in Yasuko's eyes and actions. I worried that her overwhelming desire to climb this mountain could end up killing her if she ran her race before her time. I purposely climbed in front of her to impose a more suitable pace.

The oxygen mask and goggles cover most of your face and hide your true feelings and expressions. All morning I had been bothered by bad stomach cramps. They were growing so bad, I was regularly doubled over in pain. To everyone else it would have looked like the normal resting position for high-altitude climbing, leaning heavily on your ice axe for support. It was becoming a threat to my position as a guide and my summit chances. Some members of the Fischer group, including the guide, Neal Beadleman, had passed us while we changed our oxygen cylinders. At the base of a steep rise leading directly to the South Summit we caught up to Neal who was about to fix a rope to this difficult section. I intended to help uncoil the rope for Neal and belay him but a sudden attack of stomach cramps stopped me in my tracks. Bent over in pain I seriously contemplated heading down. 'Tie this end to something solid will you,' yelled Neal as he tossed the end of the rope. It fell across my back as I was fearing losing control of my bowels. Impatient at my seemingly unhelpful attitude Ang Dorge snatched up the rope from my back and secured it to something solid. Fifteen minutes later I started up the rope that Neal had just fixed. I was feeling marginally better. It was 10.00 a.m. when I arrived at the South Summit. Jon was not far behind and while I waited I passed on the good news of our progress and position to Helen and Caroline who were monitoring our radio calls at BC now 3.2 kilometres below us. I remarked to Jon that we had only 80 metres to go; in fact, we could almost see the summit. I was barely able to control my temptation to push on. Rob, however, wanted us to regroup at the South Summit and assess the situation from there. Yasuko arrived next, followed by Andy, with Rob and Doug not far behind, but the steep unrelenting climb to the South Summit had taken its toll. Two hundred metres below us Stuart, John and Lou had reached their highest point at around 8600 metres before descending with one of our Sherpas. I felt sad for my friend John but he had climbed as far as he could and that is all one can hope for. I hoped he could salvage some satisfaction from this fantastic day we were experiencing. At this stage I don't remember any comment on Beck. He had, however, succumbed to problems with his sight and Rob had instructed him to stay near where we first changed our oxygen bottles until we returned. The attrition rate for both teams had been very high by the time we reached the South Summit. As the remaining members of both teams regrouped there, they became well and truly mixed together and it was difficult to tell who was who behind the oxygen mask and goggles.

The standing arrangement was that both teams of Sherpas would swap leads in fixing the sections of rope on the trickier sections. This system had not worked with Ang Dorge doing most of the trail breaking and Neal fixing the odd piece of rope. The Sherpa from the Fischer group had not materialised so at the South Summit Ang Dorge, and rightly so, considered he had done his share and refused to do any more. The question now seemed to be who was going to relent and do that little bit more. The sections to fix were not overly difficult with only a couple of short sections between us and the summit and I felt inclined to fix them myself, but Rob had given me instructions not to get involved. He would rather I stayed with our group. Precious minutes ticked by at the accountable rate of 2 litres of oxygen per minute. A rest of fifteen minutes was acceptable, given the time of day, but it was now starting to extend past that. I fought an internal battle, should I ignore Rob's instructions not to fix ropes and for the team to regroup at the South Summit by heading for the summit now? The wind was also playing heavily on my mind, it had increased in strength making it difficult to decide if we should go up or down. Repeated calls on the radio to Rob for help to answer my dilemma were met with silence. No doubt he was climbing in the transmission shadow cast by the South Summit. Finally the problem was solved when Neal and Anatoli, two guides from the American team, decided to fix the ropes themselves.

Another call to Rob revealed he was just below the South Summit and he said those of us waiting should go on up to the summit. I had been watching Jon who reminded me a little of myself, although I never really got to know him. For an American he was quiet, almost reserved. It seemed he preferred to listen and think about an ongoing conversation, contributing a little only if he had to. During our forced delay on the South Summit Jon and, to a lesser degree, Andy could not hide their eagerness to continue. I knew the feeling well from 1993, but this year I had none of that driving ambition. Andy, with his usual thoughtfulness for others, suggested Jon and I should go on ahead but I knew the importance of an Everest summit for Andy and told him to go instead. The two of them would make short work of the distance to the summit; besides, he had some rope which might be useful above the Hillary Step. This would leave me to discuss with Rob my concern about the rest of us continuing. Yasuko had slowed dramatically leaving me to wonder if she had the strength and speed to reach the summit before our turn around time of 1.00 p.m. Doug was certainly dragging the chain too. Rob remained out of radio contact.

The wind on the South Summit continued to increase but was certainly very mild compared to the wind on the summit ridge of Kangchenjunga. I was checking the oxygen supply in Yasuko's bottle when Rob arrived. 'Where are the others?' he asked.

Had he forgotten our chat just a few minutes earlier or had I misunderstood him? I pointed in the direction of the Hillary Step and offered no explanation for letting Andy and Jon go ahead, preferring instead to change the subject.

'What about this wind?' I asked. He considered my question carefully before he answered.

'It'll be all right, provided it doesn't get any worse. Why don't you and Yasuko go to the summit, while I wait for Doug. He's not far behind.'

The corniced and narrow ridge connecting the South Summit to the Hillary Step seemed more difficult this year than I remembered it, perhaps because there was less snow, so we took our time over this airy traverse. Every foot placement had to be spot on and backed up with our ice axes driven as deeply as possible into the hard-packed snow. Yasuko had regained her gritty determination and by the time we had overcome the final obstacle of the Step itself, Andy and Jon were returning from the summit. Meeting them on the narrows of the summit ridge created a delicate passing manoeuvre and Andy wanted to make our meeting even more memorable by greeting me with the 'high five'. He was justifiably pleased with his summit and he knew we were only minutes away from ours. His parting words were lost in the confines of his oxygen mask.

Yasuko and I went on to summit at around 2.15 p.m., just ahead of some members of the other team. The view did not compare with the morning's but it was still better than in 1993. The usual low-level cloud for this time of the day had flooded the valleys as the warm air of the plains rose to meet the cold air of the mountains. Yasuko's spirited arrival at the summit meant she had now reached the highest points on all the seven continents. I was pleased for her but personally felt little emotion. The summit had come too easily this time with the use of oxygen, and even though Everest was the highest point in the world, it felt like just another summit. I was not even interested in taking photos, but Yasuko was, so I tried to capture the moment for her: a panoramic shot of her sitting on the summit and a second filling the frame with her delighted smile.

Rob arrived on the summit as we were packing up, and he said that Doug was not too far behind. I gained some pleasure from this unrewarding achievement by shaking Rob's hand. In the short time we had known each other I had always enjoyed our partnership in the mountains and we had become good friends. I had purposely left the pleasure of speaking to Helen and Caroline for Rob as I knew that this moment was one of the highlights for Helen in her role as BC manager. No doubt they had already received a call from Andy and Jon and were waiting for the final summit tally so they could contact our family and friends. Once Rob had broadcast the good news, Yasuko and I started down as it was becoming quite crowded on the summit with five or six of the other team arriving. Rob would follow with Doug. As Rob predicted we met Doug not far below the summit just above the Hillary Step. I slapped Doug's shoulder in encouragement and said the summit was 80 metres up the gently sloping ridge. It would come into view around the next corner and from there there would be no stopping him. It has been reported that Doug didn't reach the summit until after 4.00 p.m. This meant that Rob would have waited on the summit for another one and a half hours and presumably for a lot of that time watching Doug shuffle agonisingly slowly towards the summit.

Yasuko handled the descent to the South Summit with much more ease than the ascent. I was not so lucky. Halfway down the abseil of the Hillary Step I was caught with an acute urge to have a pee. Looking down to the fly of my climbing-suit, I saw the long cord attached to the zipper was tangled in a mixture of harness straps and buckles. Bent over double I waited in vain for the urgency to pass. I would have to abseil to the bottom of the Step and untie as quickly as possible. But in my haste I lost control and a pleasantly warm flood trickled down the inside of both legs, mainly to the left boot. I realised my left foot was the warmest it had been all day. I suffered none of the embarrassment of my childhood pants-wetting days, but I did worry that any icicles dangling from the crotch of my climbing-suit might raise Yasuko's curiosity! Thanks to modern-day fabrics, nothing could be seen.

Every second step squelched to the sound of a boot full of urine; I may have found this amusing, if it were not for finding Jon slumped on the ridge beneath the Hillary Step. He was in a very distressed state, having run out of oxygen—a crippling event at such altitude, made even more critical for Jon when Andy told him there was no more. This comment by Andy signalled that he was also affected by oxygen deprivation. I unplugged my bottle and connected it to Jon's hose. The benefit was almost instantaneous and the three of us continued to join Andy on the South Summit. Here I easily located our eight bright orange cylinders that we had stashed for our return. It would have been easy for Andy, in oxygen debt and in the euphoria of a post-Everest summit, to mistake full cylinders for empty as there is little noticeable difference in weight. However, I knew that Andy was behaving irrationally and I was keen to get him back on oxygen as soon as possible. I expected the same remarkable return to normality as I had seen from Jon just a half hour earlier.

At any other place in the world these full cylinders may have been looked upon as scrap metal or useless pieces of junk, but at the second highest summit in the world, they were priceless and they represented a return ticket to the real world below. I carefully distributed the cylinders to Andy, Jon and Yasuko as if they were new-born babies. This left four full ones in the stash for Rob, Doug and two of our Sherpas, Ang Dorje and Norbu, who were now accompanying Rob. My priority for attention was for Andy, I wanted to turn Andy's flow rate up to the maximum of 4 litres a minute for five minutes so he could recover, but I was distracted by Yasuko who fumbled with her cylinder dangerously close to the edge. Her tiny hands had difficulty grasping the cylinders so I helped her change. After this I was distracted again from helping Andy by Jon who wanted me to check the flow rate on his regulator which should have been on 2 litres a minute but was on 4 litres, which explained why he had run out prematurely. By now Andy had his mask on and things seemed to be under control. I still wanted to check with him but I had now been without oxygen for some time and felt it was important for me to get back on the Os.

Many months after this climb someone asked me how I could function without bottled oxygen while everyone around me couldn't. I put this down to the fact that I had done so much climbing above 8000 metres without bottled oxygen that my system could cope better than theirs when the oxygen was gone. I also, therefore, didn't have the emotional dependency on oxygen. This was the first time I had used oxygen above 8000 metres; for the others it was their first time above 8000 metres.

With everyone appearing to be comfortable with their new bottle of oxygen I stood up to see Rob's lanky figure standing patiently at the top of the Hillary Step waiting for someone to clear the ropes. Doug was standing there too, leaning heavily on his ice axe and no doubt Ang Dorje and Norbu weren't too far away. They were in for a long wait as five or six of the Fischer group were in the process of abseiling the Hillary Step. I waved to Rob, who acknowledged with the thumbs-up signal; this visual contact between the guides was common and a short wave of the hand had meant the situation surrounding them was under control. We could have easily used our radios to do this, but we were constantly out of breath, and when we had a clear sighting of each other, a simple hand signal was all that was needed. Satisfied everything was in control, I turned to Andy and said, 'Let's get out of here. Rob and Doug are just above the Hillary Step and they are going OK.'

'Go ahead. I'll follow you in a minute,' said Andy, who seemed to be in no hurry to move. Again I should have checked on him more closely but now there seemed to be nothing outwardly unusual about his behaviour.

Yasuko and Jon followed me off the South Summit and we lost height quickly and so our line of sight to Andy, Doug and Rob. Just 70 metres above the point on the South East Ridge where we had exited from the gullies that dropped to C4, the radio inside my climbing-suit came to life with Rob's voice. I let Jon and Yasuko continue while I listened intently. He wanted to know where the spare oxygen bottles had been left on the South Summit. Before I could transmit, Andy, from wherever he was at the time, replied that there were none left on the South Summit. This I knew to be incorrect as I had personally checked and stacked the remaining four full bottles in a conspicuous place on the South Summit. I replied quickly. 'Rob, listen to me. This is Michael. I have left four bottles for you at the South Summit. Do you understand?' There was no reply. Repeated transmissions failed, only Andy's and Rob's confusing conversations could be heard. On many occasions earlier in the expedition I had spent idle minutes chatting on my radio but now, when I needed it most, it failed me. I tried BC, then C2 and finally C4, but there was no response. After more calls Caroline at BC picked up my signal and said she would pass on my message on her clear line of transmission to Rob. Content that everything was under control, I caught up to Yasuko and Jon and we continued descending with one of the Americans from Fischer's team, who was trying an unorthodox passing move in an uncontrolled tumble off to our left. From where I stood he looked out of control and in no hurry to regain it, preferring instead to slide happily towards the edge and into Tibet. He stopped abruptly in an explosion of white from a thick bed of snow 30 metres below us with no sign of injury. Jon was anxious to keep moving, so I told him and Yasuko to go ahead while I helped the American. They had only just left on their way down the gullies to C4, when on my way over to the stunned American, I picked up Rob's call again for oxygen. I did not understand why there was still so much confusion. I waited with my gloved finger poised over the call button ready to steal some time in between the now desperate calls between Rob, Andy and BC. It was obvious that my radio was not working properly as conversations dropped in and out. It was not the batteries, as I had changed them the day before. Whether it was my position on the mountain or something more technical than that, I couldn't tell. After persistent tries in between their conversations I eventually got through to Rob. I once again repeated the position of the oxygen bottles. I reassured him they were there. He seemed, however, quite convinced they weren't. He begged for help and I replied that I was on my way back up. It would take hours to get to him. I yelled to the American that the trail he needed to be on was over near me and then started to climb. It was 4.30 p.m.

I had climbed 100 metres. There was a light wind and snow fell softly settling on my shoulders. Above me I saw two people descending fast and for a few minutes I felt relieved as I believed them to be Rob and Doug—they must have found the oxygen and everything was okay. It wasn't. Our Sherpas, Ang Dorje and Norbu, materialised out of the falling snow. I asked if they had seen Rob, Doug or Andy, but they hadn't seen them since the South Summit.

'What about the oxygen? Is it still on the South Summit?'

Ang Dorje replied. 'Yes. Two cylinders are still there. We have two full ones with us.' His response only confirmed what I already knew and I wished it could be as simple as that for Rob. I had left four bottles up there. Ang Dorje and Norbu now had two of those four. Rob and Doug only needed the remaining two. I couldn't understand why they had not found them. I asked Ang Dorje where he had collected their two bottles.

'Same place as this morning,' he replied.

I grabbed my radio. Thankfully it worked and I told Rob exactly where the bottles were. This time Rob did not seem so stressed and his immediate problem seemed to be solved. He only had to traverse 30 or 40 metres to the stash of oxygen on the South Summit, whereas I would need to climb up 200 metres to get the cylinders. If Rob now knew where the cylinders were, I saw no sense in continuing up, so I followed Ang Dorje and Norbu in their hasty descent. The fact that they had been with Rob and had come down indicated that things weren't as desperate as I thought they might have been. On reflection, I believe my call to Rob came at a moment when things were coming slightly back under control for him. There was a calmness in his voice and perhaps Andy, who was closer to Rob than me, had returned to the South Summit to help. He was certainly more lucid. However, it was never going to be quite that simple. Rob and Doug had been without oxygen for far too long and the three of them were still extremely high at a depressingly late hour of the day.

It continued to snow. Lower down the ridge the American who had passed us with such haste was amazingly only just getting to his feet after all this time and moving again, veering dangerously close to the wrong side of the mountain in a series of drunken flops into the snow, one of which could end up over the edge into Tibet. I detoured off my path to get close enough to speak with him. I could see that his oxygen mask had slipped off beneath his chin and clumps of ice hung from his eyebrows and chin. Lying half-buried in the snow, he was giggling—a result of oxygen debt to the brain. I told him to pull his oxygen mask over his mouth. In a fatherly sort of manner I then coaxed him closer and closer to the ridge crest, and as I did so I was interrupted by calls from BC. Every attempt to respond failed and from then on I heard no further talk on the air waves.

With the American now following me closely, we continued down the ridge a little way until we reached the exit point into the gullies that led down to C4. 'Now, see those two climbers down there in red? Just follow them,' I said pointing to Jon and Yasuko still visible in the gully below. He stepped off the ridge in such a haphazard manner, I wondered whether he cared if he lived or died. Concerned about his judgement, I decided to stick with him. All this time Beck Weathers had gone unnoticed standing beside me.

'Is that you, Mike?' The Texan accent startled me. Beck was camouflaged perfectly in a light sprinkling of fresh snow. He must have been standing still for some time, judging by the amount of snow that had settled on him. He looked like a tatty scarecrow, his bulky down suit pushing his arms awkwardly out to the sides.

'What are you doing here, Beck? I thought you would have been well and truly back at C4 by now.'

'I can't see, Mike. I have been waiting for you to come down.' He didn't have to say any more. I knew we were in trouble when I looked into his blank and unfocused eyes.

'How bad is it, Beck? Can you see anything at all?'

'Everything is a blur. I can't seem to focus,' said Beck in a remarkably calm voice, considering our position.

'Okay, Beck. We'll see how you go on this first bit, which is fairly easy. I have a rope if you can't manage. Follow me if you can.'

A year or so earlier Beck had had radial keratotomy to improve his failing vision. The sudden drop in barometric pressure, however, severely impaired his now delicate eyes.

Within the first few metres I knew I had a difficult task on my hands to get us both down alive as Beck fell over twice on easy ground. I pulled a rope from my pack and hastily tied it to Beck's harness because from here on the gully became much steeper and more difficult to negotiate. Just 2 metres of tight rope separated us, and just one wrong move separated us from certain death. I directed our progress from behind, 'Left! Right! Stop!' were the only words I used for the next couple of hours as Beck often balanced dangerously close to walking over the edge with many a step into thin air. I tried to predict his falls by bracing myself and driving my axe deep into the snow. This worked well, considering my disadvantage in weight—64 kilograms to Beck's 80 plus. On several occasions, however, caught on bare rock slabs, I was pulled forwards, my crampons scraping across the rock, and only just managed to stop Beck from toppling over the edge. There was no doubt that I was more nervous than Beck, for he could not see the exposure below us. I knew if there was any lapse in my concentration, Beck would pull us both over the edge. For one instant I thought of my friend, Lobsang, who had fallen from around here in 1993. I quickly put it out of my mind.

For hours I shouted my instructions to Beck as we weaved our way down through the endless rock and ice gullies. It was just on dark when we stumbled thankfully onto the easy snow slopes that led to C4, but they were still steep enough for Beck to sit and slide while I lowered him. I stopped for a few seconds to get a bearing on C4; we now looked across to it rather than down on top of it. Under normal conditions it would have taken half an hour, but for us it would be at least an hour. Here a few members of the Fischer group caught up with us, the only one that I knew being Neal Beidleman.

By now Beck was exhausted. It was still snowing and in the last few minutes of fight I got my visual direction on C4. If we kept our bearing, we would walk straight into it, but the distractions were many as I shouldered a good deal of Beck's weight to try to make any sort of progress. The falling snow now had a sting to it brought about by a steadily increasing wind, and with Beck's regular requests for a rest I soon lost any sense of C4's position.

A few metres further on we came across Yasuko sitting in the snow. Neal had found her first and was removing her oxygen mask as her supply, like ours, had run out. No amount of persuasion could convince her that she had run out as she persisted in putting her mask back on, which only suffocated her more. Finally we ripped the straps from her mask and shoved it into her pack. Thankfully Neal and his group were able to descend with her, while I continued very slowly with Beck. Visibility was now down to a few metres as high winds lashed the upper slopes of Everest and with it came the energy-sapping cold. I was afraid we would lose sight of the others.

'Come on, Beck. We have to keep up with the others,' I yelled.

'Mike, I need to rest. Just a short rest,' he begged.

I relented, silently cursing with every second that passed. Beck was going nowhere without a rest. Meanwhile the others were moving further away from us.

Quickly the situation became critical: we lost sight of Neal's group and any shouting to contact them was carried off by the wind. Beck and I were alone. I had done everything I could to keep up with the others, but our pace was far too slow. I sat Beck down as the 70 to 80-kilometre-per-hour winds threatened to blow us off our feet and snow stung my eyes, temporarily blinding me. At best I could see 3 or 4 metres. I used my radio to call C4 but there was no reply on my useless piece of junk; nevertheless I continued my transmission in the hope that they could hear me. Even if they did respond it would have been difficult to hear them above the roar of the wind. We wanted a direction, a light, a voice, a familiar sound, anything to help guide us in.

It's not in my nature to beg, but that night I begged Beck to keep moving—every minute we delayed for a rest put another nail in our coffins. The wind was increasing rapidly and the temperature was dropping to an unbearable level. I shouldered Beck's weight for as long as I could, now ignoring his requests to stop in our relentless pursuit for shelter. Again I tried calling C4 on my radio; still there was no reply. A beam of light flashed in front of us; for a moment I thought it was help from C4, but as we came closer we found Neal and Yasuko who were as confused as we were. Neal was trying to regroup his team who had scattered in all directions. You didn't have to go far in these conditions to be totally lost. Slowly they regrouped and I allowed Beck to sit. I did not get involved in the yelling match about where C4 was—I was just as confused as the rest of them. My only contribution was a request that we all stay together and there was a unanimous agreement. Finally a direction was agreed upon and Neal led off hopefully; it was as good a direction as any. Beck leaned heavily on my shoulder—he could lean as much as he liked, so long as I could keep us both moving.

When I tripped over two old oxygen bottles, my spirits soared; we were obviously close to C4 and I told Beck this. Only a couple of head-torches were working now, and their criss-crossing beams often silhouetted the distressing sight of clumsy figures struggling to stay upright. I tried not to think that Beck and I would have looked equally pitiful. Neal stopped to allow us to catch up, all the time encouraging his team-mates to stay together and to keep moving. He asked if I had any idea of the direction of C4, but I confessed that I didn't as the constant attention to Beck and the white-out conditions had distracted any sense of it. Others also voiced their opinion, but they often conflicted. Today, looking back, I realise we had staggered depressingly close to C4 before veering away in the opposite direction.

I struggled with Beck but the dread of losing the others was enough incentive to keep moving. I was tempted to try my radio again but the fact that it had been malfunctioning made me think it was a waste of time. We continued to chase the others in their search. Up front the two leaders had come to an edge, their head-torches shining into a black void. Between us and them lay four or five exhausted climbers, some were kneeling, some had collapsed and were lying motionless in the snow. The edge marked the most significant landmark we had found in the last couple of hours, but was it the edge leading into Nepal or was it the edge dropping into Tibet? No-one knew, although there were some wild guesses. The situation was seriously grim now. Beck had lost one of his gloves, leaving a bare hand exposed to the elements; I searched in the snow and rocks in the immediate area, but no doubt the wind had carried it off, so I gave him mine and then checked on Yasuko. She was still standing, still keen to push on, but she was incoherent, unable to tell left from right. Now I had a chance to use my radio. It worked! Stuart answered my call from C4. I asked him which direction the wind was blowing from at C4, as it might help me get some idea of where we were on the South Col. If I had been warm and rested with a sea level supply of oxygen, I would have easily made use of the small amount of information he was able to give me, but tonight it made little sense at all. Once Stuart had picked up my call, he wasted no time in coming out to look for us, banging metal and shining his head-torch in wild arcs into the night sky to give us the best chance of seeing him. But he could only travel a short distance from camp for fear of becoming hopelessly disoriented too. Stuart tried desperately to find us before having to return to his tent to recover from the cold. He came back out time and time again, but all to no avail.

I moved closer to the edge to look for any clues. There was nothing but a black hole where only the wind dared to go. It could easily have been the edge of the earth. I stepped back quickly; it was no place to stand braced against the gale. For a moment I paused, confused. I had to try to think of a new plan of action but that action was more or less decided for us, because lying on the rocks at our feet were the pitiful figures of three or four climbers who had been pushed beyond their limit with the torments of the cold and exhaustion. We desperately needed to find C4, but we were going nowhere, we had nowhere to go. Neal yelled to a couple of his team-mates who were still standing to lie low to try to shelter from the bitterly cold wind that was showing us no mercy. He asked if I agreed with his decision to shelter as best we could and I nodded my agreement. There were maybe twelve of us altogether and Yasuko lay down among the other climbers on the rock and ice, tucking her hands in between her legs and pulling her knees up to her stomach. My fingers had long since stopped performing any delicate tasks and had become useless attachments. I grabbed a handful of Beck's clothing and pulled him to the ground beside me, unapologetic for the way I was handling him. I didn't want to lose sight of him now, as I doubted I had the energy to repeat any unnecessary action. Up until now the uncertainty of whether or not I'd find C4 had remained a finely balanced question but now the broad expanse of the South Col as jet stream winds blasted across it bringing crippling temperatures well below −40°C. Any sense of control over the elements was lost to me. I was trapped in a giant wind tunnel, that was equal to the most desolate place in the world.

I lay on my side in a small depression and pulled Beck in behind me to protect him from the wind. From this position he was able to put his frozen hands inside the chest pockets of my climbing-suit where I tried to rub some warmth into them. Although I had run out of oxygen some time before, I kept the mask on to protect my face from the cold. This prevented me from speaking clearly to anyone, but the wind made sure of that regardless. The wind was now unrelenting in its bid to drive the cold deeper into our bodies and for hours we shivered uncontrollably. I felt totally alone and, even though I had no intention of dying, my thoughts did turn negative from time to time. It did not bother me to think about it for I have had plenty of practice over the years. Unfortunately freezing to death doesn't happen quickly; it torments your mind and body with a slow and painful suffering for hours before finally showing some mercy in allowing you to go to sleep, never to wake again. For long and wandering periods I thought of Judi, and of our hot and humid holiday in Fiji just a few months earlier, when a sudden and uncontrollable shiver made me lurch from my rocky resting place. With this sudden movement came a terrible stinging pain to my right ear. I had been using my pack as a pillow and my ear had become glued to it with ice. I rubbed the palm of my gloved hand up and down the length of my pack to feel if the top part of my ear was stuck to the pack, but I came to the drowsy conclusion that I couldn't care less; it would be just another body part lost to frostbite. Now that I was sitting up, I had a look around, it looked like doomsday, everyone seemed dead until I heard some moaning coming from the motionless bodies scattered around me. Someone was crying, someone else was begging not to be left to die like this. I saw Yasuko shaking from the cold but otherwise lying silently behind one of the Americans. It was a hopeless situation and I lay back down, the pain from my ear being just another discomfort in the whole miserable affair. I tried to pretend it was only a nightmare, that it would all go away.

I tried my radio again, first to C4, then to BC, but no-one responded. I turned my attention to Beck.

'Beck, how are you going?'

'I'm very cold but I'm OK,' said Beck. His distinctive Texan accent was slurred and only just recognisable above the roar of the wind. For me it was a small but comforting thought to know he was still alive because I did not know how much longer I could last protecting Beck from the full force of the gale. I could only hope that Yasuko was equally protected in her hollow. It was a long night and I was starting to surrender to the temptation of eternal sleep.

Throughout the night the roar of the wind brought numerous false alarms when we thought someone had found us, which sent our small group into an excitable frenzy only to be miserably disappointed. It was after midnight when the alarm was raised again. I think it was Neal who saw it first and I rose, fully expecting to be disappointed again. A gap had appeared in the cloud that was whipping across the Col and left a short but adequate sighting onto the south-east slopes of Everest. To get a better view I had to break away the ice that hung from my eyebrows and around the rim of my hood. From this unmistakable landmark we were able to gain some idea of where we were in relation to C4. We were too far east—closer to Tibet than Nepal.

Neal gathered those in his team that could still walk and headed off in the direction he thought C4 should be in.

I pulled Beck to his feet. Yasuko had managed to get to her feet with the other climbers. Beck had lost his glove again and as my head-torch had expired because of the cold, I had to search the ground with my hands. Luckily I found it stuck to Beck's cramponed boots, otherwise it would have surely blown away with the wind. Beck suggested that if he had his head-torch on, the beam might give him some direction to focus on. I shoved my frozen hands into his pack in search of it, but it was a fruitless effort as my hands had no feeling.

All this had consumed precious minutes and by the time we were ready to move, the others were out of sight. Yasuko had tried to go with them but had collapsed not far in front of us. She stood up again, swaying precariously on her feet as if she had been hit with a knockout punch. Staring stubbornly into the teeth of the storm brought no answers for her. There were three more bodies in our vicinity sitting in the snow. At first I thought they were dead, but one of them started crying. It was a female voice and again I heard the plea. 'Don't leave me. I don't want to die here,' she begged.

I ignored the pleas for help as I fought against the wind to gather in Yasuko before she wandered off into the night.

By this time Yasuko had collapsed again, so I pulled her back onto her feet and removed the rim of ice around her hood so she could see. By now the three Americans had moved off and disappeared. I stretched Beck's left arm around my shoulder and supported his weight as best I could, but I had become so incredibly weak in the last few hours that we swayed like two old drunks. Yasuko fell yet again. Leaving Beck to stand unsupported like a statue, I picked up Yasuko; this time as I stood her up, her arms moved in a swimming fashion, so I pulled them down to her side and held them there, yelling at her to follow Beck and me. 'Camp Four is not far away,' I said for encouragement, but I doubt she understood me. I still had no idea where C4 was.

The three of us began to move, leaning heavily into the full force of the gale. After a few metres Beck needed to rest. This time I was thankful as he was becoming far too heavy for me to support any longer. Yasuko stumbled and fell face down. I didn't dare let go of Beck as I knew I would not have the strength to lift him to his feet again.

'Come on, Yasuko. Keep moving. Follow me,' I yelled, but I expected little response from her. None of us was able to walk a straight line as we teetered on the edge of total exhaustion. Only the recent sighting of the upper slopes of Everest gave me some motivation to keep trying. Step by step we moved on if ever so slowly.

We had been out in the elements for twenty-six hours and I doubted we could last much longer. If the wind increased its intensity, it would bring the wind chill factor down to an unbearable level and this would finish us off quickly. Beck, Yasuko and I had stumbled just 15 metres when we encountered the three Americans again, two of them had fallen to the ground and the other was pleading with them to keep moving. Here Yasuko stumbled and fell. The American male and I both knew that we were not going to make it under these dreadful conditions and he asked if I could go and find C4 and bring back help. I hesitated, pretending for a second or two that I hadn't heard his request, but it seemed like our only chance for survival.

Yasuko was now lying motionless behind us; Beck stood, barely, and my fellow path-finder had his two companions lying semi-conscious in the rock and snow. I only agreed to go on the condition that all of them stayed put and did not separate. The American agreed and I slapped Beck hard across his shoulder to make sure I had his attention before I explained my request.

'Stay here with Yasuko. Don't let these people out of your sight.' I immediately felt stupid, as I had forgotten Beck could not see.

'OK,' mumbled Beck. I repeated my request to the more able-bodied American. It was even more important that he understood my instructions concerning Beck's and Yasuko's condition.

My frozen hands made it extremely difficult untying the rope that bound me to Beck. I was very reluctant to leave Beck and Yasuko behind while I went in search of help. The short piece of rope had forced Beck and me to work as a unit and now I felt I was giving up on him. On the other hand it was our only choice, if anyone was to survive. I propped Yasuko up against a rock. Of all of us she was probably the closest to death. I yelled my instructions to stay with Beck and the others directly into her face. She nodded agreement but she didn't stop nodding as I walked away—I doubted she had understood any of it.

I drew on the limits of my reserves to make some headway into the wind. I leaned heavily into the gale and protected my eyes from the high-velocity ice particles that had the sting of a thousand needles. It dawned on me that the people I had just left could well be the lucky ones. Perhaps the others who had left us about twenty minutes earlier had already found C4 and were sending back help; perhaps I would be the one who remained lost and alone; perhaps in the near-zero visibility I would walk over the edge, never to be seen again. I had no idea where I was going and every second rock looked like the outline of a tent.

My crampons skidded uncontrollably across the rocky terrain of the South Col; each stumble only confused my sense of direction even more. At some stage I stopped and stared at two head-torch lights bobbing and weaving high up on Everest, somewhere in the vicinity of the gullies that led down to C4. My immediate thought was that it was Rob and Doug making their way down, but on reflection I know it wasn't; I suspect I was longing for the lights to belong to them and therefore imagined it. In my lonely search I stopped to rest, believing I had been wandering for hours and that soon it would be morning. I even considered stopping altogether because I couldn't remember what I was searching for. By now I had lost all sense of urgency. I had forgotten about Beck, Yasuko and the others, the wind no longer bothered me and, worst of all, I felt comfortably warm. As far as my body temperature was concerned, I could not have been more seriously cold.

I wanted a nice place to sit and wait for morning. This special place couldn't be just anywhere; it had to be big enough for two of us. I sensed his powerful presence: Lobsang was with me now and we had a lot to talk about since we said goodbye on the summit ridge of Everest in 1993. As we looked for a place that would give us the best view of the sunrise, a sudden clearing in the turbulence of the wind-driven snow and ice extended my visibility to 40 or 50 metres.

'There it is!' I said to Lobsang. 'Over there!' I had just spotted the unmistakable outline of our wind-crushed tents at C4, and I suddenly remembered the reason I was here alone.

I don't know why but I went past the first tent, preferring instead to go to one in the middle of the huddle. There was a long moment of disbelief on both sides as I crouched outside the door belonging to Stuart and Jon. Did they know who the ice-encrusted apparition was? Or was I the one that was dreaming? I am not sure if I spilled out the speech that I had so carefully rehearsed in my mind during those crazy hours of wandering around on the Col. If I did say something, it probably sounded like a drunken slur. Whatever I said, I hoped I gave some accurate directions and instructions to help find Beck, Yasuko and the others.

I was convinced that as a result of whatever conversation took place between us, rescuers would be rounded up to help me get Beck and Yasuko back into camp. Somehow I was confronted with another closed tent door. Had Stuart closed the door on me to prevent the tent being filled with snow? Or had I just imagined my conversation? Or was this a different tent? If anything was clear to me at this moment, it was that I didn't have a clue where I was. I only remember kneeling outside the tent trying to unzip the door that I had thought was open. Stuart may have even directed me to my tent. It was a frustrating exercise in coordination, a skill I no longer had. If Stuart was playing a joke, it was a bad one. I yelled for help and Frank responded from inside the tent. I was trying to remember where the full oxygen bottles were to take back for Beck and Yasuko, but Frank operated with the efficiency of a battlefield medic and pulled me inside the tent. It was then I gave up trying. Frank swore at me and I thought he was abusing me for being late. Before I knew it I was being wrapped and buried in a sea of down sleeping-bags. The questions continued while he broke away the ice from around my face. If I answered them, I answered very few.

Everything seemed to be happening in slow motion, most likely because the cold had drained every ounce of energy. Speaking was difficult and confusing. I tried to sit up to answer a voice that I thought came from outside the tent—it was probably Stuart wanting to confirm directions for Beck and Yasuko—but I couldn't even find the strength to sit up. At some stage Frank went outside, leaving me in the hands of John, an anaesthetist by profession. I was not an easy patient for him that morning as I shook uncontrollably while he tried to keep an oxygen mask on my face. I settled down slowly, and in the belief that a search party had gone for the others.

The next thing I remember it was early morning on 11 May and high winds continued to batter our tent. I immediately looked for Yasuko, hoping to see her dark eyes peeping out from the bulk of her over-filled sleeping-bag, but there was nothing except a shambles of ice-encrusted gear littering our tent. John told me that Frank had gone to keep Lou company, as his tent-mates Beck, Doug, Andy and Rob were still missing. I asked what had happened to Beck and Yasuko—they should have been here by now—but John had no answer.

In the meantime I continued to drift in and out of reality, with one dreamlike conversation after another. The few real events I remember were John's persistent efforts to supply me with more and more drinks—a difficult task of coordination and strength. However, in the back of my mind I was still aware of those unaccounted for. I tried to gather my wits and strength to get up to at least look for Beck and Yasuko but John, who could judge my condition better than me, said there was nothing I could do. I suspect he knew everything that could be done in these dreadful conditions was being attempted.

It is my understanding that after alerting Stuart he set out alone to find Beck and Yasuko but once again, like so many times before, he found himself in danger of becoming hopelessly lost in the blizzard conditions. The guide Anatoli, who was Neal's counterpart in the Fischer group and who had returned to C4 from the summit by late afternoon, was alerted by Neal's desperate arrival at C4 with a few surviving members of his team. In a long and sweeping search of the South Col Anatoli found no-one and returned to the tent. Undaunted by his fruitless search he set out again. This time he found the three Americans, and Beck and Yasuko who lay motionless, he presumed they were dead.

At dawn Stuart and Lhakpa Chhiri went out in search of Beck and Yasuko. Later Lhakpa Chhiri and Ang Dorje made a determined but hopeless attempt to reach Rob, who was still trapped up at the South Summit. Too weak to move, Rob was known to be still alive due to his intermittent radio calls that had been picked up by BC and Jon and Stuart who had our spare radio.

Throughout the expedition I had felt uncomfortable about using the Sherpas to do the back-breaking work; their tireless efforts and cheerful attitude made me feel lazy and guilty. Without them our expedition would not have existed and they were as much a part of our team as anyone else. I found out that these rescue attempts were being made when I regained some degree of consciousness, and I was crushed by a heavy weight of guilt as I lay incapacitated in my tent. No amount of persuasion or money had made Stuart, Ang Dorje or Lhakpa Chhiri do what they were doing; it was their nature to do so.

I learnt later that the Fischer group had left C4 that morning in an effort to get to safer ground. How they made progress under those conditions, I do not know. Stuart and Jon had our only working radio in their tent and they kept Helen and Caroline at BC informed of our situation and of the high winds that continued at C4.

Jon thought he had last seen Andy Harris only a stone's throw from C4 just before 5.30 p.m. of 10 May, when Andy made a sudden turn to the right towards the Lhotse Face saying, as he disappeared, 'I'm going straight to BC.' Jon, however, has since changed his mind and thinks that, in the confusion of the moment, he saw someone else. An expedition that summited much later in May found Andy's ice axe at the South Summit. It is widely accepted that Andy was behaving abnormally from hypoxia and could easily have left the South Summit without his axe just as he believed there was no oxygen on the South Summit. However, I believe he returned to the South Summit to help Rob. This explains why Rob sounded in control of the situation when I made that final call to him from below the South Summit: Andy had returned to help. Sadly, we will never really know.

The struggle of someone wrestling his way into the tent woke me from my hazy existence. It was around mid-morning, 11 May. I was alarmed at the sight of Stuart, exhausted and wind blown. Above the roar of the wind that continued to hammer our tents he yelled out that he had found Beck and Yasuko. He said that in the time it took for him to return to the tent, Yasuko would most likely be dead but Beck might yet be alive. To make things worse, he said they were close to an edge, perhaps the Kangshung Face—not where I remembered leaving them. It was a risky proposition for anyone to venture out to get Beck. Stuart asked me what I wanted to do.

I was coherent enough to understand what was going on and the implications of Stuart's question. Without doubt it was the most difficult question I have ever been asked. Lhakpa Chhiri and Ang Dorje had been beaten back by violent winds higher up; Stuart had done everything he could for Beck. Who among us had the strength to go out again and operate a rescue? Was it worth risking other lives to rescue someone who would most likely be dead when found or would die soon after? I couldn't ask another to go if I couldn't go myself. This was the ruthless way I had to look at it. My priorities had to shift to the surviving members of our team. It was crucial for me to regain some control of the situation and get our team out of C4 and descending as soon as possible, otherwise more would die. John's antidotal comment about decisions being made in the Vietnam war to save the lives of surviving soldiers by abandoning their less fortunate and critically injured teammates was only mildly comforting.

Around early afternoon there was a lull in the gale, which allowed a rescue party to reach C4: Pete Athans and Todd Burleson were members of an independent expedition. Their mission was two-fold, to lend assistance to us and to try and rescue Rob. They tried to coax me into getting the rest of my team down to a lower camp, preferably to C2 as soon as possible. It was the correct decision but it was not possible—I was barely able to sit up in my sleeping-bag or think clearly, let alone descend to C2; also Lou was snow-blind. I nearly suggested that Pete and Todd take the remaining members down while I stayed, but Lou would most likely have to remain too and I did not know if I would improve enough by the morning to get myself moving and to help a blind person down. Both of us would need assistance, and we needed more time to recover to be able to help ourselves down. Time at this altitude, however, was also a killer. I asked Stuart to count the remaining full oxygen bottles. There were enough for the six remaining team members and our four Sherpas to survive one more night and descend the next day.

I explained our situation to Todd and Pete; considering the late hour of the day, I felt we would be moving too slowly with our disabilities to reach the safety of a lower camp before nightfall. I believed it was better for us get an early start the next morning. There was a risk, however, that the jet-stream winds might intensify and pin us down even longer at C4. I made the assumption that Lou and I would have recovered enough to be able to descend the next day without assistance and if the winds did increase, it would be up to the individual disabled climber to struggle down into the shelter of the Western Cwm without hindering the others. Pete and Todd reluctantly agreed to let us stay one more night and they set up a tent next to ours.

Around mid-afternoon Jon and Stuart brought the radio into my tent. They had been maintaining contact with Helen and Caroline at BC, who were relaying the information, most of it not good, to Madeleine, Rob's personal assistant at the office of his guiding company in New Zealand. It was not a clean and simple connection of two phones—all the guides had two-way radios which allowed us to speak to each other and to BC. At BC the incoming phone calls could be patched to the incoming two-way radio calls via the satellite phone. Madeleine then had the unenviable task of giving news of our individual team members to their families. I was warned by Jon that an earlier conversation with Rob, who was still trapped on the South Summit, had revealed that Doug had gone. No explanation was given, none was asked for; we all knew what it meant. When Rob came on line, all the radios between BC and C4 tuned into his channel. I managed to get through to him only once before I was cut off by another caller, and in a hopeless effort of persuasion to get him moving in our direction, I told him we were all waiting for him at C4 to come down. It was the last time I spoke to him and no amount of encouragement by anyone else could make Rob move. The radio conversation gave little hint of the real misery he was suffering. Why hadn't he made an effort to continue? Perhaps the answer lay in my own condition—exposure to the cold had sapped all my energy and the motivation to move. I thought of the time a couple of years earlier when Rob, Veikka and I had to fight our way down from the high camp on K2 in conditions similar to these. I was trying to think of what to say next when the radio crackled into life with the sound of Rob's wife, Jan, speaking via telephone from New Zealand. We listened for only a few seconds before turning off our radio. It was the last time I heard Rob's voice. Outside the deafening roar of the wind continued to trash our tents; inside a sad silence formed an uncomfortable barrier between us all. Rob was dying.

Murphy's Law prevailed. That night the terrible wind picked up in strength and it became the toughest night yet at C4. I placed my pack to the windward side of the tent and pushed hard with my feet to prevent the tent collapsing in on top of John and me. Much-needed sleep and rest were impossible under such conditions. Unlike earlier in the day I was now conscious and fully aware of our situation. My thoughts tended to wander between those who were missing or dead and our immediate danger. I already had all my gloves on to keep my frost-bitten hands warm and had tucked my boots into my sleeping-bag in case the weather turned into a full-on storm and the tent ripped open or was ripped from its tie-down points and blown away with us in it. Whose tent would we go to, if ours exploded like a balloon? What would we do if all the tents ripped open? Fortunately though, I had experienced far more serious storms than this, and I knew what to expect. I guessed the temperature to be −30°C and the winds to be blowing at 70 to 80 kilometres per hour. They had the potential to return to their normal velocity of over 200 kilometres per hour at any moment. A shrapnel cloud of ice and rock could shred the tents in minutes. If this happened, it would be no good praying. The emergency actions for our team's survival filled my mind until the cold, grey hours of dawn and the eventual subsidence of the life-threatening gale to nothing more than a nuisance.

It was 6.00 a.m. on 12 May. The wind had punished us severely for daring to stay another night at C4. Our once-cosy tent was a shambles of displaced food, drinks and frozen pee-bottles. John lay shaking in his ice-coated sleeping-bag. I assumed he was cold from the amount of ice on his bag, so offered him my down vest, but the cold wasn't the problem—he said he was worried about our chances of getting out of this mess alive. I assured him we would be on the move to safer ground in less than an hour and to start packing.

'Bring only the essentials. Abandon everything else and leave room in your pack for a full bottle of oxygen,' I said.

Before I put on my boots, I checked my feet for frostbite. I could see the tell-tale signs appearing on both feet, and the left was far worse because it had been swimming in my urine that had since frozen. Thumbs and fingers on both hands had more advanced frostbite, with the tips of some turning a dark blue-purplish colour.

I dressed and ventured out to the other tents to pass on the same message. My instructions were simple: be ready by 7.00 a.m. with a full bottle of oxygen. In passing from tent to tent, I saw that the night had been tough on the others as well by their bewildered faces: the last forty-eight hours had not been a bad nightmare but reality. I took in the devastation of our hostile environment—torn and twisted tents were everywhere and for a few moments I couldn't help but think of the others who were still unaccounted for, and I knew there would be casualties from other teams as well. For the moment, though, I had to deal with the more immediate problems. I only looked towards the summit of Everest once that day; it was still lashed by jet-stream winds. Somewhere between the summit and me were Doug, Andy, Rob, Beck and Yasuko—all dead. I didn't look that way again.

It took some time to speak to everyone as each tent had some little problem to sort out. Our team of Sherpas had been a strong and tireless bunch and had worked unselfishly to get us in a position to try for the summit, but now they showed signs of exhaustion and were understandably saddened by our losses. I was not used to having Sherpas on the mountain with me and because of this I knew just how much they had done for us. Now my only request was that they get down the mountain as far and as quickly as possible. Casting back the door of one tent I came face to face with Arita, bug-eyed with fear and alone with the disorder of his tent. His look of absolute terror scared me, causing me to deliver my instructions quickly, none of which he could understand. I called over Lhakpa Chhiri to help pacify Arita and explain the reason for my urgency. He soon resolved the misunderstanding I had caused. Lhakpa Chhiri, who is always good-spirited, rallied his team-mates into packing their belongings. It was a difficult and tricky path back to my tent: a tangled web of tent guy ropes formed a high-altitude obstacle course and it required considerable effort and coordination not to trip up. I was in mid-stride when something urged me to look in a particular tent.

There was no obvious reason to go to the tent as it belonged to the Fischer group, but I went anyway. It showed signs of having been left in a hurry as the doors at both ends of the tent flapped wildly, allowing the wind to tunnel through. Kneeling down to look inside I was confronted by a pair of climbing boots. At first I was startled by the sight of a body dressed in a red and black climbing-suit lying on its back, with a sleeping-bag covering the face and upper body. It was impossible to tell who it was by the clothing as every second climber was dressed in one of these particular climbing-suits. Besides I had no desire to know the true identity of this casualty of misadventure in the mountains—I had seen many like it over the years. Because the body was in the American team's tent, I believed that it belonged to one of the Fischer group. I called by Todd and Pete's tent to let them know that we would be heading down soon. Pete smiled, perhaps with a sigh of relief. It was a smile that I remember well as no-one had smiled in a long time and it helped relieve some of the pressure I was under. However, I startled Pete with the news of the dead climber I had just found. With no reply from him I returned to my tent to finish packing.

Everyone was ready: Lou, Frank, Jon, Stuart and John were crouched outside their tents making last-minute adjustments to buckles and straps, while Ang Dorje, Norbu, Lhakpa Chhirri, Arita, Chuldum and Kami finished the last of their packing. I had insisted that we abandon everything except our sleeping-bags. The clouds had cleared, leaving a bright but windy day. I guessed from previous experience on the South Col that we would be out of the worst of the wind by the time we dropped off the end of the Geneva Spur down to C3. Everyone was

moving slowly from exhaustion so I had plenty of time to pull out
the fixed rope that lay buried under the snow drifts. From our vantage point at 1.5 kilometres above the Western Cwn I could see the
entire length of the Cwm and I noticed some movement down near
C2—small black dots moving up towards C3. At about this same time
our Sherpa team overtook us and continued down to C3 and later to
C2, all in amazingly good spirits now that we were heading down.

The Yellow Band is the last obstacle before reaching C3 and it involved
a number of short abseils to reach the bottom. Here I let the others pass
so I could wait for Frank, who was the last in our line. Stuart and I shared
a small rocky ledge, both of us clipped in to the same anchor, waiting for
the rope to clear below us before Stuart began his abseil. Here he told
me the incredible news. Beck was alive at C4! I learnt that the partially
covered body I had found in the tent was Beck. Pete and Todd were
bringing him down. Stuart abseiled away from me shortly after this,
leaving me deeply upset and shaken. I was standing in roughly the
same place where I had been cleaned up by the avalanche in 1991; even
when you are used to it, it is still a dizzying fall from all that way to the
valley floor. Luck had been with me then as it had been with me during
the last two terrible days, but now as the missing pieces gradually fell in
place, I was regretting surviving at all. Stuart's reaction was one of relief
and happiness that Beck had miraculously survived; I was grateful too,
but I also felt a deep sense of failure: I had helped Beck all that way
down the mountain but in the ensuing complications had failed to
bring him home. In the isolation of my airy ledge, I hoped for another
avalanche to sweep me away.

My initial reaction was to show that I truly cared by waiting for Beck
and helping him down, but below me, strung out on the fixed rope,
were the remaining members of our team, all treading a fine line
between safety and carelessness due to exhaustion. As the only surviving guide, my responsibility remained with them as I knew Beck
was in the excellent hands of Todd and Pete.

I found out later that Beck had stumbled into C4 around 5.00 p.m.
on 11 May. He recounted later that he had woken from some sort of

reptilian sleep, decided he was not going to die and started to crawl into the wind, the only way he could keep a sense of direction. When alerted to Beck's arrival Todd and Pete attended to his immediate needs. I was not told of Beck's miraculous appearance and I can only assume that it was because of my condition at the time and they did not want to burden me with the added responsibility. On reflection I believe they had my best interests in mind.

If there were ever such a thing as a ghost town in the mountains, our C3 was it. I sat between the two tents that once accommodated Rob and Doug in one and Andy, Yasuko and myself in the other, and felt desolate. The others had continued down to C2. As I rummaged through the personal belongings in our tent, I was overwhelmed by the haunting memories of the once friendly chatter that filled the air between the tents that sat so precariously on this narrow ledge. Andy, Yasuko and I had shared this tent on more than one occasion. Andy and I had even planned our next climbing trip from this very tent, and I got to see the funny side of Yasuko as we tried to trick her with English jokes, only to find out that she understood everything we said. I prised my personal belongings from the pool of ice that had formed in the floor of our once happy home. I freed Andy's jacket from the ice and absent-mindedly turned to pass it out the door to him before I remembered. This had become our normal packing procedure— someone inside passing various belongings through the door to the other to be packed into a different rucksack. By the time I was finished I had respectfully folded two neat piles of gear: one for Yasuko and one for Andy; these would be collected later.

We may have arrived at BC in April as a dozen different teams and a multitude of nationalities, but on 12 May there were no such barriers to keep us apart as everyone who could came up from C2 to help us down. From within a group of Sherpas and climbers who had climbed up the base of the Lhotse Face came a voice. 'Hello, Michael *Dai*. Let me take your pack.' It was Nima, a cook boy whom I had employed ten years before but who had now risen to the rank of a climbing Sherpa.

I remembered how terribly sick he was then with altitude sickness. I had fetched a cup of tea for him from our kitchen tent and, with two or three Aspros, managed to offer some relief for his throbbing headache. It was the least I could do. For the remainder of the expedition he was extremely grateful. Back then he used to call me 'Michael *Sahib'*; now 'Michael *Dai'*, which means 'Brother Michael'—a little less formal but equally respectful.

Nima eased my heavy pack from my shoulders and sat me down. Lou and Jon were there too, but the others had continued down to C2. We sipped tea silently, while the reception party rearranged our packs to carry down to C2.

'More tea, *Dai?'* asked Nima, who was offering me more than my fair share. Too exhausted to talk, I declined with an open palm.

By now it was a perfect day at 6500 metres on Everest. It was warm enough to strip down to our thin first layer. Only the jet-stream winds, 2 kilometres above us and still thundering across the summit, gave any hint of the harshness of our environment. Nima told me to take it slowly; he would look after everything now, even though he was employed by another expedition. I had no choice but to walk slowly as my feet were driving me crazy with the pain of frostbite and the usual bruising from over-activity. All I had to do was follow the relatively easy terrain down to C2.

Our large mess tent at C2 had now turned into a MASH unit to deal with the injured climbers who had come down from C4. I had not seen most of the climbers who maintained this service on the mountain before this day. I was attended to immediately and the news was not good. I was close to tears when one of the doctors told me I could lose more of my feet. Another 10 millimetres off each foot and it would be impossible to walk again. Although the true extent of my frostbite injuries was not yet known, the doctor was preparing me for the worst. He gently cleaned my feet and wrapped them in bandages, and I was then carried to my tent where I started on a course of circulation-improving drugs and an injection of pain relief that made me so drowsy I slept for the remainder of the day. This was exactly what the doctors wanted: to keep me off my feet for as long as possible to prevent further damage. The climbers who came to our aid took care of everything, including caring for the needs of the remaining members of our team. Their labour was tireless and sympathetic.

It was just on nightfall when I was woken by a ruckus in our mess tent next door. Beck had arrived and room was being made for him among the other injured climbers and medical supplies. I leaned on one elbow and listened through the walls of the tent; I would have disregarded the doctor's orders to stay off my feet to go and see him if I hadn't been tied to a drip and felt too dizzy to stand. John, who was sharing a tent with me, went over immediately to see if he could lend a hand. He returned later to say that Beck looked terrible but was in remarkably good spirits, considering his injuries that consisted of serious frostbite to his face, hands and feet. Occasionally I could hear his cheery Southern accent and, like me, he would have been in some sort of morphine haze.

My conscious state passed quickly to the morning of 13 May. I tried to remain patient as it took considerable time and energy to squeeze my painfully swollen feet into my boots using aching frostbitten fingers. More than anything I wanted to see Beck; John had warned me he didn't look good but I wanted to confirm for myself that the cheery spirit I had heard last night was really Beck. I was not to be disappointed. Although at first it was hard to recognise him, as his face was swollen and black from frostbite, I hoped a lot of it was superficial. There was nothing superficial about his hands; they were in a shocking state. Privately I gave little hope for his fingers. I felt awkward and compelled to offer some explanation for what had happened but a brief and interrupted chat was all we could manage as people pushed past in a rush to get him and an equally seriously frostbitten Taiwanese climber ready to move further down the mountain. We were all heading down to BC that day and various more able climbers from other expeditions were joining in to help get Beck and the Taiwanese climber down to the top of the Icefall, where they hoped to rendezvous with what would be the world's highest helicopter rescue.

I said goodbye to Beck. It was simple but heartfelt with none of the usual intoxicated BC or Kathmandu parties to soften the sadness of our disbandment as a team. I particularly thanked all the climbers who had lent a hand to Beck, my team-mates and me. I was given another injection for pain; it was just enough to take the edge off it and still leave some feeling in my feet. Too much and I would be away with the fairies while going through the Icefall and that was an area where I wanted to be as alert as possible. Despite the easy passage through the Icefall this season, it was still not the place to take any chances and therefore I was prepared to tolerate a lot of discomfort.

In a little over an hour since leaving Beck I stood among the towering pillars of ice in the upper reaches of the Icefall to watch Beck's helicopter labour under the heavy influence of the altitude. It reminded me of one exhausted climber going to the rescue of another. It also reminded me of John Coulton's and my experience waiting for a helicopter near Kangchenjunga and I knew how Beck would be feeling right now—anxious, exhausted and useless and maybe even regretting ever wanting to climb Everest. He would be fed up with everything and all his hopes would be focusing on the helicopter making the pick-up and getting him home. Pain, if it existed at this early stage, would be under control by his medical aids. Lots more memories came flooding back, none more memorable than my father's remark when he found out I was returning to Kangchenjunga for the second time. It was like daring 'to pull the tiger's tail twice. You're bound to get caught one day.' This time the tiger had bitten back hard and I would be scarred forever. How many more times would I gamble my life? I came to the conclusion that the key to this game of high-altitude climbing is to quit while you are in front and to resist the temptation to go back for just one more climb, but I know that will not be possible.

On 14 May 1996 I sat on a large rock about fifteen minutes walk below BC. A large dose of morphine had helped to get me here and now I stared dumbly in a narcotic daze at the large area of flat rocks that I had so meticulously levelled four weeks earlier so a helicopter could pick up one of the Sherpas who was seriously injured when he fell into a crevasse. Now it was my turn to be air-lifted out as the doctors had warned me that to walk on my re-frostbitten feet could do irreparable damage. With the exception of my fingers, no visible signs of frostbite had appeared and I could not understand the tremendous amount of pain in my feet. Although it was only a short time since they were frozen, they looked OK from the outside, but it can take a little while for the true extent of the injury to show. I was not going to take any chances. Beck had been flown out the day before; today there would be two landings by the same helicopter as it shuttled people down to a more suitable collection point in the valley before taking us all together back to Kathmandu. I would be on the second flight out. Although Beck's rescue the day before had been 600 metres higher it had never been attempted before and it will always remain something out of the ordinary. Base Camp is at the maximum level of altitude for a helicopter landing and there are only a couple of hours during each morning at BC when the cold air is dense enough to support an incoming helicopter. Any later than 10.00 or 11.00 a.m. and the air would be too warm and therefore not dense enough to support a landing helicopter at this critical altitude. Because of this tight limit in flying time the first flight also collected the body of a Taiwanese climber who had fallen from C3. The accompanying climbers had to scramble in over the top of the tarpaulined body and I was thankful to be on the second lift. It took twenty minutes for the helicopter to return for me and I took shelter behind the large rock I had been sitting on. This time the helicopter flew in large decreasing circles around BC. I was puzzled by this expensive waste of time. When it circled closer I looked up, anxiously wanting it to land, only to look straight into the barrel of a TV camera. As the helicopter flew back down the valley it did not dawn on me what had happened, but Helen, who had accompanied me to the helipad, was more attuned to the situation: news crews were trying to get into BC to do interviews. There was a standing arrangement among the various expeditions at BC that a 'No comment' response was to be given to any news crews silly enough to

fly straight up to 5300 metres without acclimatisation. We guessed a
TV cameraman, on a mission to get footage for his network, probably
offered more money to the pilot than my US$2500 ticket out of BC,
showing no regard for the sick and injured climbers desperate for
urgent medical help. Fortunately morphine has a remarkably calming
effect and I trudged wearily back up to BC with a furious Helen.

Another helicopter was ordered for the next morning and this time
John was going to come with me in case I needed further assistance to
get home. In the meantime, Caroline had found a suitable alternative
to the mind-numbing morphine, so that I could be more aware of
what was going on around me. I was also deeply embarrassed by the
trouble which Helen and Caroline were taking to get me home, but I
knew that if I lost as little as 10 millimetres more off each foot, I would
never be able to return to the mountains again. Overwhelmed by
depression I hid in my tent.

Like the morning before, it was another early start. I had little confidence that I would be out of BC that day as I limped down to the
helipad. Helen and Guy Cotter helped carry our gear. Guy and his
team-mates Dave Hiddleston and Chris Jillet, in a selfless act, had
given up their Pumori expedition to come up to our BC to help deal
with the drama that was unfolding on 10 May. They were now doing
the job that I was meant to do, packing up BC and returning with the
members to Kathmandu. For half an hour I strained to hear the chatter
of an incoming helicopter—it was depressingly silent and the helicopter was late, but once it came there was no time for prolonged
goodbyes to all those that had helped. They deserved more consideration on my part but before I knew it John and I were in the helicopter
and off to Kathmandu.

A little over an hour later we had landed in Kathmandu and under
the umbrella of the spinning rotor blades milled a pack of hungry journalists. I could see there was no escape and I prepared myself to face
international interrogation. When the door slid open I couldn't believe
my eyes: there was Nima, my erstwhile friend who has been my agent

in Nepal for the last ten years. He guarded the opening with outstretched arms before jumping up to greet me. His hug was short, his actions urgent. 'Follow me, Michael. Do not stop to talk to these people.' I could see no escape for us as John followed. I was pushed and poked from all directions and surrounded by the usual media weaponry of microphones, lights and cameras. I was bombarded with questions and the most vexing was, 'Do you have any photos of the dead? I will give you a good price.' Nima pulled harder than the rest and dragged me towards an approaching minibus. In the crowd of thirty or forty journalists I had noticed a dark-haired woman, who looked comparatively unthreatening but my manners had long disappeared in response to the aggressive crowd. As she homed in on me, hustling to get beside me, I lined her up for a hard elbow in the ribs—the fate of some equally aggressive journalists a second or two before. But before I could swing into action, Nima had hauled me into the bus. The woman doggedly jumped in beside me. Pushed beyond the limits of my patience, I turned to serve her the full strength of my anger, but found myself defending the windows from journalists outside. John had only one foot in the bus, when Nima turned to the driver and shouted, 'Go!'

'Hello, Michael. My name is Claire. I'm assistant to the Australian Ambassador here in Kathmandu. I'm here to help you get out of the country without too much trouble from the media. Unless, of course you want to speak to the media!' It was good to hear an Australian voice and I suddenly felt I was almost home.

Twenty-four hours after leaving BC I really was home, still wearing the same stinking clothes from BC. This rapid return to the real world made it feel like the past few days on Everest had been nothing more than a surreal nightmare. I allowed myself to get sucked into this pretend world for a little longer, knowing full well that I would have to deal with reality sooner or later. The next day I was off to the doctor for an injection of morphine. Some worrying patches of black had started to grow in size on the ends of my feet and fingers, but thankfully time would eventually heal all the new frostbite injuries.

• • •

Not a day has gone by since when I haven't stopped to think about the events and the friends who died. When I returned home I was convinced that everything humanly possible was done to save the lives of our friends and team-mates. But with the passing of time memories of the appalling conditions we endured fade: the incredible cold that caused crippling exhaustion, the sting of that relentless wind, and zero visibility. As these images grow dimmer with time, I have started to ask myself the question, 'Could I have done more to save lives?', 'What if I had done this or that?', 'What if . . . ?' I have experienced the same and worse conditions on other climbs, but never with such tragic results. When I first arrived at BC in April 1996 our team was one of a dozen teams attempting Everest from the Nepal side of the mountain. A record number of permits had been issued by the Ministry of Tourism in Kathmandu that season and I said to John as we surveyed the construction of a small tent city from our higher vantage point at BC, 'With this number of climbers on the hill this season, there is bound to be at least half a dozen who won't be going home.' Perhaps it was a premonition of events to come, but I think not. I am sure John assumed I was referring to the members of the other teams, making the classic assumption that it always happens to someone else. I know I was.

In Everest's long history, 10 May 1996 will go down as a disastrous day. So much for our lucky date of the 10th.

from # Climbing High
by Lene Gammelgaard

Lene Gammelgaard (born 1961) was a client on Scott Fischer's 1996 Everest expedition. This is Gammelgaard's account of her summit day.

CAMP IV TO THE SUMMIT

May 9–10,1996

11:30 p.m. It's pitch-dark here at the South Col, the only sounds coming from people already departing and from my friends handling oxygen bottles, masks and crampons. As usual I am late getting out of the tent. It took me an hour and a half to pull myself together enough to get out of the sleeping bag and into my down suit and outer boots. Even the simplest tasks demand so much of you—on every level.

Outside I am met by a starlit sky and a line of headlamps—Rob Hall's team already a half-hour ahead of us. The first part of our team is leaving camp now, and I hurry as much as I possibly can. This overwhelming intuitive feeling that I simply must stick to my group comes over me. At no point—under any circumstances—must I risk being alone on the high flanks of Everest. After clumsily getting my crampons on, I look around and catch sight of only one figure. Must be Scott. Rushing up to him, laughing, I note that his down suit is dark blue so I can recognize him on the road.

"Hi, Scott! Is it two oxygen bottles from now on?"

"Yes, it is," he laughs back. We exchange "good lucks," and I hug him big time before I half-walk, half-run after the fading line of headlamps. I must stick with my team and not fall behind.

At first I walk an almost level stretch of rock-cinder and snow. The ground is littered with old oxygen canisters, but after five or ten minutes' walk, the human debris thins out and there is only sheer blue ice under my crampons. Steep, broken blue ice, hard as rock. Crevasses all over, difficult to see in the dark. I've caught up with the headlamps and am with my group—Klev, Neal, Sandy, Charlotte, Tim, Martin—but where is Anatoli? There he is. He stays in the vicinity of the rest of us.

A steep ice- and snow-covered slope leads upward. A fall here and you . . . No, don't get scared. Concentrate on one step at a time. Focus on the person in front of you, and follow. Don't think; don't let the old fear take over. Upward, upward. Where the hell do the fixed ropes start? I've gotten used to having a "safety line" in the most hazardous places during the expedition, and now there are none at the most risky pitches. Rob Hall's and our Sherpa teams have been assigned the task of fixing the ropes so that no bottlenecks develop, delaying the ascent and increasing the risks. How stupid! In other mountains I wouldn't have become mentally dependent on fixed ropes, but here I have become unaccustomed to the mental pressure and challenge presented by climbing first on a route. But, it's okay. After all, this is my first time climbing the highest mountain in the world, and it takes a little getting used to.

Finally—a snow stake with an orange rope. Relieved, I clip the carabiner into the line and climb upward across the ice. Upward and upward. Even with oxygen, it's madly exhausting. There are ropes, but since they are secured only every 150 to 250 feet, safety is probably so-so. But what do I expect if I wish to roam in the death zone?

How am I going to get down again after many, many hours of this? How exhausted will I be? Don't think ahead, Lene. Focus on what you are doing now. There's Yasuko, from Rob's team. Our group has caught up with the advance guard. There's Anatoli, he's a little behind—green down suit, no oxygen mask. Lopsang is easily recognizable in his white Sherpa suit, which he wears over his down clothes, and he has a flag-pole sticking up out of his backpack. Between coughing fits, he manages to tell us that he and Scott have arranged for a stunt on the summit of Everest, but he'll not reveal any of the details. He's still ill, but nobody does anything about it.

How much time has passed? One hour? Two hours? The group progresses at a snail's pace up across a wall of mixed climbing. The fixed ropes have come to an end, and I am scared. Scared of falling and scared at the thought of how on earth I'm going to get down again. Now and then I climb in a beginner's style, down on all fours, just to be in close contact with the steep, rocky ground. I do not feel like free climbing at this altitude and in this terrain, but I continue and come a little more to my senses as I move. This is very real and very dangerous, but didn't I, in fact, expect something like this when I set out to climb the highest mountain in the world? If it were only a picnic, Mother Goddess of the Earth would disappoint me. She cannot do that, nor does she.

The best thing about climbing and mountaineering is that they can't be belittled. There's no getting away with a "in reality it's probably not that difficult, it's just overly hyped so that those who do it feel like heroes." The mountains are not like that. They are real, they are dangerous and they are exacting, and they show you precisely what you can and cannot do. Show you who and what you and others are.

Watching a slide show years ago, at the beginning of my climbing career, I actually thought to myself: It's surely not that difficult, it's not that steep, it doesn't require that much training, it doesn't require that much in the way of skills to make it all work out. Because I belittled the climbers' achievements, I didn't need to respect them or, consequently, envy what they did, something that I, at a deeper level, wanted to do myself, but didn't have the network or the guts for.

As I got acquainted with vertical rock walls, winter climbing and the hazardous beauty of glaciers, I found out that, yes, it is that exacting. It is that difficult. It is that dangerous. And I was scared and happy! Here, finally, was something that lived up to its own image. Something that was not idle talk. Something that commanded you fully, completely—and even more than that—if you wanted to join in. Something in which you got to know your own limitations and learned to accept that there are some things you'll never fully master, but that there is much you can train for, and that experience is the key to greater adventures. The mountains are the real thing, and they treat everybody alike. The same rules apply whether you are American or Russian or Danish. Your survival and your success depend on you, yourself. In a simple and brutal sense.

Upward, upward. The 3,028 vertical feet from the South Col to Everest's summit are estimated to take at least twelve hours, so there is no reason for false hope. Upward, upward, for a long, long time to come.

The mixed climbing comes to an end. My teammates and I are standing, slightly doubtful, on the edge of a wide snow couloir. The risk of avalanches is high here, but we must traverse to get across to the rock on the other side that seems to leap upward to the Southeast Ridge, our first oxygen depot. Suddenly we see Lopsang's white outfit over on the rock, and in the fading darkness, we catch sight of an oxygen bottle acting as a signpost in the middle of the snow field. We begin a slow plod across the steep snow field, or rather we fight through the snow, which is so deep that we sink up to our hips in several places. The traverse requires several gasping-for-breath breaks. Oh God, I have to get down through this again! One avalanche and good-bye.

Onward. Pull yourself together, Lene. The first sunbeams peek out from atop the ridge, and I can see a group of brilliantly colored spots sitting on a rock island in the middle of the snow masses. Are they birds? People? Or hallucinations? The sun is stronger now, no clouds, divinely beautiful. A view down over Nepal and the surrounding mountain ranges—I get scared, don't dare to look around too much. It is simply too vast here, too far down. I'm profoundly conscious of being in the death zone, and switch to "tunnel vision" so as not to get paralyzed by the greatness, the madness, the surrealism of my being here. I am on my way to the top of the world! It's huge, and it's scary. I fully understand how people die up here. There is more to die from than to live on, and the least bit of bad weather could make the death trap slam shut. Here, there is no safety margin.

It is probably 5:00 a.m. when our group reaches the Southeast Ridge in bright sunshine. Those brightly colored spots that played a trick on my oxygen-starved brain turn out to have been people. Sherpas and climbers in our small community exchange smiles and look up toward the ridge leading to the summit. I turn my head and gaze with awe down the side of Mount Everest we have just scaled, thinking of the biblical tale of Lot's wife, who looked back at the city of Sodom and was turned into a pillar of salt. I look out over the edge of this narrow ridge, almost two miles above the Tibetan Plateau. Mountain ranges as far as my vision reaches, sun and blue sky above. Are we up so high that I'm actually seeing the earth's curve?

Got to pull myself together—shoot some pictures and exchange my one almost-empty oxygen canister for a full one. Thanks to the efforts of our high-altitude Sherpas, there's a supply of full oxygen bottles here and, supposedly, a supply below the South Summit, one more advantage of being a member of such an expensive expedition. And one more reason I wanted to climb Everest without supplementary oxygen. Then I wouldn't have to struggle with the question of whether all this help from the Sherpas is cheating a little. But just now I'm thoroughly pleased with the luxury money can buy.

There's Anatoli. How does he manage without oxygen? Same pace as the rest of us (for once). Says nothing. Yes, he is cold. Looks a bit worn out, too. I have no problems keeping warm—so Henry Todd's advice to me about using O_2 to conserve body heat is true. I take off the mask to see what it's like without the oxygen supply—just a bit of preparation, so as not to panic if the oxygen should run out ahead of schedule. I can breathe without the mask, so I drain off the condensation so it won't freeze up or frostbite my face. I've become accustomed to the device and no longer give it a second thought—as long as it gets me to the summit.

Where is the summit? Still not visible? There is a short, sloping stretch of snowy ridge with overhanging cornices, and then we move upward—mixed climbing as far as I can see. Serious business—at this moment, I'd prefer that all those who call Everest a hike were right. But they are not.

Can't help but remember Scott's optimism a year ago: "Everest is easy. Piece of cake. Just a hike!" How I would have loved to believe him, but familiar with his enticing and contagious enthusiasm as I am, I decided to wait and see. And sure enough, Lene Gammelklog (the Danes use the adjective *gammelklog* to describe a precocious child) was right: The closer we got to departure, the more I sensed his reality adjustment. Finally Scott wrote me:

> We'll have fun in Kathmandu, we'll have fun on the trek, we'll have fun at Base Camp, and from then on, it will be one and a half months of extremely hard struggling.

The next stage I'm looking at is tough mountain climbing. It's a good thing I've improved my relationship with ridges, and this one is more dignified than most. Tibet on one side, Nepal on the other—and, both, very far down! To the summit and safe return.

To get from this comparatively safe platform of snow up onto the ridge itself, you have to balance on a cornice hanging out like a terrace above the Nepalese side of the mountain and too steep to gain a decent foothold on the Tibetan side. The middle part consists of a cracked glacier edge. Up to you to choose among these three evils. Each choice entails its own risk. I choose the Nepalese side and pray to God the snow stays in place.

It holds, and I continue up the ridge, walking on the Tibetan slope till I catch up with Martin, Sandy, Tim, Charlotte and Klev at a big boulder that marks the last rest stop before the top. I try to drink a sip of water and see that the energy drink in my bottle is almost frozen solid, even though it's been in the special pocket next to my body.

Upward, upward, using exceedingly old fixed ropes left by previous expeditions, ropes used again and again, even by expeditions with the best intentions of putting up their own. At this point, you don't care, as long as there is something—anything—to grab on to. The rock— yellow porous sheets warmed by the sun—can't be trusted, so with Tibet far below, even an old piece of rope provides some feeling of security. I'm careful not to put more weight on the rope than is strictly necessary, though.

Come to a standstill for what feels like hours, almost nodding off hanging from the jumar, until somebody up there gets his or her ass in gear so that the rest of us can get on with it. Time goes by. I am tired. How far is it to the top?

Unfortunately, I'm focusing on the notorious Hillary Step, a steep stretch of climbing near the summit that has beaten many a great climber just before the finish line. Charlotte and I discuss whether that's it ahead. What we are looking at looks difficult and perma- nent enough to be the Hillary Step, but we know we're just deluding ourselves—there is still a long way to climb before we get to it. Upward, upward.

After hours of hard, physical effort, I've fallen into a familiar trance. I'm moving instinctively—not thinking, not feeling, not reflecting— just moving, occasionally checking the bubble in the hose to see if the oxygen is flowing as it should. Carabiner into the fixed rope. Jumar on. Next length of rope. Which rope looks the least aged? I almost don't care. Upward. How will I get down these steep, yellow sheets of rock safely? Onward. A snow ridge. Could that be the summit up there? I can see some rock formations and try to force my brain to remember what the summit looked like in all the photographs I've studied. What did it look like on the video Scott made in 1994? Can't use the images, anyway, for the amount of snow constantly changes the appearance of the mountain. Slowly upward, gasping for breath. My poor lungs:

They're working like crazy. Hope they can take it. My breathing has adapted to the environment—more rapid and not very deep.

Pause and then onward. Our team sticks together. And we move at an almost identical pace. Then—STOP! Some down suits are already gathered in a small hollow—five to ten crouching people, sheltered a little from the rising winds and with a view of the Western Cwm a mile and a quarter below. I sit down, kicking my crampons solidly into the snow so as not to slide out of the hollow and down. There is the South Summit, and *there* is the Hillary Step!

It's around 11, or maybe noon. It's cold and I'm tired, so Tim helps me check the oxygen content of my bottle. Damn hard work to take the backpack off up here. You have to untangle yourself from the hose connecting the bottle to the mask, check the gauge and then do the whole thing again in reverse. It's nice to have Tim's help. "Almost empty," he reports. Have to think now. From here to the summit and back again, how many hours? Three to five—probably at high flow rate, for the hardest climbing is ahead of us. I've got to find a full bottle of oxygen among those lying scattered around here. And, of course, it must be one belonging to us. Unthinkable to take from Rob Hall's cache.

Nobody has been on the summit ridge this season, so there are no fixed ropes, only those that have survived from previous summit attempts. The other expeditions at Base Camp supported our two teams climbing first, as it will make it easier on all those coming after us this year if we've fixed new ropes, just as we're using our predecessors' ropes. I look across the cornices toward Tibet and see fixed ropes from previous expeditions hanging in open space, like telephone wires, 30 and 50 feet below me. They emerge from the snow wall in one place and disappear again in another. Wonder if I could grab one of them if I fell . . .

Everything seems to have come to a stop. It's being debated—a little desperately—whose job it is to take the lead fixing the next pitch of ropes and, consequently, who will be the rope fixer on the Hillary Step. Neal thinks it ought to have been done already. Who has rope? Who has snow stakes? Nobody. More feverish gesticulations. Anatoli sets out, followed by Neal and somebody in a blue down suit from Rob's team who suddenly shoots ahead with a rope on his arm. Who is that? He doesn't seem okay. I huddle in a crouching position, freezing in the rising wind. Charlotte, Tim and I agree to stick together. Charlotte is honest: She plain and simple doesn't like this situation.

I watch Anatoli with deep respect. The Russian man climbs deliberately up the Hillary Step, a fly at nearly 28,900 feet above the surface of the sea, his years of experience expressed in his assurance. No panic, no words, no trying to get praise. He does what needs to be done. And does it well! I hold my breath till he is safely up, but know he won't fall. He is too good.

Not many feet of rope to secure us with and no useable old ropes—they're covered by the winter snowfall and impossible to pull out. The first stretch on the ridge is an extremely exposed traverse—spooky—like walking on a tightrope in a strong wind, knowing full well there is no rescue if you stumble, if the crampons catch your trouser leg, if the ice axe's grip isn't good enough. I start out—have to turn back—return to the imaginary security of the hollow, feels so protected . . .

Must think. Is the summit worth this kind of risk? If I fall, I'm dead. I can turn back here—others have. The wind has picked up, and I can see the snow drifting across the summit ridge. There is no security beyond my own capabilities—do I want to summit that much? Contemplate what it will be like when I return home, what I will feel every time I see the summit ridge and Hillary Step in my mind and be forced to face my own defeat. Think of my promises to the sponsors. Think of the possibilities I will miss if I turn back now—as I have previously turned back.

I want to get to the top of the highest mountain in the world. I want to be the first Danish woman to reach the summit of Mount Everest. I know I have the experience to climb the next pitch, know that it's only old fears that stop me, know I have the resources in my mind to break through them. I want to get to the top—whatever the cost—so I get up and start the traverse on my way to the top of the world.

I'm climbing like a beginner—stiff, unsteady, staggering and, therefore, a real danger to myself. Lopsang sees me. He has never seen me like this before. He takes my hand, and it helps, even though I know it's more dangerous than if he hadn't. After barely a few steps, I am an adult again. The paralysis disappears, and my body moves fluently.

In goes the ice axe with the shaft pointing down; I hold on to the blade and have better support than without it. Lousy axe for climbing. What was Scott thinking of when he recommended it—has he forgotten what it's like up here? I would have felt much better with a long-handled classical axe. Well, next time I have to trust my own experience more. Up across the snow ridge. Every time I take the axe out of the snow, I make a little peephole through which I can see Tibet—there is next to nothing to walk on, but we still do it. I trust myself again and begin to enjoy the madness of being so close to the top on a dangerous stretch of climbing. I can make it. I have what it takes.

Sandy sits down in the snow. Exhausted? She has otherwise done well. There are problems getting quickly past the Hillary Step. It takes Yasuko half an hour, maybe a whole hour. I slip easily up and over, thankful for many years of rock climbing. Was that the notorious Hillary Step? Piece of cake. *Whoopee!* I did it!

Will the summit never come? How far can it be? There's Martin on his way down.

"Congratulations on the top, Martin." I'm happy for him.

Klev follows. The gentleman's dream has come true.

"Congratulations on the summit, Klev." Soon it will be my turn.

What's happening? A blue down suit sits cross-legged in the snow. Something is very wrong, but somebody is with him, and Rob Hall, who is a very careful and serious expedition leader, is right up ahead. There is nothing I can do, so I walk on. Pass Lopsang, who is throwing up. I pat him affectionately on the back and smile to thank him for his kind encouragement when I was trying to cross the frightening traverse earlier.

There is the summit! I recognize the metal survey stake from innumerable pictures. I stagger the last few feet.

I made it! I have reached the top of the highest mountain in the world! Satisfaction mixed with fear washes over me. I have to get down again—but how in the world am I going to get my ass down from here . . . The valleys I could see before are now covered with white clouds— but the sky above me is deep blue. There's a wind blowing. It's around 2:30 p.m., I think, or is it 1:30?

I made it, damn it! I have reached the top of the world! I am 29,028 feet above sea level; snow, ice and mountains below me—*everything* is below me—as far as I can see.

Am I euphoric, uplifted, overwhelmed, disappointed? No, I am not disappointed in Mother Goddess of the Earth. I am proud. Quietly, silently, massively content. And then I am tired. Maybe I'll have to climb up here once again just to enjoy the view or have enough strength left to notice whether there is one. It is too much right now. I just want to get down safely. Christ! I am really here! At the top.

We congratulate each other. Anatoli is already gone. First up—first down. I say hi to Rob, who is standing there talking to his collar. Walkie-talkie. Well, yes, some people have these. I thank him for keeping a watchful eye on me down below when I reverted to child-hood. Everybody seems happy and satisfied—in fine shape, even if we are tired, of course. Who wouldn't be after what we've been through?

Sponsor photos? I have no energy for anything, but now's the moment I have to pay back what others have given me. Off with the backpack and out with the plastic bag containing the logo flags. Neal agrees to take pictures, and nobody at the summit believes their eyes when I pull the front page of *Ekstra Bladet* out of the bag:

LENE GAMMELGAARD, FIRST DANISH WOMAN ATOP EVEREST!

Too much! I feel people gaping.

Neal took off his outer mittens to press the release of my camera. His fingers are already frostbitten, and he sanely refuses to shoot any more pictures. I've begun to feel pressed myself. I've got to get down from here. And that can't happen fast enough! Flags and camera are thrown into the backpack. Charlotte, Neal, Sandy and Tim have begun the descent, and again I am driven by the compulsion that I must not be alone on this mountain. I have to stick to the group. It is take-off time! Lopsang is unpacking his flag arrangement and waiting for Scott so that they can play their boyish pranks.

There is the man himself—Scott emerges over the ridge above the Hillary Step. Pure joy at being together again.

I hug him. "Good to see you, Scott. I made it! I'm tired. Get down safe!"

"Congratulations, Lene! You're the first Danish woman on top of Everest. I'm happy. And so tired. See you down there."

We part, heading in different directions on the top ridge.

DOWN FROM THE SUMMIT

Afternoon, May 10, 1996
I hurry to catch up with the others. It looks as if Klev is helping somebody across at the South Summit, or are they taking a break?

Down, down, keep your balance—most of those who perish on Everest do so on their way down. Set your foot precisely, place the ice axe and take just one step. Clip into that bit of rope, and get down the Hillary Step. I made it. I fucking made it! Now I just have to survive the hours to the South Col, then to Camp III . . .

Down, down past the traverse where I had to stop on the way up. Now I hardly recognize it—doesn't seem as steep. Next the oxygen cache. How is my oxygen situation? Almost empty. How many of us are there? How many full or less-empty bottles? I check several bottles in the pile: empty, almost full, full—there's no system any longer. Order has changed to chaos. I exchange my oxygen bottle and calculate that the contents of the new one will hardly be sufficient to reach the South Col, but the further down I get, the safer I will be. So down I go, onto the bad fixed ropes, round the corner, and POW!

Full gale-force winds and snow! *Fuck!* This is serious. The clouds I saw from the top must have been a snowstorm building up further down, and now we're heading right into it. Tim shows the stuff he's made of. Calm and deliberate, he proves himself capable of responding superbly whenever the situation gets truly critical. Charlotte is a lucky woman. I'm on the rope and hurry down after her and Sandy. Tim is after me.

Sandy suddenly sits down and does not want to move. Somebody shouts, "If you don't pull yourself together *right now*, you will die!" and Charlotte unzips her down suit, finds her emergency kit and gives Sandy a shot of dex, just as prescribed, in the buttock through her clothes and the whole caboodle. It helps a bit. We confer and discover that Sandy's oxygen bottle is approaching empty. As I am the strongest among us, she and I exchange oxygen containers, and I hurry on.

I want down, and it is late. I clip into the rope leading down across the yellow sheets of rock. Where there was naked rock five hours ago, there is now a covering of seemingly bottomless snow, like soap flakes. The snow is scary, like quicksand under my feet. Though I can no longer see very far, I know that there's a drop-off to the left, and that climbers have quite literally disappeared in this area without a trace. I hope the fixed ropes can stand the weight of our bodies—we have all clipped in. Neal has taken hold of Sandy. She doesn't seem to be all there, or is she?

I quickly discover it's not possible to glissade on my feet in this snow. It's too dangerous, so I sit down on my ass and slide down Mount Everest. When my speed threatens to get out of hand, I lean against the fixed rope with my whole body and try to brake a little with the carabiner. If the fixed rope snaps, I'm done for. We stagger, fall, crawl, slide, swim our way down the mountain. Our worst nightmare is materializing around us—bad weather! Sheer survival now.

It seems like it's taking forever to get down. Neal is having trouble with Sandy. Charlotte, Tim and I are in fine shape, considering. In the course of a few hours, we get down to the spot on the Southeast Ridge where we took a break at sunrise. Somebody is sitting there—Klev. He's preparing to descend the rock flank leading directly down to camp. In good weather, it would take one and a half to two hours to get back to our tents—who knows how long in these conditions.

NIGHTFALL

It's probably close to 6:00 p.m., so we simply have to be off. The body is almost finished. Exhausted. No food or drink since when? Yesterday afternoon. It feels like an eternity.

Neal is with Sandy. Tim and Charlotte are doing fine, so I hurry up and join Klev. We go directly down the snow flank, where there's a danger of avalanches—even more so now with the snowfall. Slow, exhausting. I start to struggle and discover I'm out of oxygen. *Shit!*

"Stop, Lene. Oxygen! Breathe deeply, and keep breathing. Take some more!"

Evidently, the sudden loss of oxygen made me hyperventilate. Klev can see how blue my face is. Myself, I didn't notice anything.

We work our way down, and Klev insists—despite my protests!—on sharing his remaining oxygen with me. For some time he climbs down, and I continue sliding on my ass. My down suit tears, and the down creates its own snowfall. It doesn't matter now—a down suit can be replaced, and I feel safest going down this way. The visibility is getting worse and worse as darkness falls and the snowstorm increases. Sliding on my ass, I at least won't trip over my own legs.

There's a fixed rope, so we are at any rate in a place where people have been before. Who's that in front of us, emerging from the storm? It turns out to be Yasuko Namba on her way down the rope. It gives us hope to see someone else. I am glad she's on her way down. After some time, Klev and I pass her.

It's almost completely dark now. I have a spare headlamp battery in my backpack, but neither of us considers it worthwhile to struggle with changing the battery right now. The advantage of the headlamp is that you can see better within the field of the light beam; the disadvantage is that your eyes adjust to the light and you no longer can see the outlines of the landscape around you. For me, it's a matter of weighing how best to find my way—with or without a light. The light seems to reflect off the snow, turning the whiteout into a snow wall, so for now, it's best without it.

"Klev, I think we should keep to the right at the couloir—don't you see something down there that could be the lights from camp?"

"Yes, let's head for that."

We struggle downward. The whiteout and gale-force gusts make it almost impossible to get our bearings. Every outline of the landscape has been blotted out. Fatigue and lack of oxygen don't help either. Mountain climbers have lost their way up here before because of bad weather. Many simply lose their orientation and walk over the edge of the precipice on the Tibetan or the Nepalese side. The roar of the storm prevents us from hearing any yells from Camp IV and Klev and I are reluctant to tax our decreasing resources by crying out ourselves.

Cool calm pervades us both. Survival!

LOST ON THE SOUTH COL

"What is that over there to the left?" Klev and I can feel the ground under our crampons becoming less steep, a sign we've probably reached the outskirts of the South Col and are down from the steepest descent. We're trying desperately to find or recognize something that will give us a hint of the camp's location. Why didn't anyone think of fixing ropes all the way down the steepest part? And a rope ought to have been tied to our camp! But it's easy to be wise after the fact, and it doesn't help us now. We stop and talk about the best possible way of finding our way back to camp so that we don't end up as permanent inhabitants of the South Col.

"Quite a bit of light over there. But I think the camp is to the right."

"I totally agree."

But still, we decide to investigate the lights to the left and begin to struggle through the rising storm. Enormously exhausting just to find a foothold and move my boots forward in this lunar landscape.

The lights turn out to be our teammates—Tim, Charlotte, Neal, Sandy, two Sherpas—and two down suits, one of which I think is Yasuko. Klev and I defer to the Sherpas' experience. After all, they've been here before. Looking for known terrain, they poke their ice axes down into the layer of new snow and examine what lies under it—rock or ice.

How long do we all follow the Sherpas—a quarter of an hour? half an hour? longer?—before we realize they are lost? Now they don't seem to have the slightest idea where they are and begin to walk around in a bewildered way and without any apparent plan.

It's very dark now, stormy, a blizzard, really. If the Sherpas can't find the way, it means the worst has happened: We are lost.

"Okay, what now? We need to stay together and agree on an action plan so we don't waste energy." I think of a phrase I carry with me—it sounds like a joke, but it helps you stay calm in situations like this: "No, I am not lost; I just don't know where I am right now."

Klev and I are in agreement. We hardly need words to know what the other thinks, and we do what we consider most expedient. I leave it to Klev to talk with Neal. Calmness is the only thing that works in catastrophic situations.

We begin to search the South Col, sticking together. Yasuko is clearly on the verge of losing consciousness, but there is nothing we can do other than try, to the best of our ability, to get her to follow the rest of us. We progress at a snail's pace in the blowing snow. Can't see anything, do anything. A little upward, a little downward. It takes the utmost effort just to stay upright, let alone move our feet. It's a difficult terrain to walk in. Nobody is allowed to sit down or fall behind. We know that equals death up here. The storm, the hope of rescue, the unreality of this living nightmare make us exclaim again and again, "There's light. I can hear voices." But again and again—disappointment.

The Sherpas are no longer with us. Where are they?

The terrain under my feet feels all wrong. Too much rock, too steep and at the wrong angle. Last night, when I started out, I was walking on ice, and there's too little ice here and too few empty oxygen bottles for this to be even in the vicinity of the camp area. I think several of us realize we're headed toward the abyss of Kangshung Face, and we decide on emergency plan No. 2. We have now walked around and around, using survival energy in our search for the camp. We haven't succeeded, and instead of using further energy, our best chance to survive is to find a hollow, a boulder, something—anything—that can give a little bit of shelter against the raging snowstorm, and then huddle together and hope for a break in the weather later tonight. Or, worst case scenario, keep each other warm enough and awake so that we have a chance of surviving the night. At least some of us.

I lie next to Klev, no, half on top of him. Klev has one arm around me. Neal and Tim are on our right. Up against my body, Sandy lies moaning, "I know I am going to die. My face and my hands are freezing off." Charlotte lies next to her, lifeless. She has given up. Some time ago she said, "Just let me be, I just want to die in peace." A little further away in the darkness is the Yasuko bundle and her unknown companion. I don't know anymore where the Sherpas are.

"Keep moving your hands and feet. Say something, shout, keep the guy next to you awake!" Neal, Tim, Klev and I take turns shouting, moving. Klev shakes me. I shake him and kick Sandy every few minutes: "Are you awake? You must not go to sleep. Hold out!" Sandy moans, "I just want to die."

Tim is nothing less than fantastic. He does all the right things in the right way and takes care of everybody in the group. Calm, deliberate, in control in spite of the circumstances. Neal tries to guide, but I sense fear underneath his words.

The gale continues to blow. It's even darker now as most of the headlamp batteries have given out. Everybody's oxygen has run out.

"Charlotte, are you awake?" Tim shouts mercilessly. Charlotte is lifeless.

Snow is starting to pile up on top of Klev and me. Soon we will be just another bump in the landscape. I get halfway up and brush most of it away. Snow crystals begin to penetrate my down suit, collecting in the seams and melting—soaking through my last armor quietly and inevitably. I debate with myself if I have enough strength to take off my backpack. The buckle broke on the summit, so the hip belt is tied around my waist. I'd have to take off my gloves and mittens and work it loose with my bare hands . . . but it might be worth the risk, for at the bottom is my wind suit. That would keep out the gale for some time . . . but I'd also have to get the climbing harness off . . . and crampons . . . I don't have strength for so much, and the risk of losing a glove or . . . too huge . . . so I lie down again.

"Sandy, wake up. You are not going to die."

"My hands," the yellow suit next to my body cries. "They're freezing off."

How tragic. Has Sandy reached the summit she aspired to for so long, just to die or end up maimed?

I fear for Yasuko and her bundle over there. Absolutely no sign of life.

How long have we been lying here?

I know I'm not going to die tonight. I just know it . . . I am not scared. I realize our situation, without fear or panic. My turn has not come yet . . . I am not going to die now . . .

I can still move my toes inside the boots. I guess they are all right—bending them—stretching—bend—stretch—on and on . . . My fingers are cold . . . I move them, beat them against each other when I have the energy for it . . . Bend, stretch . . . Damned gloves. Not good enough for Everest. The outer cover is stiff as a board. Frozen to ice. But it protects against the gale. Try to put the mittens under my armpits to protect my hands against the storm. But too much snow collects—making me still colder . . . Bend, stretch . . . bend, stretch . . .

"Klev, are you awake?" Of course he is.

Kick at Sandy.

"Sandy, check if Charlotte is awake."

Tim works tirelessly. He and Neal try to get Charlotte and Sandy to sit up. Anything, the smallest sign of a will to live rather than apathetic surrender. Yasuko has long since stopped responding. She is blessed, in a way. Is the person sitting next to her dead?

Bend, stretch, bend, stretch . . .

I lie across Klev shaking uncontrollably from the cold. My teeth chatter in my mouth, and the shaking is not of this world . . .

Bend, stretch, bend, stretch . . . make fists of my hands inside my mittens. Move my toes.

How long have we been lying here . . . one hour, two hours?

I don't know how, but through wordless communication, Klev and I collect what is, very likely, our last strength. Somehow we know, without discussing it, that our only chance—and, consequently, the group's only chance—to get out of this situation alive is to perform the impossible right now: to get up and find the camp. Neal has come to the same conclusion, and just then, the weather gods look upon us with mercy. The gale and the snowstorm pause just long enough for a mountain massif to emerge at our right. And I think there is a star. Neal believes he has some direction now.

The trio begins to stagger forward. Klev tries to drag somebody. Yasuko? Charlotte? There's nothing he can do. He has to shake the person off his arm, otherwise he will die here. It takes everything just to keep upright and more than that to move our feet.

"I know where we are, and I know where the camp is," says Klev, and the sense of focus in his voice and the certainty of his movements make me believe in him. Neal is on my other side. He seems to be quite affected by the efforts he has made and the lack of oxygen. He's confused, but struggles to stay in control.

I know I have to stay on my feet, not stumble and disappear. Walk! Now I see Everest to the right and Lhotse? To the left . . .

"Klev, light! Ahead, to the left . . . I'm quite certain."

CAMP IV

May 11, 1996
Hope . . . stagger along . . . to survive . . . the survival instinct is all there is . . . the will to live.

There's a tent, two . . . I need to pee, so I pee in my down suit. There is nothing I can do about it. I am exhausted.

And there is Anatoli. It was his headlamp we saw.

Neal disappears into his tent. Klev tumbles into ours, falling to the ground like the trunk of a tree.

I look at Anatoli through the storm. He looks at me—knows it is serious—bends down and takes off my crampons.

"Anatoli, the others are out there. They're dying."

"Where?"

"Not far. Walk straight ahead. That way."

from # The Climb

by Anatoli Boukreev
and G. Weston DeWalt

Jon Krakauer in his 1997 best-seller Into Thin Air *criticized climbing guide Anatoli Boukreev's role in the 1996 Everest tragedy. Boukreev's (1958–1997) response to such criticism included passages such as this one from* The Climb, *co-authored with G. Weston DeWalt.*

Gammelgaard remembered that initially she and Schoening led the attempt to find Camp IV. "Klev and I just sort of stick together. Neal is wandering a little bit here, a little bit there, and then he is sticking together eventually, too, and . . . I don't know where camp is at this point, but I say, 'Okay, I can as well trust Klev . . . it's as good a possibility as anything.' Then at a point I see light, and there I sort of take over and say to Klev, 'This is light from the camp. We have to turn left. It's there!' And we go there and it turns out it's Anatoli's headlamp."

Like all the returning climbers, Gammelgaard was teetering on the edge of total exhaustion, keeping upright out of the sheer exhilaration of having survived. Boukreev, she said, "looked at me, but we didn't have to speak. He just knew it was serious and he bent down to take off my crampons."

The events from that point, as remembered by Boukreev, were dictated to his coauthor, Weston DeWalt, within days after his arrival in the United States from Nepal. In the interest of maintaining his voice and the immediacy of the events he experienced, his words as spoken in English and without benefit of an interpreter are presented here. They are interrupted only for clarification.

Q: *What did you do when you saw them coming in?*
A: I saw exactly these lamps come and I saw Lene and Klev come. And I saw them with lots of ice around the face, impossible to see [oxygen] mask because is just ice. I take off crampons of Lene and put outside of tent. I see people was not able to do nothing, just I get crampon, everything, and help for Lene and for Klev go inside by crawl. And I saw what is happening, very serious. People said . . .

Q: *Did you give them any oxygen?*
A: Yes, I gave some oxygen from like what is I have, three bottles—one Martin, one Klev, one Lene. From tent. And I give for people this, and this is situation. I understand I need to be ready. I began take my shoes, but it is not so easy. Also I tried to find the shoes, I found the shoes, take over my shoes, big shoes. It was before I was without the shoes. And then was ready go out.

Boukreev had already given one of the three oxygen canisters he'd received from Pemba to Martin Adams. The other two he had given, one each, to Schoening and Gammelgaard. The shoes for which he searched were his overboots, which he would need to go back out into the storm.

Q: *So you put on your climbing boots again?*
A: Yes. Probably—I cannot say what time people come. Now it is difficult to say. People talk like . . .

Q: *Twelve to twelve-thirty?*
A: I take my shoes and maybe I started go out. It is one o'clock. I think maybe like eleven-thirty people come or eleven o'clock. I was very slow because I was with Klev Schoening, I spoke with people, I gave tea, I gave oxygen, I gave sleeping bag, everything. There's lots of time, is like probably eleven-thirty the latest time clients come, I think, because now I tried to understand just for myself. I think like eleven to twelve o'clock. But I start go out exactly like around one o'clock.

Q: *What did you understand about the condition of the clients?*
A: Lene she say—Sandy is dying, maybe Charlotte also dying, and I think, "Okay, these people frozen, you need to hurry, maybe . . ."

Q: *She said Sandy and Charlotte were dying?*
A: Very close, like, "Sandy very close. Maybe if you will find, you will find her dead. And you need hurry." Also Klev understand—you need just make direction, no go up, just go, just cross this big square of South Col, and you will find people on the end, near of Kangshung Face. Not go up. I said, "How long time?" Probably fifteen minutes. I said, "Oh, very close, if people fifteen minutes, for me maybe five minutes or ten minutes." I ask, "For you or for me?" "Oh, for you it is maybe fifteen minutes." Okay, for me it is fifteen minutes.

Boukreev attempted to get from Schoening and from Gammelgaard directions on how to reach the climbers who had been left behind. With no landmarks to reference, no sighting point to walk toward, they were trying to guide a blind pilot to the field.

Q: *Did you ask for help from Neal?*

A: Neal go inside of tent with crampon. I get off his crampon, because I said, "Oh, he will cut this tent." And I get off his crampon. And he just collapse.

Q: *He's in his tent at this point?*
A: Just half of his body probably in tent, half of body outside of tent. And when I spoke with Lene, I said, "How Neal?" And she say, "Maybe some problem with Neal." Mostly Lene, she was more talkative for this situation. Klev, I don't know what was situation, but Lene just talked. Maybe Klev have some problem with his head. And I go inside of tent, I tried to speak with Neal Beidleman, but he was very cold, impossible for him—no possible talk with him, and I understand. He began just use oxygen inside of tent.

Boukreev, on going to speak with Beidleman, found him half in, half out of his tent, his crampons still on. Concerned that his crampons could rip the tent fabric and expose him to the cold winds that were at times at hurricane force, Boukreev removed Beidleman's crampons and helped him into his tent. His condition was such that Beidleman could barely talk.

Q: *And then?*
A: I go again inside of my tent. Lene and Klev already in sleeping bag, and I check with her again to make sure I don't need go up. Lene and Klev told me, "You don't need go up. You need go just cross what is flat place." Lene told, "You don't need go up." Pemba go inside and he said, "Lopsang tell you, you need go up." Why, where, I need go up or I don't need go up? And I am responsible about life. I understand this—before, I hoped it is okay, these people have guides, people have Sherpas, people probably have some oxygen, it is okay, just not visibility.

Now this situation, people just come, maybe people get frostbitten, and just all news come very quickly for me. I get this very upset very quickly. I get this power from upset.

Q: *Adrenaline?*
A: Yes, that is word.

Boukreev, in his first exchange with Klev Schoening, had been told that he didn't need to "go up" the mountain, but "across" the South Col. Given that the directions meant that the stranded climbers were considerably off the course of a normal descent, Boukreev wanted to check again what he'd heard.

As Boukreev was talking to Gammelgaard and Schoening, trying to get the best instructions possible, Pemba came to Boukreev's tent and said that Lopsang had returned to Camp IV with news that several hours earlier he'd had to leave Scott Fischer just below the Balcony. Out of oxygen, delirious, suffering from what appeared to be cerebral edema, Fischer had been unable to move without the assistance of Lopsang. Despite Lopsang's heroic efforts he'd not been able to get Fischer down. Desperate to get help for his friend, Lopsang wanted Boukreev to climb up to him, to take oxygen and hot tea to him. Boukreev was thoroughly confused by the conflicting bits and pieces of information that were coming at him through the climbers' hypoxic haze. Was Fischer with the clients? Were they in the same places? Where on the South Col did he need to go? Up or down or across? He was trying to sort it all out.

Q: *Did you speak with Lopsang?*
A: Pemba said Lopsang come and he spoke with us, and I jump out of tent and wondering where is Lopsang? I don't know. I go inside of tent where is Neal. Neal has collapse. And I help little bit him, and then outside of tent I heard some voice of Lopsang. He said, "Anatoli you need go up."

Q: *You don't see him? He's yelling at you from his tent?*
A: Yes, yes. Just—"Anatoli, you need go up." And I understand Scott is have difficult situation.

Q: *So what do you do then?*
A: I go again inside of tent and I said again, "Lene, Klev, I need go up or I need just cross this flat place?" They say, "You need just cross this flat place." "Scott is there?" I'm asking. "No," they say, "Scott not." So, okay, now I am begin understand. Scott is up the mountain. Clients are down, different places.

Q: *So, is it after that that you go into the tent, to the Sherpas' tent, to get some oxygen?*
A: I went for Lopsang and say, "Lopsang, you need go together with me, some our clients probably died, we need carry our clients." And I didn't see him. He said again, "Anatoli, you need go up, Scott said he wait you, he respect you, he expect you help him like this, and you need carry oxygen and hot drink for him."

Q: *But you don't see him when you're having this conversation?*
A: Just at vestibule of tent, just I hear his voice. I think he need understand whole situation. "Lopsang, we need carry some clients, maybe fifteen minutes—are you able?" He said me again, "Anatoli, you need go up."

Q: *He doesn't answer, he just talks?*
A: Just talk directly what he have this idea inside of head, he didn't understand what I talk, he just heard my voice and told me just exactly what—all the same, repeat. And I need helping five people—I am one. I go inside of his tent, Sherpas' tent. I ask Pemba about oxygen. And I understand from second talk with Lene about Beck Weathers and

Yasuko Namba. And I ask, "Okay, Pemba, you need to find for me oxygen. I will go for another tent, for Rob Hall's tent, maybe somebody will help me." And I go inside and maybe another camp—for Rob Hall's expedition, open one door. And I try, "Hey, somebody, can you help me?" No answer. I say, "Yasuko Namba, Beck Weathers, need helping—somebody—are you ready to help me?" No answer. Another tent, same. Another tent, same. And then I go inside—I saw some Sherpas' tents of Rob Hall. I open and somebody talk with me. And I say, "Yasuko Namba and Beck Weathers need help. Some power from your expedition go together with me help for our clients." And I say, "Okay, you need to be ready." And then I go Taiwan tents—nobody. No answer.

Lopsang had made a promise to Scott Fischer when he had to leave him behind. He'd told him, "Okay, please, you stay here. I . . . leave you here. You stay here. I send some Sherpa and oxygen and tea." Groaning in pain, Fischer had told Lopsang, "You go down. You go down." Leaving Fischer, Lopsang had reassured him, "Please, Scott, you never walk anyway; you stay here. I send some Sherpa and Anatoli. I send up oxygen and tea."

Like Boukreev, Lopsang could see that the Mountain Madness Sherpas could not or would not go up the mountain. He was counting on Boukreev, but Boukreev had reports of five clients down, three of them with the Mountain Madness expedition. He couldn't do it all; he needed help, so he made a quick round of the expeditions tented nearby: to the tents of Rob Hall's clients, to the tents of Hall's Sherpas, to the tents of the Taiwanese.

Rob Hall's expedition's members were either asleep, unable or unwilling to lend support to Boukreev's effort. One of them, Lou Kasischke, was totally incapacitated, still snowblind, still alone in his tent. His tentmates, Andy Harris, Beck Weathers, and Doug Hansen, as of 1:00 a.m., still had not returned to Camp IV.

The failure of Boukreev to get assistance from the Rob Hall expedition members at Camp IV was the second time that evening that a plea for help had gone unheeded. Mike Groom, who had left Beck Weathers and Yasuko Namba behind in the dogpile and returned with the Mountain Madness climbers, Schoening, Gammelgaard, and Beidleman, had about an hour earlier pleaded with various of the Adventure Consultants' team members to attempt a rescue of their fellow climbers. He'd had no better luck.

Likewise, from the Taiwanese, no assistance was offered. Nobody could or would help.

> Q: *With no help, what do you do?*
> A: I come back again to Pemba. "Pemba, do you have hot drink?" "I have hot drink." "Where is oxygen?" He says, "I didn't find oxygen." "How you didn't? I need oxygen, some bottles; clients need oxygen." He said, "All bottles empty." I tried to find oxygen also at this time. I hurry. I know somebody can die, and I hurry, hurry, hurry—check for bottle of oxygen—no I find—no. I go again inside of tents of our Sherpas. And I saw quiet. People just understood— maybe Anatoli wants us go out, but is dangerous—like quiet, stillness. And I say, "Lopsang, somebody need . . ."
>
> Q: *Are you raising your voice with him?*
> A: Yes, big strong wind outside, very cold, lots of problem come, and I upset with him in this situation.
>
> Q: *What do you say to him?*
> A: Nobody answer. Very quiet, like all people get collapse after hard work. I understand this very difficult.

Boukreev, when he discovered that Pemba could not supply him with any oxygen, was incredulous, angry, impatient, and desperate to get to the lost clients. Fifteen canisters of Poisk had been left at

Camp IV before the assault bid. He'd gotten three canisters earlier. Somewhere, he reasoned, there were more, but Pemba was saying, "No oxygen."

Q: *So, you had no oxygen to take with you?*
A: Lene told me, maybe very bad situation with Sandy—you need hurry. Now I lose lots of time to try to find support of somebody who can help me. And now I didn't have oxygen, I have just my mask and reductor. And inside of [Mountain Madness Sherpa] tent, nobody speak with me. And I saw Lopsang, and I saw he used oxygen. And for me this is little upset and I saw he used oxygen and he said many time, "I don't need oxygen," and just I take off his mask and get his bottle of oxygen. And I say, "I need this oxygen," and take this oxygen.

Q: *You took his oxygen?*
A: Yes, everything, and put in my pack.

Q: *Did he try to get it back?*
A: No, not answer. He just was very quiet. He don't like. I say, "Somebody need help and we need carry somebody." I was very hurried, just very fast. I get oxygen, I know I have some oxygen, I have some tea, and I have this oxygen together with mask, reductor, I didn't—I know, just off, and I think maybe I need hurry very soon—fifteen minutes, I try to find Sandy—what is happening with Sandy. And just I take this and I understand if I will try again to find support. And I run out. I get strong wind, no visibility, I begin keep my direction and go out.

Q: *So, you get the oxygen off Lopsang, you have the tea from Pemba, and you head out. So how do you decide which way?*
A: People say, not go to up. And I understand this. Actually,

I remember what is—how it is South Col, plan of South Col. And I didn't get crampon, because I was very hurried and people said you don't need go up. I leave camp, just little walk, and just go direction from wind, I keep this direction and I cross the South Col, and I didn't see—I cannot see nothing, just my headlamp little bit just through white. And this is—I don't know, maybe fifteen minutes already. I was fifteen minutes, I saw watch, it is like began like fifteen minutes past one or twenty minutes past one. Now I began just saw this watch because I began work, I began hurry. And I get fifteen minutes, just begin recognize just this big rock. And then after this rock began small part from right side and go down to Kangshung Face. And maybe thirty meters before, from this big rock, small rocks, and I didn't see nothing. And I didn't see nobody. I try go up, but without crampon, impossible. I think maybe I need little go up. And I think maybe these people get mistake. And I came back to camp.

Boukreev, walking with the wind to his back, had headed in the direction he thought Gammelgaard and Schoening had directed him, but in the elapsed time they said the trip would require, he had found no one. Thinking that Gammelgaard and Schoening had been mistaken in the description of where he could find the dogpile, he had headed in a direction that led him up the mountain. The route was too steep to be negotiated without crampons, and Boukreev returned to Camp IV, steering directly into the wind and blowing snow.

Q: *Did you go to Lene and Klev again?*
A: Yes, I look in the tent, I spoke with Lene and Klev. I said, "I didn't find nobody. Where is? I need maybe go up." People said, no. But I said I cross already—nobody, just rock finish—and people say probably you need to go down little bit. I said, "Okay, maybe it is small mistake, maybe I need go down little bit." I said, "Okay, I will try."

Q: *Did you go back to the Sherpas' tent at that point?*

A: It is probably all together like before two o'clock, the time now—before two o'clock. And I go out from my tent and I go inside of Neal's tent and spoke with Neal. Neal began just little speak. And he also talk me about Kang-shung Face and how he go down. But when I saw Neal, I didn't ask about can you help me. For me, it is exactly—it is look like—like, I didn't ask Klev because Klev come and Klev cannot able, but I saw Neal and I saw his face. He just get terrible time and just frozen and shaking and just inside of tent he was very poor.

Q: *Did he ask you about Scott, or did you ask him about Scott?*

A: He didn't talk. He didn't talk nothing about Scott. I understand situation. I already understand. I try to find about various people—where is Sandy, her situation. And again then I go to tent of Sherpas. It is there quiet. Sherpas like clients get collapse. All Sherpas inside. And I go outside again for another tent, for Rob Hall expedition.

Q: *So you looked in the Sherpas' tent, and everybody's out of it?*

A: Out. And no possible. I saw the situation. I go again inside of Sherpas' tent from Rob Hall expedition and I ask somebody can help me. I said, "You need to go out together with me." This Sherpa try he say maybe to go out, and saw weather, and he said, "Okay." I saw he get out his pack. I said, "Okay, I go in my tent and I waited you." Maybe five minutes he will be ready. And then I go inside of my tent with Lene and Klev tent and little keep myself from wind and waited five minutes—nobody came. And then I just open my tent and try to go out—I saw the Sherpa come. And he said, "Actually, I don't like go out together with you because this situation, no other Sherpa go together with me, and also I don't like situation." I say, "Why you don't like?" He say, "No one other Sherpa come. Why I need go to risk? Just me and no one ready go together with me." I cannot say who is this Rob Hall Sherpa, but some Sherpa. And when I heard this, I understand. Again I run out, take my oxygen, and try to go out to find these people.

Q: *Did you try to find more oxygen or did you still have just the one canister you got from Lopsang?*
A: No. This is situation. Was very hurry. When next time I get close to same place, think, I saw some lamp, maybe Tim make this lamp. And I saw somebody make this light from headlamp. This is maybe after two o'clock. And I found the people. Very close together. I come and I say, "How are you?" and people was very slow, not able, just frozen voice, just very slow, somebody like Tim, very slow. Charlotte, she didn't able talk.

Returning to the same area that he had searched before, but staying on "the flat" and scanning the landscape, Boukreev spotted Tim Madsen's headlamp approximately thirty yards from where, on his previous trip, he'd diverted up the mountain.

Boukreev found Madsen, Pittman, and Fox huddled in a close circle; Yasuko Namba lying on the ground, appearing unconscious; Beck Weathers nowhere in sight. Tim Madsen has said that at some point Weathers had wandered away from the dogpile.

Q: *They're on their feet or . . . ?*
A: No, like sit down. Nobody, just like . . .

Q: *On their butts?*
A: The butts. But people have some packs and people sit down on them. And this situation—when I saw this situation, I take oxygen, I first time I open my tea . . .

Q: *You have one canister?*
A: I have one bottle of oxygen. I have one thermal bottle tea. And I give for tea, some cup. Charlotte, Sandy, and Tim. And then people drink tea. Just I saw the situation. I am one person and this is three people, and I saw Yasuko very close, maybe two meters from people. And I put mask for face of Sandy.

Q: *Was Sandy talking at all?*
A: No, nothing.

Q: *How was she behaving?*
A: Just little bit, just she is frozen. Just Tim can little talk.

Q: *Making any noises, Sandy?*
A: She can little talk. Sandy—for me, it was very difficult talk. Strong wind, I am tired. I cannot remember exactly about—but people, just Tim say, "Where is another people?" I said, "Just I am alone. Nobody can able to help." And just I have just one bottle of oxygen. And somebody can't come together with me. Sandy couldn't tell nothing. Charlotte, nothing, just frozen people. Very frozen, very small power. And Tim, very slow; he can little talk. I understand. And I understand these people not able without helping. I said, "Maybe somebody ready to go together with me." And Charlotte said, "Yes, maybe I like go." I said for Tim and Sandy, "Okay. This is one bottle of oxygen. You can share this oxygen. And, Charlotte, I take you." After one minute I take my pack again and I take Charlotte and we begin walk. I have some crampons now, and very strong wind just directly on our face. Impossible to see—nothing, just—I tried to help for Charlotte to stay on her feet.

Q: *Was it hard for her to stand?*
A: Yes. Just she can able little walk, but without me, no way. Just for me, very hard. Every time I tried to make this—equilibrium.

Q: *Her balance?*
A: Her balance—keep this balance. But very strong wind. And I understand, without my hands she will fall exactly.

Q: *Your right arm around her?*
A: Yes. She get her other [left] hand above my shoulder.

Q: *She's on your right side?*
A: Yes, and I hold to the left hand and we walk. And very strong wind for me. Actually I am frozen, she is frozen, she wasn't able talk very much, but very slow, step by step we go. But it is four hundred meters and step by step. Sometimes we stand, if I understand this is good place for make some rest, because another place, if I saw some stone little bit, I put Charlotte—little sit down. Because from ground it is very difficult to help her stand up, but from stones it is possible. And little, maybe three, four times, we made this stopping. Then I began recognize this place, some garbage . . .

Q: *Some empty oxygen canisters?*
A: Yes, very old bottles. My crampon is hitting metal, I can feel, and I understand is very short distance for camp, probably two hundred meters.

Q: *Is Charlotte trying to talk at all during this time?*
A: No, no. She just talk little—just she say "too hard" or something. Very hard for her. It take long time, more than for me when I go, maybe forty-five minutes. She just robot,

walk like robot, I think. Me, too. We cross the South Col
and I saw some lamps inside of tents, Pemba probably . . .

Q: *No blinking lights?*
A: No. This is around three o'clock probably already. And
when I get to camp, maybe it is around three o'clock. And
I get her [Charlotte Fox] out of her crampon, harness, everything, and she crawl inside of Neal's tent. And I ask Neal—
he is much better; I saw the situation. He used oxygen, he
just began grow up. And Neal, I said, "You need help for
her." And I take mask from his face, put for her face because
just like robot I work. And now again for this situation, I go
for Sherpas' tent. This time I ask again every tents to help
me. I tell I saw this Yasuko Namba . . .

Q: *You went again to Rob Hall's and the Taiwanese tents?*
A: Yes, and I ask again. I go, just I need relax, I work very
hard, and I use my time for little relax, for rest, go just one
tent, another tent, and tried again to help. Because first
time I was hurry. And then I ask some Sherpas of Rob Hall,
I talk about Yasuko Namba, and I come back, I tried again
talk with our Sherpas, with Pemba, with our Sherpas, very
quiet, like collapse people, didn't say nothing. And I go
inside of tent, also opposite of my tent is Taiwan tent. I
open some and ask—no, quiet. And then I go inside of
tent. I was very tired. It is three o'clock. And also I ask
Pemba, give some tea for Charlotte, and I waited some tea
and Pemba bring more tea for Charlotte and Neal, and
then he bring some tea for me.

Q: *Are Lene and Klev asleep now?*
A: Lene also drink little tea and I tell her about Charlotte
and say, "Now, here's Sandy used oxygen and I have now
big problem with Yasuko Namba." Somebody, like nobody

help me. And it is very difficult for everybody. Also I have not oxygen. And now people have one bottle oxygen. Pemba couldn't find, didn't find, and I didn't find oxygen.

Q: *Did you speak again with Pemba about oxygen?*
A: This is situation, just I waited little time—maybe somebody can be helping me—I checked all tent from Rob Hall's and I waited. I was very tired and also I understand nobody can be responsible to help me. I go out again and I go inside of tents of our Sherpas; I took again just mask and some oxygen from another Sherpa, put in my pack, and run out for my clients. And when I get, it was around four o'clock probably. Maybe four-fifteen, four-ten. Just begin light. Because in five o'clock it started to get light. Five o'clock, possible to see, little bit.

And I went out and I found these people, Tim and Sandy, and they used oxygen maybe one hour already, maybe one hour. And people spoke with me. Sandy began spoke with me. And I ask, "How are you?" And people said, "Okay." And Sandy began talk with me and I understand. Now, it is much better for her.

Q: *What was she saying?*
A: I said, "How are you?" She said, "I am okay." I said, "What is happening with Yasuko?" because it is two meters. And I didn't ask people gave for her tea or people didn't. It is for me what I had, what I carried, I gave for tea. I didn't ask people gave her oxygen or tea because just one bottle, three people was together. And for me, this is very close situation. I will be very empty, without power. And for me, just I work like robot also. I take Sandy Pittman and same situation like Charlotte Fox.

Q: *You had another canister of O's?*
A: I give this for Tim.

Q: *What did Tim say?*
A: He just took mask and nothing. Also this situation, also I have carried some second bottle of tea, I think. I have very little drink; I gave some drink and we begin start walk. And probably around five o'clock it is begin light. Just no impossible to say sun come, but it is begin light and around probably I think like four-forty, four-forty-five we come. I was very tired, empty, and had just help for Tim, for Sandy, go inside of tent, ask again tea. And then I need rest already. And I say, "Pemba, I wait tea for me," and I go inside of my tent. Just I put Tim Madsen and Sandy inside of tent, help for people get out of crampons, like harness, everything, packs, help for people put inside of tent, closed, talked with Pemba, go inside of my tent, keep warm. Lene was near and she little talk about it. "Anatoli, you need rest. You need oxygen. Look for your face, you are very terrible." I say to her, "Okay, don't worry about me—what is happening now with Scott?" I think he get very difficult situation. Now all our clients in the tent, just without Scott. I think he have difficult situation. Now just problem with Scott. But I believe Scott is guide and maybe he can survive much better than these clients. And when Pemba come, we drink tea and I told Pemba now what is situation. Now I saw storm lose power and begin light. And we need send two Sherpas with oxygen to go up for Scott. And do you understand. And he say, "Yes, I understand." I say, "Try to talk with Lopsang and two Sherpas—we need to send for help, for Scott with oxygen." Try to find oxygen. I go inside of sleeping bag and drink little tea and just what I think about Scott—I understand this is problem, and I don't remember much from there, like two hours I slept.

• • •

Lene Gammelgaard, recalling Boukreev's return to their tent after shep-
herding Pittman and guiding Madsen, who was able to move under his
own power, said, "I think about five o'clock in the morning I wake up,
and he's back in, and it's light, and again no words. He's just sitting
there and he's absolutely empty. There's nothing left in him. And I sort
of think, perceive, whatever, understand that he's got Charlotte, Tim,
and Sandy in, but I also have the feeling that he's been out there and
not been able to do anything for Yasuko and the other one [Weathers]
who was sitting out there. At this point I didn't know."

from # Above the Clouds
by Anatoli Boukreev

After surviving the 1996 Everest tragedy that killed guides

Scott Fisher and Rob Hall and several other climbers, guide

Anatoli Boukreev turned his attention to neighboring

Lhotse, the world's fourth-highest mountain at 8,516

meters. Boukreev himself died on Annapurna some 19

months later, leaving journals that included this account of

his Lhotse climb.

Lhotse

When I returned to Base Camp, I experienced a turbulent flood of conflicting emotions. Coping with Scott's death and my adrenaline-soaked nerves and muscles left me restlessly exhausted. Concern for my physical state prompted our expedition doctor, Ingrid, and Neal to try to help me, but the medicines they gave me triggered an allergic reaction. My emotions released in a torrent during the memorial service, but there was no psychological relief in weeping.

Neal assumed the responsibilities of expedition leader. At the memorial I spoke with him about climbing Lhotse. He and Ngima, our camp sirdar, were occupied with the details of getting our climbers and gear to Kathmandu. In early March, Scott had put my name and that of several interested clients on a Lhotse permit and paid for our share of the cost. The impulse that compelled me to climb after such a tragedy may be impossible for some people to understand. It may seem a vain and ambitious act. It is difficult to explain. Mountains are my life. At the time I remembered the standard that Scott had set for all of us when he'd climbed Lhotse and Everest back-to-back. Repeating his achievement, demanding of myself the price in effort he had once paid, was a way I could express my respect for him as a mountaineer. I wanted to say farewell to him that way. Neal told me to go; he understood.

Tired and a little crazy, I left Base Camp on the night of May 16 at 8:30 p.m. By midnight, I reached Camp II, where I rested an hour and drank some tea before heading up to Camp III. The dark, enormous slope blended into the night sky, and the boundaries between earth and heaven disappeared. Anxiety binding me to the tragedy was pulled out of me and released into space. The night gifted me with strength and tranquillity. The emotions that bound me to the earthly world slipped away. Weathering the cold, at 4 a.m. I arrived at a tent where I expected to find my friend the Danish climber Michael Jörgensen. I drank tea, closed my eyes, and slept like a stone for four hours. Leaving at 8 a.m. I saw evidence of strong winds ripping across the South Col; snow was brushstroked up toward the sun rising over the peaks. The sky was clear. The weather was good enough. It, the altitude, and technical difficulties on the route were my adversaries.

Gusting wind noticeably impeded my rate of ascent above the 8,000-meter mark. The effects of the previous days' work told on my performance. I stopped to stash my small backpack at the beginning of the steep couloir that leads to Lhotse's summit. Into the roomy pockets of my down suit I stuffed essentials—a headlamp, a flask of water, and a thermos of tea. My heavy Nikkormat camera hung around my neck. Alone, without belay, leaning over my ice ax, I climbed the acute angle of the couloir. In the narrow neck I fixed twenty meters of 8-mm climbing rope. Down-climbing that section in darkness would be more dangerous than ascending. The rope protection would speed my descent. I emptied the flask of water, leaving it as well, thinking to spare myself the effort of carrying more weight. The snowy couloir became wider and ended with a shallow gully. A metal stake for anchoring rope protruded from the snow at the top. Climbing the last meters, I left the protection of the steep walls. The wind buffeted me, trying to rip me off the mountain. I dug my crampons into the snowy névé slope and leaned low over my ax to maintain my balance. Terrible hurricane-force gusts deviled my progress. I took the left route up the last slope and reached the summit at 5:45 p.m., slightly more than twenty-one hours after leaving Base Camp.

Through breaks in the clouds, when the wind permitted, I looked over at our route to the summit of Mount Everest. Somewhere on the rock shelf about 8,300 meters was the body of Scott Fischer. His spirit is now in the sky somewhere higher. Everest's summit is a springboard for those who dream of rising above earthly concerns to examine their lives, expecting the height of this mountain to provide a vantage point that allows them to understand themselves better, hoping that when they descend, something will have changed inside.

There is no simple answer to what went through the minds of Scott Fischer and Rob Hall as they waited for help that never came. Perhaps they were able to understand something essential about themselves, about our drive to get to these summits. My thoughts during the last few ascents have evolved. When climbing the last meters or even stopping on the summit's snowy ledge, my understanding of the meaning of the achievement has changed. My sense of joy in the accomplishment and my satisfaction with being on the top is overshadowed by the wonder that one could make such an effort for the transitory reasons of human vanity. It is as though, arriving at the top, something has been forgotten or lost, and without that it is impossible for me to understand why I am standing there. A great emptiness fills me, and I experience tranquillity, knowing that when I go down, the world will be easier for me.

On the Lhotse summit, gazing at the route from the South Col to the highest point on the planet, it was important for me to believe that our ascent, achieved at such enormous cost and effort, had some lasting meaning. Something should change in the lives of those who aspire to climb to the summits covered with snow and rock. A human can be transformed by the effort that it takes to breathe the atmosphere above the clouds.

The wind intensified. Loss of ambition accelerated my desire to descend into the windless space. Reasons that down below had seemed so important had evaporated. Off the summit's rocky point, I reached the protected slope of the couloir and relaxed. Abruptly, the hurricane wind ceased; my surroundings became perfectly still. Had the wind understood that its efforts to push me into the abyss were useless? The summit of Everest was absolutely calm in the clear evening air; blameless, every reality was quieted by the advancing coldness of the darkening sky. I was amazed by the overwhelming tranquillity of that moment. My consciousness relaxed, tension left me, and exhaustion rolled over my body and through my muscles.

As I descended one of the steep sections in the couloir, my crampon slipped off its rocky support. I lost my balance and flew down the slope. With the strength in my arms and legs spent climbing up, I could not arrest my fall with my ice ax. Gaining speed, I slid fifteen meters down the incline. Some force stopped my flight. My crampons stuck solidly into the névé on a shelf no wider than my feet. Where did the strength come from that allowed me to hold my ground after the sudden stop? Below me, my trajectory dropped several hundred meters into a rocky funnel where there would have been no possibility of arresting my fall.

I felt no fear, nor did adrenaline give power to my movements. I wondered, "What kept me from dying this time?" As though every bit of strength had been used to make the stop, slowly I made a downward traverse to better footing. Absolute darkness enveloped me at the base of the couloir. I was wrung out physically as never before in my life. In the place I remembered leaving my backpack, I searched the ground, primitively coveting the bivouac sack, stove, and food it contained. Again I lost my balance, slipped off a steep, rocky shelf, and came to rest on a gentle slope of snow. As I fell, my down suit caught on a rock. The weak beam of my headlamp illuminated the finest-quality down feathers floating into the night air as I watched dispassionately. My excellent down suit! Analyzing myself carefully after the fall, I gave up looking for the pack; it might have been just a few steps away. I reached the fixed ropes at 7,600 meters and slowly continued my descent.

Sometime late in the night I arrived at Camp III. There was no wind; the sky held a blanket of enormous, bright stars. The same perfect sky had covered us one week before as we started out for the summit of Everest. My friend Michael Jörgensen, the Danish climber who had been with me on Everest in 1995, was waiting for me in the tent. I drank a cup of tea and slept.

I woke late the next day. There was no strength to follow the impulse to retrieve my backpack from above. I hardly had the power to make the short descent to shelter at Camp II, where I crawled into a sleeping bag in a sun-warmed tent, drank some tea, and slept until the next morning. My physical exhaustion caused me no concern. It was a relief that I was calm inside and that the oblivion of sleep came to me as a pleasure. The sad reality of Everest had drifted away and did not weigh on my brain and consciousness. My nerves relaxed and my heart became lighter, as if I had paid debts that had oppressed me for a long time. Physical labor had healed my suffering soul.

On May 19 I made my way down to Base Camp. No trace of the Mountain Madness expedition remained on the glacier. I borrowed a backpack from Michael and stuffed it full of my high-altitude equipment. After tea in the Himalayan Guides mess tent and reassuring friends that I was okay, about 6 p.m. I set out for the village of Namche Bazaar. Under a canopy of stars, I walked slowly down the Khumbu Valley, arriving at my destination, the Himalayan Lodge, early in the morning. Abruptly, I abandoned my cup of tea in Mingma's kitchen when I heard the distinctive sound of a helicopter flying up the valley to Syangboche airstrip. Shouldering a heavy pack, I rushed up the hill to the airstrip. I found our team preparing to board the waiting helicopter. I felt as if I were running to catch a moving train, and that train was called Life.

SUMMIT
Daybreak stars interface time with space.
On the summit's altar
Light falls like rain from black sky,
Pouring down purifying my body,
Washing my soul with serenity.
Will and every act of kindness emanates
Traveling for centuries
Carried on cosmic winds.
Life is a trifle
And you have risked all earnestly.

Earthly compassion,
Conscious comprehending
Strength overcoming
Mindfulness discerning good and evil.
Live fully heart at one with the Earth.

Returning home, I breathe easier.
My life appraised from the vantage of Himalayan slopes
Healed are the doubled agonies of my bloodless wounds.
No summit is gained without pain.
Walking a knife-blade ridge to the summit
Cold steel light illuminated your image.
Next to me, climbing with me were a troop of men
Their past lives marching.
Lives cut short by love that was true.
Songs left unfinished
They could not tell you why love
Sacrificed life for the blue mountains.
I came down to you

Bearing thoughts and dreams
To live their unfinished melodies
So you would hear and understand them.

—Anatoli Boukreev

acknowledgments

Many people made this anthology.

At Thunder's Mouth Press and Avalon Publishing Group:
Thanks to Ghadah Alrawi, Tracy Armstead, Will Balliett, Sue Canavan, Kristen Couse, Maria Fernandez, Linda Kosarin, Shona McCarthy, Dan O'Connor, Neil Ortenberg, Paul Paddock, Susan Reich, David Riedy, Simon Sullivan, and Mike Walters for their support, dedication and hard work.

At The Writing Company:
Nate Hardcastle helped with editorial research and oversaw permissions research and negotiations. Nat May, Mark Klimek, Taylor Smith and Wynne Parry took up slack on other projects.

At the Portland Public Library in Portland, Maine:
The librarians helped collect books from around the country.

Walt Unsworth's *Everest*, near-essential reading for Everest freaks, was a valuable resource.

Finally, I am grateful to the writers whose work appears in this book.

p e r m i s s i o n s

We gratefully acknowledge everyone who gave permission for written material to appear in this book. We have made every effort to trace and contact copyright holders. If an error or omission is brought to our notice we will be pleased to correct the situation in future editions of this book. For further information, please contact the publisher.

b i b l i o g r a p h y

The selections used in this anthology were taken from the editions listed below. In some cases, other editions may be easier to find. Hard-to-find or out-of-print titles often are available through inter-library loan services or through Internet booksellers.

Anker, Conrad and David Roberts. *The Lost Explorer: Finding Mallory on Mount Everest.* New York: Simon and Schuster, 1999.

Bonington, Chris. *Quest for Adventure.* London: Hodder & Stoughton Ltd., 1981.

Boukreev, Anatoli. *Above the Clouds: The Diaries of a High-Altitude Mountaineer.* New York: St. Martin's Press, 2001.

Boukreev, Anatoli. *The Climb: Tragic Ambitions on Everest.* New York: St. Martin's Press, 1997.

Coffey, Maria. *Fragile Edge: A Personal Portrait of Loss on Everest.* Seattle, Washington: The Mountaineers Books, 2000.

Conefrey, Mick and Tim Jordan. *Mountain Men: A History of the Remarkable Climbers and Determined Eccentrics Who First Scaled the World's Most Famous Peaks.* Cambridge, Massachusetts: Da Capo Press, 2002.

Gammelgaard, Lene. *Climbing High: A Woman's Account of Surviving the Everest Tragedy.* Seattle, Washington: Seal Press, 1999.

Gilman, Peter. *Everest: The Best Writing and Pictures from Seventy Years of Human Endeavour.* London: Little, Brown and Company, 1993. (For "Absent Friends" by Chris Bonington.)

Gilman, Peter. *Everest: The Best Writing and Pictures from Seventy Years of Human Endeavour.* London: Little, Brown and Company, 1993. (For "All the Winds of Asia" by Peter Boardman.)

Groom, Michael. *Sheer Will: The Inspiring Life and Climbs of Michael Groom.* Sydney: Random House Australia, 1997.

Leamer, Laurence. *Ascent: The Spiritual and Physical Quest of Willi Unsoeld.* New York: Simon and Schuster, 1982.

Morrow, Patrick. *Beyond Everest: Quest for the Seven Summits.* Ontario: Camden House Publishing Ltd., 1986.

Noyce, Wilfrid. *South Col: A Personal Story of the Ascent of Everest.* New York: William Sloane Associates, 1955.

Roberts, David. *Moments of Doubt.* Seattle, Washington: The Mountaineers Books, 1986. (For "Messner and Habeler: Alone at the Top".)

Tabin, Geoff. *Blind Corners: Adventures on Seven Continents.* Merrillville, Indiana: ICS Books, 1993.

Venables, Stephen. *Everest: Alone at the Summit.* New York: Thunder's Mouth Press, 2000.

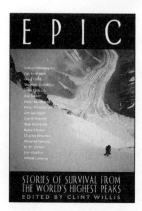

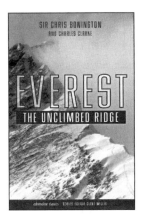
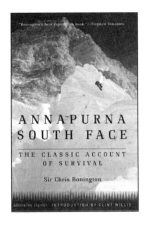

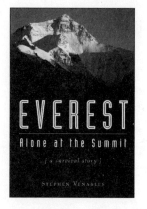
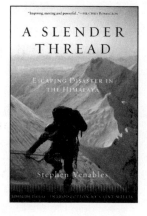